Reading the Book of the Twelve Minor Prophets

Reading the Book of the Twelve Minor Prophets

EDITED BY

DAVID G. FIRTH

BRITTANY N. MELTON

STUDIES IN
SCRIPTURE
& BIBLICAL
THEOLOGY

LEXHAM
ACADEMIC

Reading the Book of the Twelve Minor Prophets
Studies in Scripture and Biblical Theology

Copyright 2022 David G. Firth and Brittany N. Melton

Lexham Academic, an imprint of Lexham Press
1313 Commercial St., Bellingham, WA 98225
LexhamPress.com

Print ISBN 9781683596561
Digital ISBN9781683596578
Library of Congress Control Number 2022937369

Lexham Editorial: Derek R. Brown, Allisyn Ma, John Barach, Mandi Newell, Kelsey Matthews
Cover Design: Brittany Schrock
Typesetting: Abigail Stocker

Contents

Abbreviations

AB	Anchor Bible
ABD	*Anchor Bible Dictionary*. Edited by David Noel Freedman. 6 vols. New York: Doubleday, 1992.
ApOTC	Apollos Old Testament Commentary
AYBC	Anchor Yale Bible Commentary
BDB	Brown, Francis, S.R. Driver, and Charles A. Briggs. *A Hebrew and English Lexhicon of the Old Testament*
BBR	*Bulletin for Biblical Research*
BKAT	Biblischer Kommentar, Altes Testament
BHHB	Baylor Handbook of the Hebrew Bible
BSac	*Bibliotheca Sacra*
BZAW	Beihefte zur Zeitschrift für altorientalische und biblische Rechtsgeschichte
CBC	Cambridge Bible Commentary
CBQ	*Catholic Biblical Quarterly*
ConBOT	Coniectanea Biblica: Old Testament Series
FOTL	Forms of the Old Testament Literature
HBM	Hebrew Bible Monographs
HCOT	Historical Commentary on the Old Testament
HThKAT	Herders Theologischer Kommentar zum Alten Testament
IB	*Interpreter's Bible*. Edited by George A. Buttrick et al. 12 vols. New York, 1951–1957.
IECOT	International Exegetical Commentary on the Old Testament
Int	*Interpretation*
JBQ	*Jewish Bible Quarterly*
JETS	*Journal of the Evangelical Theological Society*
JHS	*Journal of Hellenic Studies*
JSOT	*Journal for the Study of the Old Testament*
JSOTSup	Journal for the Study of the Old Testament Supplement Series
JTI	*Journal for Theological Interpretation*

LAI	Library of Ancient Israel
LHBOTS	The Library of Hebrew Bible/Old Testament Studies
LW	The Works of Martin Luther
MT	Masoretic Text
NAC	New American Commentary
NIB	*The New Interpreter's Bible.* Edited by Leander E. Keck. 12 vols. Nashville: Abigdon, 1994-2004
NICOT	New International Commentary on the Old Testament
NIDOTTE	*New International Dictionary of Old Testament Theology and Exegesis.* Edited by Willem A. VanGemeren. 5 vols. Grand Rapids: Zondervan, 1997.
NIVAC	NIV Application Commentary
NSBT	New Studies in Biblical Theology
OBO	Orbis Biblicus et Orientalis
OTL	Old Testament Library
OTS	Old Testament Studies
RevExp	Review and Expositor
RTR	Reformed Theological Review
SBLDS	Society of Biblical Literature Dissertation Series
SOTSMS	Society for Old Testament Studies Monograph Series
SWBA	Social World of Biblical Antiquity
TBC	Torch Biblical Commentaries
THOTC	Two Horizons Old Testament Commentary
TOTC	Tyndale Old Testament Commentaries
VT	*Vetus Testamentum*
VTSup	Supplements to Vetus Testamentum
WA	*D. Martin Luthers Werke, Kritische Gesamtausgabe: [Schriften].* 73 vols. Weimar: Hermann Böhlaus Nachfolger, 1883-2009
WBC	Word Biblical Commentary
ZAW	*Zeitschrift für die alttestamentliche Wissenschaft*

1

On Reading the Twelve Minor Prophets

David G. Firth and Brittany N. Melton

In the last thirty years there has been a shift in Old Testament scholarship toward reading the Minor Prophets as a collection. When read in light of one another, canonically as a distinct subgroup, they are referred to as the "Book of the Twelve." However, this designation significantly predates the current emphasis and is not adopted by all or without criticism. So how did we get here?

Prior to this more recent shift in scholarship to read "the Twelve" together, scholars tended to search for the historical context of the prophet himself in order to uncover the history or background of each minor prophetic book. In other words, there was an attempt in modernity to discover the "world behind the text." More recently, interpreters have tended to focus on the "world of the text,"[1] largely in its final form, to consider if the message of the text might be gleaned more directly. Let us now examine in more detail the influences of this shift.

---

1. The now widely used distinction between the "world behind the text," "the world in the text," and "the world in front of the text" can be traced back to the influential study by Paul Ricoeur, *The Conflict of Interpretations* (Evanston: Northwestern University Press, 1974). While the earliest reference in biblical studies came in Bernard C. Lategan's "Current Issues in the Hermeneutical Debate," *Neotestamentica* 18 (1984): 1–17 (3), it was popularized by the following works: Robert Morgan and John Barton, *Biblical Interpretation* (Oxford: Oxford University Press, 1988), esp. 184, 189; W. Randolph Tate, *Biblical Interpretation: An Integrated Approach*, 3rd ed. (1991; repr., Grand Rapids: Baker Academic, 2008).

Since the latter part of the twentieth century, a trend sweeping through biblical studies is a move toward reading texts as whole units. This may in part be a reaction against an earlier generation who focused on the identification of often very small textual units and the removal of what were deemed to be later accretions to the text. Along with the focus on small units, this older model was often interested in separating textual elements that had previously been received as a single unit. This was most obviously seen in the study of Isaiah, where specialists would focus on the different layers of the text following the division of the book into Proto-, Deutero-, and Trito-Isaiah. This approach could also be seen in the study of Psalms. Here, instead of seeing the Psalter as a unit for interpretation, the focus was solely on individual psalms and sometimes part psalms once it was determined on form critical grounds (as was often done with Psalm 147) that what was presented as a single poem was in fact two discrete works.

A crucial change can be tied to the work of Brevard S. Childs.[2] It would be too much to claim that Childs singlehandedly changed the landscape of Old Testament studies. But there can be no doubt that, for all the debates it generated, his work appeared at a time when this change was beginning to emerge and was the most cogent early representative of it. Childs's work emphasized the importance of the final form of the text rather than putative earlier stages, though he retained an interest in these earlier stages.[3]

Within a decade of the publication of Childs's *Introduction*, important works had begun to appear that explored the importance of reading texts as wholes rather than focusing on their sources. Early fruit of this was evident in Gerald Wilson's work on the Psalms, where he developed an approach which was influenced by Childs in outlining how the Psalter as a whole might work.[4] Not everyone was convinced by Wilson's specific proposals. Although some critics of the whole model remain, it is now possible to point to an important shift in focus, so that a good deal of exegesis now addresses the Psalter and not just specific psalms.[5] Studies of Isaiah, likewise, began

---

2. Most notably in his *Introduction to the Old Testament as Scripture* (London: SCM Press, 1979).
3. See his *Exodus: A Commentary* (London: SCM Press, 1974) where he frequently explores this element.
4. G. H. Wilson, *The Editing of the Hebrew Psalter*, SBLDS 76 (Atlanta: Scholars Press, 1985).
5. See E. Zenger, "Psalmenexegese und Psalterexegese: Eine Forschungsskizze," in *The Composition of the Book of Psalms*, ed. E. Zenger (Leuven: Peeters, 2010), 17–67, and Beat Weber, "Von der Psaltergenese zur Psaltertheologie: Der nächste Schritt der Psalterexegese?!

to consider the unity of the book, even if most studies exploring this have continued to work with the tripartite division of the book as at least a heuristic tool. Here, particular attention should be given to a pioneering essay by R. E. Clements,[6] though the decisive work was probably that of H. G. M. Williamson.[7] Again, there is much that is debated about the appropriateness of the conclusions that are reached, but it is now clear that a significant body of research is concerned with how the book works as a whole.[8]

Given these wider trends, it is not surprising that similar concerns have arisen in the study of the Minor Prophets. In this case, there is the long-standing Jewish tradition of referring to them as the "Book of the Twelve," a label which has recently been understood to encourage reading them as a unit based on ancient witnesses and unifying elements. In this respect, the work of Paul R. House should be noted as a crucial early contributor to this discussion.[9] House argued for the unity of the Twelve by looking at their genre and seeing elements of narrative within their prophetic form. From this he explored their structure, plot, characterization, and point of view, all of which, he argues, supports reading them as a unit. This approach has been taken up and developed by others, notably James D. Nogalski[10] and Aaron Schart.[11]

But these works throw up specific challenges that are unique to them. Most notably, there is a fundamental ambiguity in the term "Book of the Twelve"—is it simply a convenient scroll on which to gather a group of

---

Einige grundsätzliche Überlegungen zum Psalter als Buch und Kanonteil," in Zenger, *Book of Psalms*, 733–44.

6. "The Unity of Isaiah," *Int* 36 (1982): 117–29.

7. *The Book Called Isaiah: Deutero-Isaiah's Role in Composition and Redaction* (Oxford: Clarendon Press, 1994).

8. See H. G. M. Williamson, "Recent Issues in the Study of the Book of Isaiah," in *Interpreting Isaiah: Issues and Approaches*, eds. D. G. Firth and H. G. M. Williamson (Nottingham: Apollos, 2009), 21–39.

9. *The Unity of the Twelve* (Sheffield: Almond Press, 1990).

10. See *The Book of the Twelve and Beyond: Collected Essays of James D. Nogalski* (Atlanta: SBL Press, 2017).

11. See *Die Entstehung des Zwölfprophetenbuchs. Neubearbeitungen von Amos im Rahmen schriftenübergreifender Redaktionsprozesse*, BZAW 260 (de Gruyter: Berlin, 1998). See also the *Interpretation* 61, no. 2 (April 2007) series of articles on the subsections of the Book of the Twelve: Aaron Schart, "The First Section of the Book of the Twelve Prophets: Hosea—Joel—Amos"; Mark E. Biddle, "Obadiah—Jonah—Micah in Canonical Context: The Nature of Prophetic Literature and Hermeneutics"; Julia M. O'Brien, "Nahum—Habakkuk—Zephaniah: Reading the 'Former Prophets' in the Persian Period"; Paul Redditt, "Themes in Haggai—Zechariah—Malachi."

otherwise short works, in which case we might stress "the Twelve," or is it intended that the book itself provides a key hermeneutical guide to the reading of the parts, in which case the stress is on "Book"? Even within the Book of the Twelve there are still clear markers that point to the relevance of each of these prophets (most notably that all twelve are named), meaning that although there are elements which push us to read them together, there are also aspects which encourage us to read them as distinct works. This ambiguity is not present in either Psalms or Isaiah, though each has its unique issues. But this immediately raises an important question that can only be answered through a close reading of the texts themselves—does the content of these texts push us as readers toward reading them as an integrated collection, or are they intended to be read as discrete works?

When we turn to the history of interpretation it becomes clear that both approaches can be seen. The dominant approach in critical Old Testament studies has been, until recently, to focus on this as a collection of Minor Prophets (a group of shorter works gathered largely for convenience). Nowhere is this seen with more clarity than in Gerhard von Rad's work.[12] For von Rad, the canonical order of the books (which varies between MT and LXX and remains a significant issue when considering the Book of the Twelve as a whole)[13] was of no significance. Instead, his concern was to explore the message of each of the prophets by placing them in their historical sequence, at least as he reconstructed it. Each of the Minor Prophets received a chapter of its own (though, typical of the time, the various parts of Isaiah also received a chapter), with each interpreted as a complete work. The Book of the Twelve was not considered a significant hermeneutical factor. Reading these works as Minor Prophets can be traced back at least to Augustine,[14] so von Rad stands in a long exegetical tradition. But it is also possible to understand Sirach 49:10 as seeing the work as a unity since Sirach treats the Twelve in the same way as Jeremiah and Ezekiel (Sir 49:6–9). Admittedly, this latter reference is not conclusive since he mentions

---

12. See *The Message of the Prophets* (New York: Harper & Row, 1972).

13. See John Goldingay's essay in this volume as well as Marvin A. Sweeney, "Sequence and Interpretation in the Book of the Twelve," in *Reading and Hearing the Book of the Twelve*, ed. James D. Nogalski and Marvin A. Sweeney, SBL Symposium Series 15 (Atlanta: SBL Press, 2000), 49–64.

14. *The City of God*, 18.25.

the "bones" of the Twelve and thus looks to the individual prophets who are included, but at the same time he allows a unity to their message.

Although this is far too brief an overview, it demonstrates that unresolved questions persist. Are we reading a Book of the Twelve or is it a collection of Minor Prophets? Even the nomenclature adopted says something about the exegetical approach that is taken. If the former is in view, then the emphasis falls more on how these books interact with one another, an approach that might serve to limit some of the more specific points of emphasis found within the various individual "books." If the latter term is adopted, then the main focus is on each prophetic book as a discrete work (although there may be some attention to the question of whether it is possible to speak of a consistent message across these works).

There are also mediating positions, which fall between these two basic positions on a continuum of intentionality. For example, David L. Petersen takes a moderate position in his preference for regarding them as a "thematized anthology."[15] It should be noted that neither position represents the extreme end of the spectrum since those who read them as the Book of the Twelve still recognize distinct textual units with multiple authors and redactors, and it is not as if those who regard them as the Minor Prophets always disregard the other eleven entirely when interpreting an individual book. Therefore, what governs the key difference in position is the question of intentionality: Were these twelve texts intended, by authors, redactors, compilers, and recipients,[16] to be read together? The degree to which one discerns intentionality and at which point(s) in the text's production decidedly informs the interpreter's approach. For instance, if it appears that allusions to other texts within the Twelve are inseparable from the message of one "book," then it can be argued that reading that individual book alongside the others was intended and therefore critical for interpretation. There are also instances when it seems the awareness of some of the other eleven occurs at points in the text less integral to its core message or in places less clearly penned at an early stage in production. When this is the case, the interpreter must decide how much weight to place on redactional

---

15. "A Book of the Twelve?" in Nogalski and Sweeney, *Reading and Hearing the Book of the Twelve*, 3–10 (10).

16. Of course, these cannot be so readily distinguished from one another, a point of critique Sweeney has leveled in response to E. Ben Zvi's "reader-centered strategy" ("Sequence and Interpretation," 50).

connections. Furthermore, if the reason(s) behind intentionally placing these texts together can be ascertained, this also influences one's interpretation. This point relates to suggestions concerning balance—does Jonah's message or the framing "domestic" metaphor[17] soften the judgment texts? And can smaller books truly stand alone (e.g., simply reading Obadiah as an oracle against the nations), or do they require the context of the larger Book of the Twelve? Finally, might the possible evidence of such intentional shaping lend itself to further interpretive considerations, for example, the repeated reference to the credo of Exodus 34 or themes that are deemed significant for the entire collection?

All of this requires that we return to the text(s), keeping in mind both the history of interpretation and what emerges from a close study of each part. The essays that follow attempt to do precisely this. Most, though not all, were originally presented at the 2018 meeting of the Old Testament study group of Tyndale Fellowship in Cambridge, UK. It should be stressed that no final answers are given to the question of how we are to read the Minor Prophets/Book of the Twelve. In fact, it will be seen that quite different perspectives emerge. But each in its own way wrestles with this essential question. While scholars have approached these twelve texts in two distinct, though not mutually exclusive, ways during the past century, the benefits of each should be recognized. Although the question warrants continued debate, the contributions of both approaches yield valuable insights.

---

17. John D. W. Watts, "A Frame for the Book of the Twelve: Hosea 1–3 and Malachi," in Nogalski and Sweeney, *Reading and Hearing the Book of the Twelve*, 209–17.

2

Hosea: Marriage, Violence, and Yahweh's Lament

Isabelle M. Hamley

Few books have the capacity to divide opinion as much as that of the prophet Hosea. You can open one commentary and find a glowing analysis of the gracious, forgiving, ever-patient love of God for his people. Or open another and find a searing indictment of a vengeful, abusive God who promotes marital violence and rape. The marriage-breakdown metaphor of Hosea is not for the faint-hearted. It divides, it tugs at the heartstrings, it calls on some of the deepest human experiences: love, hatred, fear, betrayal, despair, intimacy, and more. It is perhaps unsurprising that the marriage and divorce metaphor is one that has been used in many ways over the years and is still being used today, in all its complexity. Headlines in the British and European press have consistently labeled Brexit as a "marriage gone wrong" or "the great divorce," with accusations of improper conduct on both sides. That such a metaphor is still used, particularly at the national level, suggests it has a particular draw and effectiveness. In Hosea, it also directs our attention to *how* the text means, as well as *what* the text means. The metaphor goes beyond representation and becomes embodied in a human couple, which magnifies its pitfalls and the culturally bound notions behind it.

The book of Hosea uses emotionally loaded language for the relationship between Yahweh and Israel as the metaphor unfolds between Hosea and his wife Gomer. Language and metaphor become problematic when violence creeps in and the metaphor turns to threats of domestic abuse. Feminist readings have highlighted the problematic nature of the book and advocated for reading "against the grain," recovering Gomer's perspective, condemning Yahweh/Hosea as abusive, and refuting traditional readings that stress the depth of love and relentless grace extended by the "husband" to his "wayward partner."

Reading Hosea responsibly demands that we pay attention to the destructive nature of the portrayal of marital abuse and disfunction. A simple reading of the metaphor could seem to legitimize the use of violence within marital disputes and both reflect and reinforce the vulnerability of women. In this surface reading, Yahweh (and Hosea) appear to display what is now currently described as "toxic masculinity." However, a close reading of the text also reveals a complex picture of the use of gender and gender categories: both Yahweh and Israel shift between male and female imagery in ways that undermine simple categorization and challenge gender stereotypes, including Israel's self-characterization as mighty warrior whose identity derives from Yahweh as almighty God.

I will take feminist readings as dialogue partners, consider seriously the accusations they make, and evaluate their conclusions against the text. I will, however, also seek to ask further questions of interpretation that go beyond acknowledging the destructive potential of the text for contemporary audiences and explore reading strategies that can help acknowledge the difficulties of the text, yet explore its own ambivalence and possibilities for redemptive readings.

THE HOSEA PROBLEM

Hosea's marriage is an extreme example of dramatic prophetic action. He marries a "woman/wife of whoredom"[1] (אשת זנונים) and has "children of whoredom," whose names embody Yahweh's attitude to Israel: Jezreel, Lo-ruhamah (No-compassion), and Lo-ammi (Not-my-people). The prophetic sign is not restricted to Hosea's marriage; instead, the word of the Lord instructs him to start a whole family, or household, "of whoredom." What "whoredom" means in this instance is not entirely clear: was Gomer a prostitute or a promiscuous woman? And once she is married, given the first child is attributed to Hosea, is she a "wife of whoredom" because of her past only, or because she continues to perform sexual favors for other men

---

1. Scripture quotations are taken from the NRSV unless otherwise noted.

(for whatever reason), even though she is now married? Or is she only symbolically a "woman of whoredom" because she worships local deities? The usual idiom for marriage, "take to yourself a wife" (לך קח־לך אשה) is used here, suggesting a socially sanctioned relationship, regardless of Gomer's possible past. The ambiguity itself is awkward, as it works best in patriarchal contexts with certain expectations of the role and behavior of women.

The use of an embodied metaphor is problematic: is it right for both Hosea and Yahweh to use a woman, and even more so, her children, as teaching props, in an object lesson that vilifies the woman as a whore and stigmatizes the children with names of rejection? Here, of course, we need to ask whether the metaphor has been fully implemented by Hosea, or whether the entire book is metaphor, including the instructions to the prophet. Given the matter-of-fact description of other prophetic signs in Jeremiah, Ezekiel, and Isaiah, with specifically semiotic intent, it is not unreasonable to place Hosea in the same category and assume that readers are meant to think this is actually what the prophet has done. Inscribing the woman's and children's labeled identities into a public text is in itself an act of exposure, similar to the threatened physical "uncovering" of chapter 2. While an argument may be made about Gomer's moral responsibility in the matter, the children are instrumentalized in a way that, today, we would consider psychologically damaging. One might also wonder about the status of Hosea himself. Does knowingly marrying a "wife of whoredom" make him a "husband/man of whoredom"? Does he stand as a signifier for the state of the people, intermarrying and sharing intimate life with those who do not follow Yahweh? Hosea occupies an ambiguous position, as both a man of Israel—thereby in the "Israel" pole of the Yahweh-Israel metaphor—and the embodied image of Yahweh in the marriage metaphor. Interestingly, this means that he participates in both male and female imagery.

Beyond the issue of appropriating Gomer and her children for the sake of a prophetic exercise, feminist and womanist critics have decried the text of Hosea for promoting domestic violence. Detailed analysis of the text and its problematic aspects can be found in the works of Sherwood,[2] Weems,[3]

---

2. Y. Sherwood, *The Prostitute and the Prophet: Reading Hosea in the Late Twentieth Century* (London: T&T Clark, 1996).

3. R. J. Weems, *Battered Love: Marriage, Sex and Violence in the Hebrew Prophets*, Overtures to Biblical Theology (Minneapolis: Fortress, 1995).

Fontaine,[4] and Baumann,[5] with accusations of unfounded jealousy, violence, sexual abuse, financial abuse, child abuse, and more. These issues are concentrated mostly in chapters 1–3 (considered the "primal text"[6]). The metaphor is complex and ambiguous because of its double referents: if we keep Israel as the principal referent, the images bring out echoes of its history and well-known theological motifs; but if we abstract the embodied metaphor of Gomer from these wider meaning and associations, it becomes highly problematic. Hosea/Yahweh consistently displays what we would today describe as a controlling pattern of domestic abuse,[7] with at least a fantasy to restrict and contain Gomer/Israel. Radical feminist readings tend to assert that Hosea displays unfounded jealousy and control of a woman's sexuality (i.e., she should be able to access lovers if she wants to, regardless of the marriage covenant she has made).[8] These readings however take us far beyond the imaginary world of the text. One of the conundrums facing readers of Hosea is how to read within the imaginative and historical framework of the text, recognizing the basic assumptions without which the text does not make sense (e.g., the sacredness of a covenant; Yahweh's perspective disclosing truth) without necessarily endorsing other parts of this scenario which may be abusive or radically misread within a different cultural context.

Questions are raised about Hosea's financial treatment of Gomer as he complains she received gifts, maybe even payment, from her lovers, instead of living from the produce and wealth of the household. Once again, feminist readings attribute this to domestic abuse:[9] women should be allowed to have an independent financial existence, and the precariousness of women's lives in the ancient world meant that prostitution was one of the only

---

4. C. R. Fontaine, "Hosea," in *A Feminist Companion to the Latter Prophets*, ed. A. Brenner (Sheffield: Sheffield Academic, 1995), 40–59. C. R. Fontaine, "A Response to 'Hosea,'" in Brenner, *A Feminist Companion to the Latter Prophets*, 60–69.

5. G. Baumann, *Love and Violence: Marriage as Metaphor for the Relationship between YHWH and Israel* (Collegeville, MN: Liturgical Press, 2000).

6. Baumann, *Love and Violence*, 85.

7. For internationally recognized definitions and markers of domestic abuse, see the Duluth model of working with domestic offenders, https://www.theduluthmodel.org/; the program is the best and most widely recognized intervention model based on current research.

8. E.g., N. Graetz, "God Is to Israel as Husband Is to Wife: The Metaphoric Battering of Hosea's Wife," in Brenner, *A Feminist Companion to the Latter Prophets*, 136; Fontaine, "A Response to 'Hosea,'" 63; T. Connolly, "Metaphor and Abuse in Hosea," *Feminist Theology* (1998): 60.

9. Connolly, "Metaphor and Abuse," 60; Sherwood, *Prostitute and Prophet*, 318–20.

ways to achieve this. This observation, however, does not take into account the social organization of Israel. In a rural society organized around the household, men and women both contributed to the economic welfare of the household, each in different ways, and the health of the household depended on the functionality of the relationships within it.[10] Gender-based tasks enabled the development of technical skills and expertise that were essential to survival, and women would have had power due to their technical contributions to family subsistence.

Another set of questions are raised around specifically sexual threats toward Gomer, particularly to expose her nakedness or to uncover her shame by taking away her wool and her flax (i.e., her clothes). Both concepts are highly sexualized. Nakedness was a source of shame and embarrassment. Being uncovered by another against her will alters the dynamics and changes the sexual intimacy of nakedness with her lovers to sexual shame. At the level of Israel, however, the text echoes Genesis 3: Adam and Eve being ashamed of their nakedness and God making them clothes. In this way, Hosea 2:9 still forms a theological interpretation of the state of Israel's relationship to the God who provided for them, rather than a literal threat to Gomer.

The vision of reconciliation comes under fire too: does the woman come freely? Is this a reciprocal change in the relationship, or what domestic violence workers call the "hearts and flowers" cycle, whereby an abuser turns loving and tender in order to ensure his partner does not leave following an episode of abuse? The wilderness vocabulary adds intertextual ambiguity: Israel went to the desert to escape Egypt but soon doubted her decision. The wilderness was both the place of closeness to Yahweh, of intimacy and disclosure, and the place of rebellion, doubt, and idolatry. A vision of reconciliation set in the wilderness has deep undercurrents of doubts about the sustainability of the relationship and the capacity of Israel to hold fast to its commitment.

---

10. C. Meyers, "Women and the Domestic Economy of Early Israel," in A. Bach (ed.), *Women in the Hebrew Bible*, ed. A. Bach (New York: Routledge, 1999), 33–44. For further reading, see C. Meyers, *Rediscovering Eve: Ancient Israelite Women in Context* (Oxford: Oxford University Press, 2013). For the economic possibilities open to women and the extraordinary range of work they performed, see also M. L. G. García Bachmann, *Women at Work in the Deuteronomistic History* (Atlanta: SBL, 2013).

Problematic images, therefore, abound in Hosea 2, and gradually diminish in the rest of the book. The marriage metaphor is sporadic beyond chapter 3, and when it reappears, it is no longer embodied and is mixed with others, such as Israel as a recalcitrant child. Yet the rest of the book is still replete with disturbing threats toward the nation, though most commentators do not extend the embodied Hosea/Gomer metaphor to encompass them.

HOSEA AND FEMINIST CRITICS

The charge against the book of Hosea is serious. Baumann neatly puts the case together by arguing that the book reflects a culture where domestic violence is normal, hence the metaphor is recognizable and accepted by hearers; second, the book "not only *uses* gender roles but *cements* them, even under changed circumstances."[11] In a world where "every three seconds somewhere around the world a woman is being beaten, and every three minutes somewhere a woman is being raped,"[12] we cannot ignore language that alludes to such violence. Furthermore, Hosea not only uses the marriage metaphor, but sets it within the realm of sacred speech, within which Yahweh, by association with Hosea, legitimates abusive behavior. Weems argues the marriage metaphor is a rhetorical ploy to arouse strong feelings because of culturally available associations of right and wrong, disgust, shame, and contempt,[13] which come naturally in response because they relate to real-life fears and emotions. Furthermore, she argues this is particularly relevant because the misbehavior of women threatened the whole of society and patriarchal identity. While there is truth to this allegation, it is also fair to highlight that men's sexual misbehavior in the Old Testament is also seen as threatening (albeit differentially) and is subject to many strictures in Leviticus and Deuteronomy as well as being linked to the welfare of the land and its people.

Weems makes two widely quoted claims. First, that marriage was an obvious metaphor to draw on because of the cluster of issues of power, propriety, property, and purity around it. She places the significance of the metaphor onto the *institution* of marriage but diminishes the aspects of relationship and covenant. Second, she argues the parallel works because in

11. Baumann, *Love and Violence*, 97.
12. Weems, *Battered Love*, 10.
13. Weems, *Battered Love*, 2.

marriage a man had the right to punish his wife, which legitimizes God's punishment of Israel, because men were the dominant partners while women were subordinate. That men were the dominant partners is easy to deduce from Scripture—it reflects a patriarchal world, organized around heads of households, with a greater control of women's sexuality. It is not clear, however, that men had the *right* to punish or be violent within the home or marriage. In legal texts that speak of marital disputes, women had little voice or recourse, but men were not encouraged to dispense "justice" directly—instead, a legal process was followed. Furthermore, there is no narrative instance of these laws being put into practice. Instead, the few narratives that depict family violence are associated with a picture of corrupt public life and deteriorating morality in Israel. Therefore, Weems overstates the case, though of course, just because there is no legal right for men to be abusive does not mean that it was not widespread and socially accepted.

The text itself is clearly written from a male perspective, with the concept of "woman" as a concept of otherness. The metaphor is effective because by portraying Israel as a woman, and, moreover, as the woman whom men fear, the men of Israel are themselves forced into the position of the other. Instead of being in the dominant place and identifying themselves with their male deity, they become the one they consider "other." It would not be entirely accurate to say they become "woman": as a text written by a man within the grammar of discourse of a patriarchal world, there is little *actual* feminine presence in the text. Woman as depicted is the woman whom men imagine, the concept of a woman created by the male psyche. Continental philosopher Luce Irigaray argues that within this logic of discourse, women are not truly "other" but "other of the same," an inverse reflection of male identity, a looking-glass reflecting the opposite of who men are and therefore encapsulating some of the fears and threats to their identity.[14] If one's identity is predicated on being not-woman, then the one who is woman can easily threaten masculinity. Interestingly, the move of defining identity through otherness and the other being a mirror image is found most powerfully in Gomer's children: Not-my-people and No-compassion. The woman and her children embody complete otherness: the otherness of femininity and the otherness of being cast away by God, hence no more

---

14. Luce Irigaray, *Speculum: de l'autre femme* (Paris: Editions de Minuit, 1974) 19–21.

the "chosen people." Israel is being doubly othered, as the other to the man whose identity shapes the household, clan, tribe, and nation, and other to their constructed Israelite identity as the people of God. It is an effective rhetorical strategy—but one that rests on the erasure of actual women, and on the fundamental tenets of a patriarchal world. Some critics would go further and argue that the text "seems to express a dualistic and gendered religious vision within which female sexuality becomes the symbol of sin and all that is 'other' to the meaning of the sacred within biblical religion."[15] It is not immediately obvious, however, that it is *female* sexuality that is at issue in the text, rather than disordered sexuality, breach of covenant, and, indeed, widespread injustice and oppression. Scripture as a whole does not represent sexuality negatively, nor does it exclude any sense of the right expression of female (or male!) sexuality, as we see, for instance, in the Song of Songs. To make the text of Hosea a polemic against female sexuality per se lacks specific textual support, especially since male sexuality is also portrayed as disordered (e.g., Hos 4:14, "I will not punish your daughters when they play the whore, nor your daughters-in-law when they commit adultery; for the men themselves go aside with whores, and sacrifice with temple prostitutes; thus a people without understanding comes to ruin").

Feminist critics largely agree that the text is written by a male prophet for a male audience and therefore uses "popular norms and attitudes about women, their bodies and sexuality" to get a male audience to experience dread and desire.[16] The challenge for readers is how to approach the text: from within its own logic, which risks compounding the abuse and erasure of women, or from a critical external perspective, which risks doing violence to the text. Radical feminist readings place themselves firmly outside the text and argue that reading with the grain leads women to "identify against themselves."[17] It is not entirely clear why this should be the case; the portrayal of one woman as sinful does not necessarily entail the portrayal of all women as sinful. Indeed, if we examine Scripture for a portrayal of women as a whole, Gomer does not stand as a "typical" woman. Many critics want to argue that Gomer is every woman in Israel and Hosea every

---

15. A. Keefe, "The Female Body, the Body Politic and the Land: A Sociopolitical Reading of Hosea 1–2," in Brenner, *A Feminist Companion to the Latter Prophets*, 70–100.

16. Weems, *Battered Love*, 2.

17. Graetz, "God Is to Israel," 138.

man—that they are nothing but types;[18] yet this is not how we read every text in Scripture. A specific incarnation of man and woman may shed light on underlying social constructions of gender and configurations of relationships, but it does not have to stand for the majority, the norm, or the ideal. The problematic component here is the use of the couple as a metaphor, which lends this relationship added weight. Sherwood argues the problem of Hosea is that we have only two women, both out of man's imagination: "One is a patriarchal nightmare of rebellion, the other is a dream of submission; one is 'woman as we perceive her,' and the other 'woman as we desire her to be.' "[19] The question is: does drawing on stock images necessarily invalidate the message of the text? Does a portrayal drawing on these categories preclude the possibility that some people, some of the time, may reflect them? Just because men are afraid a woman may be unfaithful does not invalidate the possibility that a woman might be unfaithful and behave in ways that seem to match a stereotype. The strategy of Hosea may be precisely to draw on a stock fear of the men of Israel and say, "Look, you yourselves, not the women, are the very thing that you fear the most."

This strategy still leaves Gomer/Israel without a voice of their own and the text open to the accusation that only the male is a subject, while women are the object of the text, because Gomer is not allowed to be the maker of her own identity.[20] This is a reasonably common, yet puzzling, assertion. If a text is written in the voice of one person, does that mean that no other character within it can ever be a subject? Does being the object of the prophet's message mean that Israel and Gomer have had no possibility of being subjects? Is identity only created independently, or together with those who influence it? An issue here is whether we consider that Israel and Gomer have any existence outside the text that would enable the text to reflect who they are—albeit through the lens of the male prophet's gaze. As characters in the story, Gomer and Israel also have agency: to leave Hosea/Yahweh and find other lovers, to seek an independent existence. The text portrays them as independent moral agents who have made specific choices which affect others. Paradoxically, denying the possibility that this is who they are and the choices they have made further pushes them out of the text

---

18. E.g., Connolly, "Metaphor and Abuse," 58.
19. Sherwood, *Prostitute and Prophet*, 309.
20. Sherwood, *Prostitute and Prophet*, 289.

and leaves their identities malleable, this time, not to the prophet, but to commentators keen to reshape the portrayal of Gomer. Gomer is threatening to both men and women. To men, for embodying their worst fears, and to women, for embodying the kind of woman that would legitimate men's irrational fears. Therefore, both try to erase her. The complexity of the text is that it requires readers not to jump to stereotypes, yet to consider the potential damage that stereotypes and the theologizing of violence can cause and consider the story that it tells as a story of people who are not just fodder for a metaphor. Holding together both a potential "real" couple and the metaphor they are required to bear is not an easy task.

Here we need to be wary of the overuse of Gomer as a "type." Many argue that the metaphor is based on fear of female sexuality; this may be so, but could the fear played on be the more universal fear of betrayal, particularly betrayal by an intimate partner? Isolating the concept of "female sexuality" is somewhat anachronistic; Fontaine more convincingly locates the fear not within a discrete category of sexuality, but within the entire social organization of the patriarchal household.[21] The household was the fundamental unit of society, within which women and children were completely dependent. Men benefited from the system, and therefore the thought of women rising against them or moving away was frightening. Women's sexuality was guarded because reproduction was at the heart of the transmission of property, status, and power. A woman who turned away from her husband, therefore, threatened the social order, lessening and shaming her husband by implying he was unable to provide or keep his household in order. Fontaine's more complex explanation is more satisfactory, though it still tends to caricature gender roles by not acknowledging the fundamental role of women within a rural, household-based economy.[22] In addition, while the system did work to the advantage of the male heads of households, not all men were direct beneficiaries (let's not forget younger sons, servants, male slaves, strangers), and the ecosystem of the household *as a whole* depended on its stability. The threat behind the text, therefore, is not just to one individual man, but to an entire social system, hence the link in

---

21. Fontaine, "Hosea," 54.
22. See N. Aschkenasy, *Eve's Journey: Feminine Images in Hebraic Literary Tradition* (Philadelphia: University of Pennsylvania Press, 1986), 109, and C. Meyers, *Rediscovering Eve*.

legal texts that speak of sexual immorality (from both men and women) as polluting of the land and threatening the entire nation.

Ultimately, putting Hosea on trial for his relationship to Gomer is a vehicle for putting Yahweh on trial. If Hosea's behavior is deeply reprehensible, then Yahweh's parallel behavior is too, so that the text becomes a misguided apology for both human and divine violence. This position is arrived at in a variety of ways. First, it does so through positing that Gomer never tells her side of the story and that she should be allowed to voice wanting to have an independent existence, her own sexual choices, ways of making a living, and the right to leave her husband and have other partners if she desires. From there, metaphorically, why shouldn't Israel also make its own choices for freedom and asserting its own identity? Graetz asks, "What if Israel is thoroughly fed up of Yahweh's outstretched arm?"[23] while Sherwood argues that we should take man/Yahweh as the problem and woman as a standard for judgment.[24] Connolly further argues that "the woman's actions can only be considered sinful if one concedes that a woman should not provide for herself, nor allow any man but her husband to give her anything, and also that a woman's sexuality is under the control of a man"[25] (she therefore sidesteps Gomer's infidelity as irrelevant). These two positions take us completely out of the text's imaginary world by removing some basic assumptions underlying it. First, it sets the questions within our contemporary libertarian culture, post-sexual revolution. The notion that sexuality is an individual's possession, rather than an expression of interdependent relationships, with consequences far beyond a specific couple, is alien to the text, for both men and women alike. Second, this moves the text completely away from questions of covenant; even in our more permissive contemporary culture, covenant matters. The central question in Hosea is linked to betrayal and breakdown of covenant; to move the discussion into one that argues for complete sexual autonomy and freedom is to have a completely different discussion from the one initiated by the text. At a deeper level, this critique also undermines a basic assumption about the nature of God. Underlying the text of Hosea is the assumption that Yahweh is completely other, that he is trustworthy and just. This does not mean his actions cannot

---

23. Graetz, "God Is to Israel," 136.
24. Sherwood, *Prostitute and Prophet*, 255.
25. Connolly, "Metaphor and Abuse," 60.

be questioned (see the book of Job or the Psalms of lament), but that there is a fundamental recognition of the gulf between fallen humanity and holy divinity. In Weems's and Sherwood's logic of interpretation, the divine and the human are collapsed into one another, so that Yahweh is no longer other but simply another character, with just a little more power. It puts human beings and their judgment and desire for power and autonomy at the center of the text and its interpretation and removes the ability to trust the "story"—that a man is grieving for his unfaithful partner.

Feminist and womanist critics highlight real and deep issues that the text poses, yet these interpretations raise problems of their own. We are left with two equal and opposite dangers: the traditional danger of failing to recognize the toxic portrayal of some of these texts, the danger of overidentification of masculinity and God, and the symbolic damage of associating God with domestic violence. And on the other hand, the danger of taking the metaphor literally, of failing to attend to complexity, of dismissing the text without listening to it, of reading everything according to a predetermined grid that has already judged the prophet guilty. Yet, does the text carry within itself the seeds of a more fruitful approach? Does the text itself carry the possibility of deconstruction of toxic masculinity? I want to explore now possibilities for responsible readings from within an orthodox faith position that nonetheless take to heart the concerns rightly raised by feminist and womanist critics.

READING HOSEA RESPONSIBLY

A responsible reader of Hosea needs to acknowledge the dangers of the metaphor but also the reality of a patriarchal context—in its many horrors *and* in its complex reality. As highlighted already, marriage in biblical Israel was not a monolithic, simple concept that enshrined women as property. Marriage was not be reduced to a dyadic relationship, but was, rather, a family and social phenomenon that shaped and affected entire communities. To say that Hosea rests on a marriage metaphor is misleading, given the vastly different cultural assumptions we bring to the word "marriage." In fact, the text is much more of a family/household metaphor, as we see with the way in which children are affected and used between the disagreeing parents and the setting of the relationship breakdown within the wider realm of household economics and prosperity. Shifting understandings of family and its internal and external relationships mean that the metaphor today makes a very different statement. In addition, one may ask what is this metaphor a metaphor *of*, exactly? Is the metaphor primarily about marriage, or about relationship, or about covenant? These things are interrelated, but not coterminous. If, like Weems, we take the metaphor as being primarily about a patriarchal institution that fuels male dominance with its central elements being violence and battery, this will yield a very different reading from those who take the metaphor as centering on a broken relationship, the pain of betrayal, and the ways in which different partners act out their feelings and brokenness. What is the driving force of the metaphor? Is it violence? Pain? Betrayal? Is it primarily about the human-divine relationship (i.e., how human beings relate up to God), or primarily about the divine-human relationship (how God relates down to humans, as it were)? Is it about punishment, or about persistent love despite the odds? Or about a combination of all of these? And how do we weigh different elements?

The metaphor in the text is slippery, and the language moves swiftly, without clear signposting, from talking about Hosea/Gomer to Yahweh/Israel. The setting of the book makes it clear that we are to read the explicit Hosea/Gomer passages as metaphorical for the Yahweh/Israel relationship. But when the text moves to talk in ways that are either ambiguous, or more explicitly about Yahweh/Israel, should this then be read back onto Hosea and Gomer? Many feminists argue that it is inevitable, even if unintended.[26] Interestingly, they do not apply the same logic to the couple's children and the frequent metaphors of Israel as a recalcitrant child. While it is easy to collapse the two poles of the metaphor into one another, this does not warrant dismissing the text as irredeemable. Rather, we need to read responsibly, paying attention to the direction in which the metaphor is working and not overextending it. Sherwood argues that commentators have tended to gloss over the human pole of the metaphor and focused on covenant and marriage as abstract ideals rather than "the strained coupling presented in this text."[27] This isn't entirely fair. The story of Hosea and Gomer may leave many gray areas, but the power of the text, for good and bad, seems to lie precisely in its realistic depiction of a broken marriage; of course, one partner's account is biased—it always is. Yet the volatile, ambivalent feelings of

26. Baumann, *Love and Violence*, 35; Weems, *Battered Love*, 13.
27. Sherwood, *Prostitute and Prophet*, 81.

the deserted partner, the fantasies of violence, the use of children in household wars, the desperate pain and anguish and longing for things to go back to the past, all of these are deeply realistic—as much today as in ages past—and could be the feelings of any deserted partner, male or female. The shock value of the text lies in transferring these all-too-human feelings and longings onto Yahweh as a vehicle for Israel to gain an insight into its situation. Just as it is dangerous to transfer elements attributed to Yahweh/ Israel only back to the prophet and his wife, it is equally dangerous to apply the metaphor too literally onto Yahweh. The metaphor is designed to move from a transactional appreciation of the broken covenant to an emotional, relational one. This makes this text a very different text from prophetic texts that center on a judicial trial motif; the aim here is to arouse emotion, pity, compassion, and bring the nation to a sense of guilt and shame for its wrongful actions. How we interpret the metaphor also depends on the assumptions we make about its audience. Weems argues the metaphor would only work to make its point for those who are in power, as they identify with Yahweh. Yet this seems a rather counterintuitive assumption, on several counts. First, the nation is not asked to identify with Yahweh, but with those who cause Yahweh's anger and pain; they are given an insight into the impact of their behavior. Second, can we argue, as Weems seems to, that most men in Israel, simply because they have more power (what type of power and how well-distributed it was among all men is debatable) will condone violence, or be happy to be voyeurs throughout the text? Even in societies where domestic abuse is widespread, it is still far from universal. Could we, instead, assume an audience where most people will recoil from violence toward those they love, but feel empathy toward those who struggle in intimate relationships? Defining audience expectation is partly about how we position ourselves and whether we assume our own moral superiority and lower levels of morality and compassion in those who lived long before us.

Overall, critics like Weems and others simplify the text through the male/female dichotomy. The text itself, however, is highly unstable in its gender associations and resists easy categorization. Yahweh and Israel are not straightforwardly associated with male and female images, respectively. In 1:6, the girl's name, Lo-ruhamah (No-compassion), echoes God's words that he will not have compassion on Israel but will have compassion on Judah. The word for compassion (רחמה) is famously related to the Hebrew word for womb and suggests the attribution of female feelings to Yahweh, while the end of the verse "or will forgive them" is literally "carry them," which evokes the picture of a mother carrying her child and a turning away from this motherly figure by Yahweh. Verse 7 then states that Yahweh will have compassion (the womb-feeling) toward Judah but will not save them by "bow, sword, war, horses or horsemen" (i.e., God repudiates traditionally male ways of salvation via war and power in his own saving action). While Israel usually is depicted as a woman going after lovers, Ephraim is depicted as a man going after lovers in 8:9, which suggests that the validity of the metaphor does not depend solely on the gendering of the different poles. In chapter 11, Israel is a son, and God is a woman loving and hugging her child (11:1, 3, 4). Over the course of the book, God is not depicted with the traditional male attributes of unwavering strength and power but as changeable, deeply affected by emotions, and unable to control his people—hardly a picture that males in a patriarchal culture traditionally espouse. The depiction of God oscillates between strength and weakness, between anger and compassion, between violence and tenderness, which suggests that the text does not readily conform to stereotypical gender norms. Men themselves are heavily criticized in the text, as men: priests who worship false gods (4:4-10), men responsible for the whoredom of their daughters (4:13), wayward sons (11:1-12). The text does not present a dichotomized view of gender as good or bad but draws on multiple metaphors and examples to build an overall picture of the relationship between Yahweh and Israel.

The most salient component of the text, however, is the fact that men are forced to identify themselves with the one they consider other, the one at fault. The text systematically depicts men in the female role. Now, on one level, this could be dismissed as a crude form of "othering," a way to shame and humiliate the men of Israel at the expense of women, who are more expendable than they are, which displaces women even further. This, however, would belie the complexity and significance of Israel being invited to see itself as the female partner—a metaphor that does not apply only to negative characterization but to positive, idealized versions of the relationship with Yahweh. At a basic level, women are told the nation can be identified with their gender, in a nation that did not even mark belonging to Israel in the body of women as it did in the bodies of men through circumcision. Hosea 2:9 has Yahweh taking back all his gifts from Israel; a Marxist analysis would rightly point to the utter powerlessness of women in the relationship. Yet, men are now reminded that they too are completely dependent; what they have is not theirs but given by Yahweh. The metaphor uncovers the harshness of a system within which women could be easily disposed of regardless of their innocence. The men of Israel are now experiencing life from the "other" side; it may, or may not, enable a degree of emerging empathy on their part.

The picture of the reconciliation of the couple has some interesting features. In Hosea 2:16, "You will call me 'my husband,' and no longer 'my Baal,' " Baal can be translated as "master." This implies a transformed power relationship of increasing equality and a challenge to traditional concepts of marriage. Is the text, through use of the metaphor, offering an implicit critique of male-female relationships in Israel? Hosea 2:18 follows with a promise of removal of the instruments of power that threaten the woman Israel—another attack on the traditional attributes of masculinity linked with war, power, and strength. The very metaphor of Hosea marrying an unfaithful woman also challenges gender stereotypes; while the unfaithful woman may be a fear in the male psyche, straying is more readily associated with men and the tacit acceptance of the prophet with the forced acceptance women normally suffered. When reading the metaphor more literally, are men invited into thinking about what their "normal" behavior entails? And just in case the men had resisted identifying with the unfaithful woman, 4:14 specifically tells the *men* they are themselves guilty. Interestingly, men would not have seen themselves as guilty of adultery simply for sleeping with a prostitute; in the legal framework of Deuteronomy and Leviticus, adultery centers on married women. Hosea extends the meaning of adultery to men straying from their marriage. The association of the men of Israel with the woman of the text undermines the construction of the identity of the men, which is predicated on their difference from women. Instead, the object of Yahweh's desire, the nation, is cast in feminine terms; the activities traditionally associated with men are problematized, and they are shown to be guilty of sins they had thought did not apply to them. In an even bolder move, the depiction of Yahweh is not straightforwardly masculine. As John Goldingay points out, men are lured into identifying with the wrathful and indignant Yahweh of the beginning, only to find that the text takes them in a completely different direction.[28] We move from fantasies of violence (at no point is it stated that violence actually happened) to an acknowledgement of powerlessness of a God who cannot force his people to love him, yet is bound to mercy by his love for them. It is the powerlessness, pain, and desperation of Yahweh, rather than his power or anger, that moves readers. The challenge for male readers is for them to accept the invitation of the text to identify with Gomer, rather than with the prophet.

The text of Hosea, in its depiction of Israel, has a strong ethical component, often set aside by those considering gender politics. Yet the text does not reduce the strain in the Israel/Yahweh relationship to straying, or in Hosea/Gomer to sexual infidelity. The book, read as a whole, contains the same call to righteousness as other prophetic books, the same condemnation of Israel's failure to do justice, the same interlinking of personal morality and failure at the level of economics and politics. To avoid discussing ethics with respect to both Gomer and the nation is to avoid one of the central drives of the book. Part of the problem is our discomfort with the notion of punishment and the appropriate fear that if we talk of Gomer's moral responsibility, we may appear to justify violence in response—to blame the victim. However, is it impossible to condemn domestic violence in all its forms as reprehensible, yet still not depict Gomer as perfect or blameless in the relationship? Or does the impulse to exonerate Gomer from blame reveal a tendency to think that any misbehavior on her part may possibly justify her abuse? This is doubly problematic. Part of rehabilitating domestic offenders, as in the Duluth program, is to explore the fact that partners may be guilty of all kinds of things but that this does not in itself justify retaliation and violence. It is crucial, in the fight against domestic abuse, to cut this link as firmly as possible. Second, to deny Gomer's moral responsibility is to deny her humanity or personhood. It is highly significant that Scripture makes no distinction between men and women in terms of their ethical and moral responsibility; they are equally human. To hold men to a higher standard of responsibility is implicitly to diminish the personhood and humanity of women. Equally, to consider the extenuating circumstances surrounding Gomer, but not Hosea, is also unfair. As it is, the text assumes that a covenant has been broken—not just by Gomer walking away,

---

28. J. Goldingay, "Hosea 1–3, Genesis 14 and Masculinist Interpretation," in Brenner, *A Feminist Companion to the Latter Prophets*, 161–68.

but by her continuing to benefit from the material goods of marriage while forming relationships with multiple partners which benefit her materially. The only way around a moral judgment on Gomer is either to try and argue she was driven to it by Hosea (which is nowhere represented in the text, and does not, in itself, justify infidelity as opposed to walking away), or to posit that covenants are not binding or do not matter as much as personal freedom and autonomy. It is difficult to see how human relationships, both intimate and at a more public level, could function without a level of integrity and respect of promises and covenantal bonds. At the level of both the human couple and the Yahweh/Israel relationship, breach of a covenant undermines the very possibility of trusting, healthy relationships. Whether the response to this breach is itself ethical is debatable, but that the breach itself is severe and has an impact on both individuals and the nation is an important part of the ethical message of the text.

The breach of covenant is even more important at the level of the nation because it signals a breakdown not just of the relationship with Yahweh, but of the very conditions that would enable Israel to flourish as an entire nation. A nation that consciously moves away from Yahweh also moves away from Torah and the consensus that undergirds pursuit of the common good. Instead, "swearing, lying and murder, and stealing, and adultery break out; bloodshed follows bloodshed" (4:2). Rejecting Yahweh was not just a religious or relational decision, it was a rejection of Yahweh's call for justice and equality through a different social organization to the nation-states around Israel. Keefe powerfully argues that Hosea has been too often spiritualized and divorced from its real-life context and concerns. It is not a book primarily about cultic issues but about the same concerns for injustice, corruption, and oppression of the poor as Amos, Micah, and Isaiah.[29] In this sense, Hosea is primarily a challenge to powerful men who are threatening the well-being of Israel as a whole—not a text primarily concerned with female sexuality.

HOSEA AS LAMENT

The book of Hosea resists simplistic explanations and sweeping statements about its purpose or main features. Instead, we find a subtle, at

___

29. Keefe, "Female Body," 73.

times contradictory, book whose depiction of God and Israel is varied and challenging at multiple levels. The language of domestic violence is deeply problematic, particularly for female readers, and yet the book holds within itself the seeds of a profound challenge to definitions of masculinity and patterns of male violence. In the end, the question remains: how are we to read Hosea as twenty-first-century readers concerned with the impact of the book and its language as we have it, regardless of what may or may not have been intended by its writer(s)? I want to suggest that the language of violence—both within the domestic sphere and within the nation—is not primarily the language of ethical or parenetic discourse, but rather the language of trauma and lament and the uncertainty and disorientation that accompany them both. While elements of ethical discourse are present, the most salient aspect of the book is its emotional tone and its outrageous depiction of feelings and fantasies of violence.

There is little consensus on the exact dating of Hosea and its relationship to the exile.[30] The language, however, reflects wartime actions, such as rape and sexual violence as part of conflict and the systematic shaming of conquered people, often through enforced nakedness (we can see some of this in the graphic depictions engraved in Babylonian and Assyrian remains[31]). From a human angle, Hosea can be seen as an attempt to make sense of what is unthinkable, to make sense of trauma within the context of providence and the promises of Yahweh. It reflects the human tendency to seek explanations, even explanations that blame those who are themselves victims of the very circumstances that are being explained. It also sets trauma within the context of God-talk and the possibility of meaning. Whose and what trauma is it? It is unclear. To a people in exile, this may provide a causal framework; to people oppressed within Israel itself, it rages against injustice and the breakdown of traditional ways of life; to all those traumatized and oppressed, it suggests both the certainty of cosmic justice and

---

30. J. A. Dearman, *The Book of Hosea*, NICOT (Cambridge: Eerdmans, 2010), 3–8.
31. E.g., *The Humiliation of the Elamite Kings*, Assyrian, 645–640 BC, Nineveh, North Palace, reign of Ashurbanipal, gypsum, British Museum, London, 1856,0909.55, 1856. *Attack on an Enemy Town*, Assyrian, 730–727 BC, Kalhu (Nimrud), Central Palace, reign of Tiglath-pileser III, gypsum, British Museum, London, 1880,0131.7, 1880 and 1848,1104.47, 1848. Multiple panels with Assyrian war scenes can be seen at the British Museum in London, many of them retrieved from Ashurbanipal's North Palace in Nimrud.

provides a framework for grace and the reaffirmation of God's relentless love for Israel. Through both justice and mercy, it promises hope.

But I would suggest there is a specific way to read Hosea: as a text of lament—the lament of Yahweh over his people, the lament of a God who cares passionately, yet sees his people descending slowly into injustice, corruption, and practices that damage the most vulnerable among them. We are used to considering human lament as a protest to God, and we somewhat easily tolerate its language. Lament is not rational; it is not reasonable. It is outrageous; it crosses boundaries and voices the unspeakable. It brings the worst human emotions before God in response to injustice, pain, and trauma, and in the very act of being voiced before God, these emotions are held, validated, and transformed. Hosea may be a different kind of lament, but it borrows the same features and language. It depicts outrageous feelings and fantasies of violence whose enactment we would never condone. But isn't this the very nature of lament? The threat to children, the desire to eradicate the other, the pain of being forgotten, the fantasies of violence, repeated imprecations—all of this is deeply reminiscent of passages such as Psalm 137. The violence that is threatened depicts the truth of a mental state. No one would suggest that Psalm 137 depicts violence that could or should be acted upon. Instead, it portrays vividly the anger that human beings feel at injustice, oppression, and abandonment.

Lament is primarily expressed in situations of disorientation, of new and terrible circumstances that traditional forms of prayer and discourse cannot quite convey. It is the language of new suffering, a language that does not solve the problem but reaches for new words, new images, new symbols.[32] Brueggemann proposes a threefold way of looking at the Psalms, categorizing them as orientation, disorientation, and reorientation. The text of Hosea neatly illustrates a movement of disorientation, caught between the former orientation of Yahweh and Israel as covenant partners, an orientation longed for in the "going back to the desert" imagery and the difficulties and hope of a new orientation of the later chapters. Yet the

---

32. See W. Brueggemann, *The Psalms and the Life of Faith* (Minneapolis: Fortress, 1995), 7–13; F. Klopper, "Lamenting the Loss of Lament," in *Exile and Suffering: A Selection of Papers Read at the 50th Anniversary Meeting of the Old Testament Society of South Africa OTWSA/OTSSA*, ed. B. Becking and D. Human (Leiden: Brill, 2008), 234; D. Sölle, *Suffering* (Philadelphia: Fortress, 1975), 5; C. Westermann, *Lamentations: Issues and Interpretation*, (Minneapolis: Augsburg Fortress, 1994), 89.

majority of the book lives within the disorientation of the present, when the former covenantal relationship is broken, and the past is unattainable, and the future yet to be formed. The language of Hosea therefore is the language of disorientation and the extreme feelings that accompany it, with changing metaphors trying to express the unspeakable. The metaphor of the broken marriage, in its horror and pain, in its oscillation between love and hate, in its dreams of violence, is the language of emotional pain and uncertainty. The book of Hosea uses a form known to Israel but flips it to encapsulate divine pathos instead. The shocking language we find in psalms of lament directed at Yahweh is here directed at Israel. This lament therefore requires an imaginative leap from readers used to treating God as an object of study (and, traditionally, impassible) to reading the text as an anthropomorphic invitation to enter into divine consciousness. It cannot be read as a dispassionate utterance of judgment or condemnation but as a cry of the heart destined to move hearers into action. The book holds many of the traditional elements of lament[33]: address (here, to the people of Israel), complaint (about Israel's unfaithfulness and lack of justice), appeal to previous commitments, expressions of anguish, accusations, and petition (that Israel would change so that the distress would be addressed). Just as in the psalms of lament when the speaker maintains his complete innocence and accuses his enemies, or, at times Yahweh, of injustice, here the speaker (Yahweh) is the innocent party. The form itself suggests that the message needs to be read in the spirit of these psalms.

For this form of address to make sense however, God cannot be an external object; he must be a dialogical covenant partner. If the human partner of the covenant can lament and take Yahweh to task for delaying help or salvation, so can Yahweh take human beings to task for their failure to uphold the covenant. The presence of divine laments in the Hebrew Bible is one sign of the true mutuality of the covenant: without it, it would not be a relationship. Westermann encapsulates the dynamic:

> The juxtaposition of God's wrath and God's grief vis-à-vis his people in these texts is almost incomprehensible. This isn't something that is said all the time, but only when life is pushed to its ultimate limit:

---

33. See Brueggemann, *The Psalms*, 70–86, and C. Westermann, "The Role of Lament in the Theology of the Old Testament," 28.1 (1974): 20–38.

to the edge of annihilation which God brings upon his own people. The lament of God is not a general statement about God; it is rather only one of those rare and extreme possibilities for speaking of God. As such, it finds its ground in the situation itself. The incomprehensible idea that God destroys his own has its corollary in that which is equally incomprehensible, viz., that the God of wrath is also the God who mourns. The meaning of such talk about a God who laments or mourns lies not in its saying something about God in himself but about his relationship to his people. It enables those who are afflicted to hold on to an incomprehensible God, one who judges and also mourns.[34]

While lament is a sign of human beings' limitations and inability to control their fate in the face of deep suffering, divine lament is a sign of Yahweh's self-limitation out of love; his people are not forced to love him. He relinquishes his power in order to form a true relationship, one within which he can be rejected. Hosea therefore makes a profound theological statement in using this form of language: a statement about the nature of Yahweh as the God of the covenant and about the nature of divine power and how it is wielded.

The ultimate function of lament however is to grasp for a change that cannot quite be imagined yet. It represents a situation in flux. It is dangerous because it is extreme and subversive. It speaks truth that is deeply uncomfortable to hear with words designed to provoke. The outrageous language of Hosea has certainly provoked much reaction. But there is one more feature central to lament that is echoed in Hosea and essential to understanding its impact. Lament uses first and foremost the language of justice and power, at individual and social levels.[35] Hence to read Hosea as primarily about cultic issues would be misguided. Here, Yahweh rails against the injustice and oppression that are unleashed by disregarding the covenant that sets up expectations for life in community. This lament, therefore, is not individualistic, or purely theocentric; it is a lament that calls for the transformation of the social order in such a way that a new order can come to life.

---

34. Westermann, "Role of Lament," 38.
35. Brueggemann, *The Psalms*, 104.

The genius of Hosea is that it uses a form of language that Israel would know and recognize, a form of language primarily used to protest injustice, and it uses it not to portray human emotions but to invite Israel into divine pathos. It rails against human injustice and abandonment. Hosea gives voice to Yahweh's lament, and in so doing, portrays in unparalleled depth the reality of the covenant as a mutual relationship.

JOSEPH ALBERANI, VIOLENCE, AND YAHWEH'S LAMENT

3

Reading Joel within and without the Book of the Twelve

Tchavdar S. Hadjiev

The opening sentence of Jakob Wöhrle's contribution to one of the many volumes on the Book of the Twelve that have been published in recent years says, "20 years ago, Old Testament scholarship found a new object: The Book of the Twelve."[1] What is intriguing about this statement is the choice of verb. Scholars did not reconstruct, propose, suggest, or hypothesize the existence of the Book of the Twelve; they *found* it. And they did not find it buried in a hitherto unknown cave or tucked away in a forgotten library. The putative Book of the Twelve has always been a part of our Bibles; we just did not realize it was there. By focusing too much on the individual writings of the Minor Prophets readers had missed the forest for the trees. Thanks to new developments in scholarship over the last twenty to thirty years, this is no longer the case. By recovering the actual Book of the Twelve, interpreters can finally understand the various contributions of the Minor Prophets not as independent literary works but as sections, or even chapters, of one large whole. The practical consequences of this claim for exegesis are immense, since it follows that scholars have been wrong to read the books of the Minor Prophets in isolation. Instead, passages from one book

---

1. J. Wöhrle, "So Many Cross-References! Methodological Reflections on the Problem of Intertextual Relationships and Their Significance for Redaction Critical Analysis," in *Perspectives on the Formation of the Book of the Twelve: Methodological Foundations—Redactional Processes—Historical Insights,* ed. R. Alberts, J. D. Nogalski, and J. Wöhrle, BZAW 433 (Berlin: de Gruyter, 2012), 3–20 (3).

can and should be understood in their interconnection with sections from another.

For many scholars the newly "discovered" Book of the Twelve is first and foremost a historical issue. Critics believe the original authors and redactors of the Twelve fashioned the text in such a way that it was meant to be read as a single composition from the start. I have dealt with this issue in greater detail elsewhere.[2] It will suffice to say that I do not believe the historical case for the existence of a Book of the Twelve has been established sufficiently. Neither the external nor the internal evidence warrants such a conclusion. Externally, the fact that some early readers, from around the beginning of the second century BC, *may* have regarded the Twelve as a single composition tells us something about the early stages of the canonical process but does not give us much indication about the way the text itself was conceived. The editors and scribes from the sixth to the third century BC could have read and transmitted the books of the Minor Prophets as initially independent scripts, and most likely they did just that.

Internally, there are no clear indications that the Twelve were composed, or meant to be read, together. The putative "book" has no recognizable structure and no unifying theme.[3] In contrast to Isaiah, which also brings together diverse materials from a variety of historical periods, the Twelve is not united by means of a single prophetic figure. The superscriptions, with their diverse terminology and forms, ascribe the oracles to *different* prophetic individuals living in *different* historical periods and so invite the reader to regard these scripts as *different* and independent from each other. The many lexical and thematic connections between the books of the Minor Prophets upon closer inspection turn out to be inadequate to provide support for a common redaction across the collection. Often these connections are just instances of coincidental repetition of common vocabulary. Even when a literary link can be established with sufficient confidence the intention and effect of this link is not to bind the different texts as parts

---

2. T. S. Hadjiev, "A Prophetic Anthology Rather Than a Book of the Twelve," in *The Book of the Twelve: Composition, Reception, and Interpretation,* ed. L. Tiemeyer and J. Wöhrle, VTSup (Leiden: Brill, 2020), 90–108.

3. For a discussion of various proposals, including the "Day of the Lord" as a possible theme of the Twelve, see Hadjiev, "Prophetic Anthology."

of a single composition.[4] From a purely historical point of view, the Minor Prophets did not begin their existence as a single composition and, therefore, do not demand to be read together.

However, it is possible to read the Twelve as a unity aside from historical reasons. Some feel that the canonical and reception history warrants such an interpretative stance, regardless of what the ancient editors intended.[5] Alternatively, a modern reader may find that such an approach provides opportunities for fresh readings and exciting new insights and decide to adopt it without any reference to redaction or reception history. It is this reader-oriented perspective on the issue that I would like to probe here. The question, then, is not if we *ought* to read the Twelve as a unity. Rather, the question becomes: granted that we *could choose to* read the Twelve as a single book, *should* we make that choice? What are the interpretative benefits and the corresponding dangers in doing so? I will explore these questions by taking the book of Joel as an example. Joel is well-suited to serve as a test case because it contains numerous literary and thematic links with other prophetic books. Because of this it provides ample material that allows one to consider the respective advantages and disadvantages of reading one particular Minor Prophet within and without the Book of the Twelve.

READING JOEL WITHIN THE BOOK OF THE TWELVE

A convenient place to start an investigation into Joel's relationship to the Twelve is the unpublished, but often quoted, dissertation by Dale Schneider. Schneider argued that Joel was written for its current literary context, between the books of Hosea and Amos, because the literary connections with these two prophetic texts are too elaborate to be explained away as the result of a coincidence.[6] Joel draws on the authority of the two older prophets by presenting his prophecy in continuation with theirs. He binds important themes from Amos and Hosea with the theme of the election of Zion, which

---

4. T. S. Hadjiev, "Zephaniah and the 'Book of the Twelve' Hypothesis," in *Prophecy and the Prophets in Ancient Israel*, ed. J. Day, LHBOTS 531 (London: T&T Clark, 2010), 325–38; T. S. Hadjiev, *Joel, Obadiah, Habakkuk, Zephaniah*, T&T Clark Study Guides on the Old Testament (London: T&T Clark, 2020), 27–28.

5. P. R. House, *The Unity of the Twelve*, JSOTSup 97 (Sheffield: Almond, 1990), 69; E. W. Conrad, "Forming the Twelve and Forming Canon," in *Thematic Threads in the Book of the Twelve*, ed. P. L. Redditt and A. Schart, BZAW 325 (Berlin and New York: de Gruyter, 2003), 90–103 (90–93).

6. D. A. Schneider, "The Unity of the Book of the Twelve" (PhD diss., Yale University, 1979), 80.

is not prominent in those two prophetic books.[7] On the other hand, Amos and Hosea fill out and emphasize Joel's call for repentance. Joel never spells out the sins from which people need to repent or what the alternative to repentance is. Yet Joel, read in its intended literary context, "calls for an end to the injustice and idolatry." He does not need to point out specific instances of injustice and idolatry because his context, "Hosea and Amos, already lists more than sufficient examples of Israel's sin."[8] Amos 4 shows the consequences of ignoring Joel's calls: lack of repentance will lead to judgment.[9] More recent studies have embraced Schneider's hypothesis that the Twelve provide the proper literary context for reading Joel and have sought to develop his conclusions further.[10] This new literary context results in an alteration of meaning that works in two directions. On one hand, passages and themes in Joel are understood differently when read in the light of the Twelve. On the other hand, Joel impacts and alters the interpretation of various passages from the rest of the Minor Prophets. This two-way influence can be perceived on all levels: individual exegetical details, larger themes and motifs, and finally the reading of the Book of the Twelve as a whole.

READING JOEL WITH HOSEA AND AMOS

Individual Exegetical Details

Joel 1:2 reads, "Hear this, O elders, give ear, all inhabitants of the land! Has such a thing happened in your days, or in the days of your ancestors?"[11] The book of Joel begins with a rhetorical question: "Has *this* happened in your days?" Most interpreters assume the demonstrative pronoun points forward and its antecedent is the locust plague (1:4-7) followed by the crop failure and drought (1:10-12, 17-20). James Nogalski, however, argues that the demonstrative pronoun points backward to the conditional promise of salvation in Hosea 14. The assumed answer to Joel's question is: "No this (salvation) has not happened, because the repentance to which Hosea 14

---

7. Schneider, "The Unity of the Twelve," 85–86.
8. Schneider, "The Unity of the Twelve," 88.
9. Schneider, "The Unity of the Twelve," 89.
10. J. D. Nogalski, *Redactional Processes in the Book of the Twelve*, BZAW 218 (Berlin: de Gruyter, 1993), 275–78; C. R. Seitz, *Joel*, ITC (London: Bloomsbury, 2016), 39.
11. Scripture quotations are from the NRSV unless indicated otherwise.

calls the people has not taken place."[12] The opening rhetorical question with its expected negative answer is not, as generally believed, a statement about the magnitude of the calamity. It is an apologetic note that explains why the promise of Hosea 14 was not fulfilled.[13]

Joel 1:8 says, "Lament like a virgin dressed in sackcloth for the husband of her youth." Traditionally, commentators have seen the virgin who mourns for the husband (ba'al) of her youth as a general picture of overpowering grief caused by extreme tragedy.[14] In contrast, Nogalski argues that the most natural way of understanding the text is to see the image in the light of Hosea 2 where Baal worship is tied up with the issue of agricultural fertility. The virgin in Joel 1:8 is "the virgin Israel" and "the verse could be paraphrased as a command to Zion to repent, as Israel had to repent for her idolatry and turning from YHWH."[15] "The phrase 'because of the Baal of her youth' offers a reason for repentance, not the picture of a suffering innocent."[16]

Joel 4:12 reads, "Let the nations stir themselves up and come up to the Valley of Jehoshaphat; for there I will sit to judge all the surrounding nations" (ESV). In Joel 4 it is not clear why the attacking nations are said to be "all round" (missābîb) God's people, especially given the universal perspective of Joel. In Schart's view, this reference becomes clear only once the reader has reached Amos 1-2. There the foreign nations that are addressed are Israel's neighbors—enemies who literally live "all around" Israel/Judah.[17]

Throughout chapters 1 and 2 we hear: "For three transgressions of [name] and for four I will not revoke its punishment" (NASB). The refrain of Amos's Oracles against the Nations (OAN) repeatedly states that because

12. Nogalski, *Redactional Processes*, 15-17.
13. This conclusion is contested by Seitz (*Joel*, 116-17), even though on the more general level he believes that "the book of Joel has been composed to respond to the scenario set out at Hosea's conclusion" (*Joel*, 55).
14. The *betûlâ* is either a young married woman or a betrothed virgin who is considered legally married; see J. L. Crenshaw, *Joel*, AYB 24C (New Haven: Yale University Press, 1995), 97-98.
15. Nogalski, *Redactional Processes*, 22.
16. Nogalski, *Redactional Processes*, 21. For a change in the details, though not the fundamentals, of this interpretation see J. D. Nogalski, *The Book of the Twelve*, 2 vols., Smyth & Helwys Bible Commentary (Macon, GA: Smyth & Helwys, 2011), 221: "The personified land is told to lament like the virgin (Israel) for the baal (lord/husband) of her youth, which, following Hosea 2, assumes YHWH as the husband who provided for her."
17. A. Schart, *Die Entstehung des Zwölfprophetenbuchs: Neubearbeitungen von Amos im Rahmen schriftenübergreifender Redaktionsprozesse*, BZAW 260 (Berlin: de Gruyter, 1998), 264.

of three and four sins of a given nation the Lord will not "revoke its punishment," but it does not specify what this mysterious "it" is. Commentators have long conjectured that "it" might denote God's wrath, judgment, or decision. If, however, Amos is read with Joel, this problem can be seen in a different light. Central to Joel is the theme of the Day of the Lord, and Joel 4 especially depicts this day as a time of judgment on the foreign nations. Since Amos 1–2 contain similar oracles against these very nations, the referent of "it" must be the Day of the Lord proclaimed in Joel 4. The devouring fire which precedes the Lord's army as it brings about the reality of this day (Joel 2:3) is the same fire which in Amos descends upon the capitals of the nations and devours their palaces (Amos 1:4, 7, 10, 12, 14; 2:2, 5).[18]

Amos 2:7 says, "… they who trample the head of the poor into the dust of the earth, and push the afflicted out of the way; father and son go in to the same girl, so that my holy name is profaned." Reading Amos 1–2 on its own, one might be tempted to think that one profanes the holy name of God by doing the things described in Amos 2:6–8 (i.e., by oppressing the poor and vulnerable members of society). However, according to Schart, the addition of Joel brings a different perspective to this. In Joel the name of the Lord is central: those who call on the name of the Lord will be saved (3:5) and those who are saved will praise the name of the Lord (2:26). When Amos 2:7 is read in this context, the focus of criticism moves away from the social injustices to Israel's attitude to "the name." The central question is no longer whether you trample on the poor, but whether you call on the name of the Lord or defile it.[19]

Hosea and the Mysterious Sin in the Book of Joel

According to the proponents of the Book of the Twelve, the link that is established between Hosea and Joel provides a clear and convincing answer to a major interpretive puzzle. It has been long noted that Joel describes the devastation of the Day of Lord and calls his readers to repentance, but he does not explain what the sins that have caused this devastation are from which the people need to repent. When Joel is read alongside Hosea this question does not arise at all. Hosea has already detailed the transgressions of the people, and Joel does not need to repeat the accusations. They are

---

18. Schart, *Entstehung*, 264–65.
19. Schart, *Entstehung*, 264.

simply assumed in his proclamation of the Day of the Lord and as he calls the people to repentance.[20] Joel depicts the divine judgment as a reversal of the happy ending of Hosea 14 and as an echo of the judgment in the earlier chapters of Hosea—desolation of grain, wine, and oil.[21] The perplexed animals of Joel 1:18 remind one of Hosea 4:3 and of the fact that lawlessness brings natural disaster.[22] He also invites later generations of readers of the Twelve to enter into the scenario envisaged by Hosea 14 and respond in the correct way: by returning to the Lord and exhibiting the wisdom of which Hosea 14 speaks.[23]

The Role of Zion in Amos

The book of Amos, like Hosea, focuses primarily on the northern kingdom of Israel. Jerusalem plays a relatively marginal role in the oracles. However, since the words of Amos were edited and preserved in Judah, this redactional history has left its trace on the text, not least in the opening hymnic section (1:2) which states that "the Lord will roar from Zion and give his voice from Jerusalem." The verse is repeated verbatim in Joel 4:16 and provides one of the most unambiguous links between the two books.

When Amos is read in light of Joel, the significance of verse 2 is blown out of proportion as the reader is invited to understand everything that follows in light of the Zion theology expounded in Joel. There we have been told that Zion is the place where the Lord dwells (Joel 4:17) and the place where people can find salvation (Joel 3:5). The people are exhorted to turn to the Lord by gathering at the temple. Therefore, as Aaron Schart has demonstrated, this Zion conception colors the way several passages are read in Amos. The injunction not to seek the Lord at Bethel and Gilgal (Amos 4:4; 5:5) suddenly acquires a completely new meaning. The Lord is not in Bethel and Gilgal, not as a reaction to Israel's oppressive and unjust practices, but because he can be found only in Zion—nowhere else. Turning away from Zion, the source of fertility and blessing, leads to drought and natural disasters

---

20. Nogalski, Redactional Processes, 17–18.

21. Seitz, Joel, 56.

22. T. Collins, The Mantle of Elijah: The Redaction Criticism of the Prophetical Books, Biblical Seminar 20 (Sheffield: JSOT Press, 1993), 67.

23. Seitz, Joel, 55–57.

(Amos 1:2; 4:6–11; 7:1–4). Those who are carefree in Zion (Amos 6:1) are not mindful of the danger of enemy attack, to which Joel 2:1–11 alerts us.[24]

The OAN in Amos 1–2

Schart and Nogalski suggest that the OAN in Amos 1–2 receive a radically new meaning when read as a continuation of Joel. The nations mentioned by Amos are no longer simply historical peoples who threatened Israel in the eighth century BC but representatives of the universal enemy who will attack Jerusalem in Joel 4. This results in a radical and far-reaching alteration of the meaning of Amos's OAN. They now deal not with the historical situation of Israel but acquire a cosmic and eschatological dimension as they focus on the apocalyptic enemy who attacks Jerusalem.[25] Thus history is replaced by eschatology and the proclamation of judgment gives way to a message of hope.

The Day of the Lord in Amos

The substitution of judgment for hope is clear in the way the Day of the Lord theme in Amos is impacted by its juxtaposition with Joel. Jeremias argues that this can be seen as early as Amos 4:6–13. At least two features of this passage are commonly seen as establishing beyond reasonable doubt a connection with Joel. First, the fivefold refrain "and you did not return to me" arguably echoes Joel 2:12 where the people are ordered: "return to me." Second, the disaster of Amos 4:9, where the locust devours the fig and olive trees, corresponds to the natural disaster in Joel 1:4, the only other place where this word for locust (gāzām) is used. It seems, therefore, that for the reader of the Twelve Joel and Amos depict two sides of the same experience. In view of the impending natural disaster, the community in Joel is exhorted to return to the Lord, but the passage from Amos makes it clear that they did not respond to the invitation. Therefore, they are threatened with the mysterious announcement "thus I will do to you" (Amos 4:12) where the referent of "thus" is left unspecified. Jeremias suggests the reader of the Twelve will take this as another pointer to the Day of the Lord in Joel. The intrusion of the Day of the Lord in Amos 4 intensifies the urgency of the

24. Schart, *Entstehung*, 263–64.
25. Schart, *Entstehung*, 264, 278–79; J. D. Nogalski, "Joel as 'Literary Anchor' for the Book of the Twelve," in *Reading and Hearing the Book of the Twelve*, ed. J. D. Nogalski and M. A. Sweeney SBLSS 15 (Atlanta: SBL, 2000), 91–109 (99–100).

proclamation and raises the question: "Has Israel already missed her last chance?"[26]

The answer to that question is found, in Jeremias's view, in the visions in Amos 7–8, read again in light of Joel's depiction of the Day of the Lord. He comments:

> Reading Amos separately, the visions show that God's patience with his guilty people has reached a definite limit. Reading Amos after Joel, the visions show that locusts and drought which may lead to the end of Israel manifest an even greater distress. Yet, this distress, though unsurpassable in the light of God's final judgment at his terrible "Day," in the end is designed to lead Israel back to God. Once the dimension of the Day of the Lord has reached this goal Israel will receive all the aspects of final salvation described in Joel 2, as well as Joel 4 and Amos 9. ... Looking back from this final objective of God's actions, the Day of the Lord, as terrible as that day appears, in the end represents an extreme means for God to lead Israel to the salvation he has prepared for her.[27]

READING THE TWELVE IN LIGHT OF JOEL

Joel is often thought to function as a "hermeneutical key" or a "literary anchor" for the Book of the Twelve. Christopher Seitz points out the vague and general nature of the language of Joel. The addressees are elders, inhabitants, priests, but they come across as generalized characters, not as specific groups of people living in identifiable historical circumstances. The description of the disaster weaves elements from different types of calamities. The temporal perspective is vague.[28] Seitz argues that the vagueness of the description is an intentional strategy, designed to paint a comprehensive picture of judgment and repentance which is not time specific and bound to a particular context but enables future generations of readers to hear the various oracles of the Twelve in relation to their personal circumstances. Joel anticipates what is to follow in the rest of the Twelve and

---

26. J. Jeremias, "The Function of the Book of Joel for Reading the Twelve," in Alberts, Nogalski, and Wöhrle, *Perspectives on the Formation of the Book of the Twelve*, 77–87 (84–85).

27. Jeremias, "Function of Joel," 86.

28. Seitz, *Joel*, 50–52.

provides "hermeneutical coordination" for appropriating it.[29] In a similar vein, Rendtorff suggests that Joel does not present one consistent message of what the Day of the Lord means but is rather a collection of different, even contradictory, views about the nature of that day. In this way, Joel prepares the ground for the rest of the collection where at various places these diverging descriptions will be picked up and developed in more detail.[30]

According to Nogalski, Joel introduces several major literary threads that run throughout the Book of the Twelve and perform a unifying function. For example, fertility-related imagery linked to the themes of repentance and punishment is prominent in Joel and will reappear again and again in the subsequent writings. With the help of such interconnections, Joel offers a "historical paradigm" centered around the themes of disaster, repentance, restoration, and judgment of enemy nations. These themes serve as an interpretative prism through which the rest of the Minor Prophets are to be read. Therefore, the Book of the Twelve, read with the help of the hermeneutical key provided by Joel, explains the past and looks to the future. It tells readers why the history of God's people has unfolded in the way it has but also offers them the hope which comes from turning to Yahweh.[31]

The proposals surveyed so far assume the chronological priority of the order of the Twelve found in the Masoretic Text (MT). Sweeney, however, argues that the order of the LXX represents a more logical, and potentially earlier, arrangement that treats the fate of the northern kingdom as a paradigm for Judah and Jerusalem. It begins with Yahweh's judgment on Israel and its implications for Judah (Hosea, Amos, Micah), followed by material on foreign nations in the middle of the collection (Joel, Obadiah, Jonah, Nahum), just like Ezekiel, Isaiah, and LXX of Jeremiah, and concludes with prophecies dealing with the Babylonian exile and post-exilic restoration (Habakkuk–Malachi).[32] Within this arrangement Joel plays a different role. It introduces the OAN of the Twelve by using Egypt and Edom to represent typologically all the nations. The following books then develop this general picture by focusing on specific historical examples: Edom (Obadiah),

---

29. Seitz, Joel, 63–64.

30. R. Rendtorff, "How to Read the Book of the Twelve as a Theological Unity," in Nogalski and Sweeney, Reading and Hearing the Book of the Twelve, 75–87 (78–80).

31. Nogalski, "Joel as 'Literary Anchor,'" 100–109.

32. M. A. Sweeney, "Sequence and Interpretation in the Book of the Twelve," in Nogalski and Sweeney, Reading and Hearing the Book of the Twelve, 49–64.

Assyria (Jonah, Nahum), and Babylon (Habakkuk). The relocation of Joel to second position in the MT serves a different hermeneutical agenda. It emphasizes Jerusalem from the outset and reflects the later concerns of the Jewish community from the Persian or Hellenistic periods.[33]

READING JOEL WITHOUT THE BOOK OF THE TWELVE

It should be clear from the examples above that the decision to read Joel within the Book of the Twelve has important consequences for interpretation. Both individual textual details and larger themes appear in a different light once this larger literary context is allowed to control the reader's understanding. I do not wish to deny entirely the legitimacy or usefulness of such readings. Undoubtedly, they can produce some fresh insights and open up new dimensions of the text. However, on its own, this approach is not particularly helpful and should not be allowed to dominate contemporary readings of the Minor Prophets. There is a lot to lose when we take the Twelve as our only, or primary, context for the prophetic books. There are dangers to this approach, not just benefits, that we need to take into consideration. In the last section of this chapter, I will substantiate and illustrate this claim with the help of a few examples from the above survey of proposals.

READING JOEL WITHOUT HOSEA AND AMOS

Many scholars feel that reading Joel in connection with Hosea and Amos provides a good solution to the thorny problem of Joel's failure to mention the sin of the people which caused the locust plague and from which they had to repent. Earlier interpreters have variously identified this sin as idolatry, overreliance on ritualistic worship, pride, or failure of the leadership. The problem with all these proposals is that they are not clearly based on the text and so remain without a strong foundation. Some scholars assume their major deficiency lies in the fact that they work within the narrow confines of the book of Joel, taken in isolation. The issue disappears once Joel is seen as a continuation of Hosea and an integral part of the Twelve. The sins of the congregation are the idolatry condemned by Hosea and the social

---

33. M. A. Sweeney, "The Place and Function of Joel in the Book of the Twelve," in Redditt and Schart, *Thematic Threads in the Book of the Twelve*, 133–54 (149–51).

injustice criticized by Amos. Hosea and Amos fill in the gaps of Joel which otherwise are impossible to fill.

There is, however, a much better way of dealing with the theological problem of the prophet's silence on the question of Judah's sin, which is viable only if we read Joel on its own, without any reference to other prophetic texts. If Joel is taken in isolation, there is only one possible way of understanding his lack of criticism of the community. The prophet did not know what the precise sins of his audience were. It is noteworthy that he also never speaks of the wrath of the Lord, even though he identifies the army attacking Zion in chapter 2 as the army of the Lord. The disasters that have befallen the people are traced back to the Lord, but they are not explicitly interpreted as expressions of his displeasure caused by identifiable transgressions. There is no doubt who is the source of the calamity, but equally there is no explanation of it. The congregation, therefore, is not invited to repent *from* a certain set of actions or a particular lifestyle. They are called to turn *to* the Lord in despair, prayer, and ritual. Turning to the Lord means seeking the Lord by entering into his presence.[34] The precise reason for the disaster remains a mystery which will never be solved. Yet, even in the midst of such mystery, in the face of their ignorance and disturbing uncertainty in relation to their current predicament, the people of Judah are not left without direction. They can still turn to the Lord and seek him, even if they do not fully understand what he is doing and why he is doing it.

Such a reading of Joel has the potential to address the modern reader in ways that are unavailable to those who want to see the book always in connection with the rest of the Twelve. After all, many readers continue to find themselves in circumstances that resemble those of the prophet's audience. People rarely know for certain why disaster strikes. Attempts to link modern-day calamities with identifiable human sins, in prophetic fashion, are fraught with danger. The book of Joel, therefore, allows us to preserve the mystery and transcendence of God without losing sight of the pastoral needs of those who undergo suffering. In times of crisis it offers not intellectual explanation but practical strategies for survival. It can only do that apart from the Book of the Twelve.

---

34. J. Barton, *Joel and Obadiah*, OTL (Louisville: Westminster John Knox, 2001), 76–80.

Reading Amos without Joel

Jeremias is certainly right when he points out that the portrayal of the Day of the Lord in Joel, with its stress on the salvation of God's people and judgment on the nations, is very different from the way this concept is developed in other Minor Prophets who focus exclusively on the judgment of Israel.[35] This more positive picture of the Day of the Lord inevitably colors how other parts of the Twelve are perceived. Amos 5:18–20, for example, rings differently when heard after the promises of Joel 3–4. The cry, "Alas for you who desire the day of the Lord," does not have the same shocking impact upon an audience who knows that "the day of the Lord is near … the Lord is a refuge for his people, a stronghold for the people of Israel" (Joel 4:14, 16). In light of Joel, the gloom portended by Amos is no longer impenetrable, and the doom he threatens is not unavoidable. As Jeremias himself notes, the Day of the Lord "in the end represents an extreme means for God to lead Israel to … salvation."[36] The sting of Amos's message has been taken out.

Admittedly, when placed in a post-judgment setting, this is a good way of looking at Amos. There is no point in beating the certainty of impending doom into the consciousness of your listeners when disaster is already a present reality. People in the postexilic period needed to know that there was hope beyond the judgment. Hearing Amos with Joel in the background achieves just that. However, constricting Amos to this one setting limits its rhetorical power and renders vast portions of the book largely useless for many readers of later generations. If we know from the start that everything will ultimately be fine, then the threats and criticisms of the original prophecy lose most of their effectiveness. Amos's capacity to address situations of oppression and exploitation, to challenge social injustice and to champion the poor is severely diminished. Joel not only transforms the message of Amos or infuses his oracles with new meaning; Joel destroys the very core of Amos's proclamation.

A good example of this are the OAN in Amos 1–2. Read within the horizon of the book of Amos, these oracles seek to establish a parallel between Israel and the foreign nations by carefully selecting the sins of which each nation is accused. There are no indictments of idolatry; Israel's neighbors are guilty of war crimes and violence against the weak and defenseless.

---

35. Jeremias, "Function of Joel," 78.
36. Jeremias, "Function of Joel," 86.

Thus, by the time we come to the eighth climactic Israel oracle in 2:6–16 we can easily see that Israel is placed on the same level as its neighbors. Its crimes are of a similar nature. It is true that ripping open pregnant women (Amos 1:13) is more horrendous than using a house servant for sexual favors (2:7), but the rhetorical power of the oracles rests in part on that incongruence. The prophet wants his audience to see that the oppression of the weak members of their own community is as shocking as the war crimes of Israel's hostile neighbors. The meaning of the series is grasped only once we arrive at the climactic conclusion about Israel. To focus on the foreign nations is counterproductive. If we do this, we miss the whole point.

Yet, when Amos 1–2 is read together with Joel precisely this undesirable outcome is achieved. As shown above, Israel's neighbors are transformed from a rhetorical device highlighting the moral and spiritual corruption of God's people to enemies of God who will be defeated in the end. And as the nations turn into historical symbols of eschatological foes, so Judah/Israel is transformed from a perpetrator into a victim. The focus is no longer on the challenge not to trample the weak.[37]

Another example comes from the heart of the Day of the Lord passage in Amos 5:18–20. The three-animal story in which a man escapes from a lion only to meet a bear and then runs from the bear to be finally bitten by a poisonous snake in the deceptive safety of his home emphasizes the absurdity of the people's conviction that they could escape from divine judgment. This conviction informs several of the oracles in the book of Amos. It is even explicitly stated in a rare quote of the audience's attitude in 9:10: "Evil shall not overtake or meet us." Amos uses all his rhetorical power to ridicule and undermine this sense of security. He relativizes the exodus from Egypt and the elect status of the nation of Israel by placing the primary salvific event on the same level as the migrations of other people (9:7). The whole of his fifth vision is an elaborate denial that there will be any place—Sheol, heaven, the top of Carmel, or the bottom of the sea—where people can find refuge from the all-seeing eyes of Yahweh (9:2–4).

---

37. The impact of Joel on Amos's OAN is clearly seen by Collins (*Mantle of Elijah*, 69) who comments: "The condemnation of Israel in Amos has once again been pre-empted by the more hopeful vision of Joel, so that in literary terms the force of the blow is softened. Everything is seen from a post-exilic viewpoint, and the broader context of the Twelve envisages the state of affairs after the punishments predicted in Amos have been inflicted on Israel and Judah."

However, just as Amos is trying to deconstruct the arrogant self-assurance of his audience, so Joel deconstructs Amos's attempts. By implying that the Day of the Lord is ultimately light, not darkness, Joel validates the self-assurance of Amos's opponents. "Everyone who calls on the name of the Lord shall be saved," says Joel (3:5). It could be argued that this is not far removed from what Amos's listeners were doing: frequenting the sanctuaries, calling solemn assemblies (just as Joel 2:15 had instructed them to do), offering burnt and grain offerings, proclaiming tithes and freewill offerings, rejoicing in the knowledge that the Lord was among them and the light of his face will shine upon them eventually (Amos 4:4–5; 5:14–15, 21–23). When Amos is read in light of Joel, its ability to challenge religious hypocrisy and smugness is compromised.

It might be argued that with its hopeful conclusion, the epilogue of Amos (9:11–15) has already achieved all that, as it provides a glimmer of hope beyond the destruction. However, the message of hope in the epilogue does not subvert Amos in the same way as reading Amos in light of Joel does. It is expressed in a way that carefully reflects and develops further the proclamation of judgment. What arises out of the ashes of judgment are not the palaces of Samaria but the hut of David (Amos 9:11). That hut, as the context makes clear, is the reconstituted house of Jacob, once all the "sinners of my people" have been retained in the sieve and executed by the sword (9:8–10). That humble edifice does not validate the arrogance of the oppressors but provides further evidence that their arrogance will be broken and transformed.

CONCLUSION

In a discussion of the canonical meaning of the Book of the Twelve, John Barton makes the following observation:

> The "canonical" meanings that emerge from the various texts of the Old Testament tend to be very much the same. Not just the Book of the Twelve but all prophets emphasise, in their canonical form, the same need for Israel to be true to its heritage, to maintain its identity by adherence to the Torah, to look for restoration and salvation beyond past suffering and present destruction. ... When Childs maintains that the specificity of each Old Testament book has been deliberately blurred by the canonizing process, we can see what he means, but the

result is such a uniform message to be found in practically every book of the Bible, that we may soon cease to find the canonical approach interesting, and yearn for the variety and diversity of meanings which old-fashioned historical criticism puts us in touch with.[38]

My exploration of reading Joel within the context of the Book of the Twelve leads me to a very similar conclusion. I wish to deny neither the legitimacy of this exercise, nor a measure of usefulness to it. However, we also need to be alert to the dangers inherent within it. Connecting Joel with the other books of the Minor Prophets can blunt their message and obscure their particular contribution. By reading the newly reconstructed Book of the Twelve as a single composition we can generate new and interesting intertextual meanings, but this cannot be our only approach and it should not be our primary mode of reading. We should still retain the habit of interpreting the prophetic books on their own terms in order to appreciate their uniqueness and individuality.

---

38. J. Barton, "The Canonical Meaning of the Book of the Twelve," in *After the Exile: FS Rex Mason*, ed. J. Barton and D. J. Reimer (Macon, GA: Mercer University Press, 1996), 59–73 (71–72).

4

The Use and Abuse of Technology: Habakkuk's Ancient Critique in a Modern World

Heath A. Thomas

INTRODUCTION

Is it possible for ancient people to reflect upon the goods and ills of technology, or does such rumination betray modern interests? This study will delve into how Habakkuk explores the use and abuse of technology in its day.

Perspectives on technology and technological advances in the literature of the ancient Israelites remains a desideratum, with only a smattering of discussions here or there in this or that work. Robert Forbes's classic multi-volume work exploring different technologies in the ancient world provides an artifactual catalogue of food, clothing, metallurgy, or other advances in the ancient world. However, it does not offer sustained exploration on biblical material.[1] Where analyses do assess technology in the ancient world, they are usually accomplished with reference to the "social world" of the Hebrew Bible or to the archaeology of the ancient Near East.[2]

---

1. R. J. Forbes, *Studies in Ancient Technology*, vols. 1–9 (Leiden: Brill, 1955).
2. Recent attention has been given to the technology of writing in the ancient world and the construction of the Hebrew Bible, but more work needs to be done to assess how the ancients thought about writing as a deployment of technology itself. See, for instance, Karel van der Toorn, *Scribal Culture and the Making of the Hebrew Bible* (Cambridge, MA: Harvard University Press, 2009).

For instance, Paula McNutt and Philip King and Lawrence Stager's analyses tap the "social world" vein of research.[3] McNutt explores the ways ironworking technology influences the symbols of the Hebrew Bible, while King and Stager lay out how various technologies (farming, warfare, construction, etc.) impact the daily life presented in its pages. McNutt is right to note that far from being peripheral in human existence, "technology mediates between human beings and their world."[4] As such, the very symbols that one finds in the Hebrew Bible are mediated, in part, by technology. She demonstrates this in the Hebrew Bible with reference to symbols of ironworking technology therein. The "iron furnace" of Egypt is exemplary in this regard, encapsulating the oppression, threat, and danger of Egyptian sojourn through the symbol of "the iron furnace."[5] King and Stager's analysis fits the model of sociological research that exposes the technologies that existed in the past as they functioned then rather than a philosophical reflection on how biblical writers or communities considered technology.

That biblical literature could reflect on technology is no small assertion. One may object that intellectual contemplation on technology only applies to material culture in a postindustrialized world. But such an objection would be short-sighted. Recent Jewish explorations have identified the vast intellectual examination, even philosophical inquiry, present in the Hebrew Bible.[6] Ellen Davis rightly exposes the ways biblical writers and communities intellectually reflected upon on the built environment and agrarian shifts in the eighth century BCE.[7] If these studies have been successful, then it is not too far a stretch to find that the biblical material could offer theoretical reflection on one of the fundaments of human culture-making: technology. At the very least, McNutt's monograph reveals that metaphors and symbols provide a window into how the ancient Israelite society envisioned

---

3. Paula M. McNutt, *The Forging of Israel: Iron Technology, Symbolism and Tradition in Ancient Society*, SWBA 8 (Sheffield: Sheffield Academic, 1990); Philip J. King and Lawrence E. Stager, *Life in Biblical Israel*, LAI (Louisville: Westminster John Knox, 2001).

4. McNutt, *The Forging of Israel*, 14.

5. McNutt, *The Forging of Israel*, 213–60.

6. Classic in this regard is Henri Frankfort, H. A. Frankfort, John A. Wilson, Thorkild Jacobsen, and William A. Irwin, *The Intellectual Adventure of Ancient Man: An Essay on Speculative Thought in the Ancient Near East* (Chicago: University of Chicago Press, 1977); but see also Yoram Hazony, *The Philosophy of the Hebrew Scripture* (Cambridge: Cambridge University Press, 2012).

7. Ellen F. Davis, *Scripture, Culture, and Agriculture: An Agrarian Reading of the Bible* (Cambridge: Cambridge University Press, 2009).

technology. This essay builds upon that basic insight, though from a different stream of biblical tradition.

In a recent commentary on Habakkuk, I argued that ancient Judahite prophetic literature reflects, and reflects upon, the limits and potentialities of technological advance in its day.[8] I carry that basic insight forward in this essay by drawing together two texts that offer theoretical reflection on deployments of technological advance: warfare, fishing, and the built environment of a city. These two texts are Habakkuk 1:15–17 and 2:12–14, respectively. They center upon Babylon, which one could argue is the apogee of technological advance in the late seventh century BCE. As Bill Arnold states concerning the reign of Babylonian king Nebuchadnezzar II:

> A new Babylonian imperialism emerged in which hegemony became the means by which the king could fulfill his obligation to rebuild, refurbish, and supply Babylonia's cult centers; the king became the protector of all humanity; and the city of Babylon became the economic and administrative center of the world.[9]

This was a time of threat for the prophet Habakkuk, and these texts critique Babylonian ascendancy and imperial policy by exposing their technological advances. This essay will demonstrate that Habakkuk does not merely disagree with Babylon's imperial policy; Habakkuk exposes their technological deployments as fundamentally wanting.

The work of Jacques Ellul will provide a partner to dialogue with in this endeavor. Ellul's analysis on technology, and more specifically *technique*, stands seminal in sociological research and remains relevant to our discussion. Set in dialogue with Ellul's insights, I shall argue that Habakkuk 1:15–17 and 2:12–14 offer an ancient critique of technology; this ancient critique provides fertile soil from which to cultivate a constructive critique of our modern world, regarding bloody states, technology run amok, the judgment of God, and the hope for our future.

---

8. Heath A. Thomas, *Habakkuk*, THOTC (Grand Rapids: Eerdmans, 2018), 95–96.
9. Bill T. Arnold, *Who Were the Babylonians?* SBL Archaeology and Biblical Studies 10 (Leiden: Brill, 2004), 96.

ON FISHING: CRITIQUE OF BABYLON IN HABAKKUK 1:15-17

In what is likely a composite text, the book of Habakkuk presents reflection on how to live well before God in light of both internal apostasy from Yahweh and the external threat of the Neo-Babylonian empire. This text, likely composed against the backdrop of the Neo-Babylonian expansion into the Levant in the latter days of the seventh century BCE, critiques Babylon as a "bitter and hasty nation" (1:6) who thirsts for imperial expansion.[10] This critique is achieved in Habakkuk 1:5-17, but the primary focus will be upon verses 15-17 for the purposes of this essay. These verses sit within the two-part literary structure of Habakkuk[11] as follows:

- Oracle (Hab 1:1)
- First complaint (Hab 1:2-4)
- First divine response (Hab 1:5-11)
- Second complaint (Hab 1:12-17; 2:1)
- Second divine response (Hab 2:2-20)
- Prayer (Hab 3:1)
- Programmatic introduction (Hab 3:2)
- The divine march to Egypt (Hab 3:3-15)
- The prophet's response (Hab 3:16-19)

Habakkuk 1:15-17 is part of the prophet's second complaint, and it centers upon God's use of the Babylonians to reprove the wayward Judahites. Verses 15-17 elaborate upon the complaint mentioned in verse 14, where the prophet asks whether God has inverted the created order: "Have you made humanity like fishes of the sea, like a creeping thing, not having dominion over it?" (Hab 1:14). The prophet questions whether God would allow the world that he created to function in a way not fitting to the divine order of things. Specifically, he asks whether humanity no longer exercises dominion over the other creatures in creation (creeping things and fish), and in asking this question he rhetorically brings his complaint to God: surely the Lord would not enable such a topsy-turvy world!

The focus of the complaint is the agency of Babylon in God's plans. The idolatrous nation of Babylon is the one exercising dominion in creation

---

10. Unless otherwise noted, all Scripture quotations are the author's translation. For a full discussion on the dating and social world of Habakkuk, see Thomas, *Habakkuk*, 24-30.

11. Thomas, *Habakkuk*, 17-18.

rather than God's own people of Judah, who comprise the covenantal partner whom God would use to exercise his rule. Moreover, this idolatrous nation (whom God has raised up) pulls up the fishes (nations) from the seas (the kingdoms of the world) and gives worship to "his nets" (1:16) rather than to God, who ordained Babylon for divine reproof against God's people. Such a reality undermines divine order in the world. Habakkuk concludes with a question: "Therefore shall he empty out his dragnet, and continually slaughter nations he does not pity?" (1:17).

Embedded in his second prayer to God in Habakkuk 1, the prophet employs an image to describe the brutality of Babylon. This concept is not unknown in the material of the Old Testament/Hebrew Bible, but it is rare when compared to other images in the prophetic poetic repertoire. He uses the image of fishing.

Fishing was not a predominant industry in Israel's history, or so scholars tell us. Roland Boer indicates it was not a major aspect of Israel's economy in any phase of her history, whether early or late. Moreover, while fishing served as a significant industry in Egypt and the city-states of the Tigris-Euphrates River valley, fishing was much less developed in Israel and Judah. This is unsurprising. The only major bodies of water are in the Galilee region (Sea of Galilee) and on the coast (the Mediterranean Sea). The Jordan is a small river by any measure, and it is minuscule compared to the Nile, Tigris, or Euphrates. Therefore, it is unsurprising that fishing was not a major industry in Israel. That said, it is clear from recent archaeological data that fishing technology was known and commonly deployed on the Mediterranean coastland, and fishing was common around the Sea of Galilee. Ehud Galili, Avshalom Zemer, and Baruch Rosen show the significance of fishing in both regions, though the technology of fishing was not popular in the region of Judah in the late seventh century BCE.[12]

Its relative uniqueness in regions outside the coastland is one reason the activity stands out when it appears in Hebrew prophetic literature. The most recent exploration of fishing in the Hebrew Bible is found in Tyler Yoder's *Fishers of Fish and Fishers of Men*.[13] Yoder identifies fishing as a trope

12. Ehud Galili, Avshalom Zemer, and Baruch Rosen, "Ancient Fishing Gear and Associated Artifacts from Underwater Explorations in Israel—A Comparative Study," *Archaeofauna* 22 (2013): 145–66.
13. Tyler Yoder, *Fishers of Fish and Fishers of Men: Fishing Imagery in the Hebrew Bible and the Ancient Near East* (Winona Lake, IN: Eisenbrauns, 2016).

in the prophetic literature to project both God's judgment and divine resto-ration. Key texts that he explores that display divine judgment are: Amos 4:1-3; Habakkuk 1:14-17; Ezekiel 12:13-14; 17:16-21; 19:1-9.[14] A key text that identifies divine restoration is Ezekiel 47:1-12.[15] Significant in his work is identifying a typically foreign industry to depict God's work among his peo-ple. And key in his discussion is the text under consideration in this essay, Habakkuk 1:15-17. This paper departs from Yoder's stimulating discussion in terms of its approach and does not attempt to reconstruct the imagery or its function against an ancient Near Eastern backdrop. Rather, I explore the fishing image in Habakkuk 1 as an indicator of technology.

Habakkuk's selection of fishing tackle in verses 15-17 is striking. Galili, Zemer, and Rosen state, "Fishing methods can be classified into three major categories: 1) manual collection without tools; 2) passive fishing based on the use of natural and human-made devices that capture fish using natural fish mobility; and 3) active fishing, based on attacking aquatic creatures by human-made devices."[16] The fishing tackle of Habakkuk 1:15-17 falls into the third category, making it the most active deployment of skill and technolog-ical reflection to capture fish.

Three terms are employed to describe the active fishing envisioned: "fishhook" (חכה, 1:15), "fishnet" (חרם, 1:15-16), and "dragnet" (מכמרת, 1:15, 16, 17). A fishhook catches one fish at a time on a line. It is unclear what kind of fishhook is in view, whether a gorge, a fishhook (barbed or nonbarbed), or a weighted fishhook. Gorges, barbed and nonbarbed fishhooks, and weight-ed fishhooks have been discovered in archaeological sites around the coast near Carmel in Israel.[17] In any design, fishhooks are effective, but not as ef-ficient as a "fishnet" (חרם). This second device is not mentioned once (as with fishhook) but twice in verses 15 and 16. Fishnets are more efficient and effective than a single hook as they garner more fish while expending less time and labor for fishermen. These likely are round nets that are thrown out by one or two persons to attempt a greater catch of fish than could be ac-complished with a hook or spear. But dragnets are the most efficient of all.

---

14. Yoder, *Fishers of Fish*, 60-101.
15. Yoder, *Fishers of Fish*, 154-63.
16. Galili, Zemer, and Rosen, "Ancient Fishing Gear," 146.
17. Galili, Zemer, and Rosen, "Ancient Fishing Gear," 149-50.

The term "dragnet" (מכמרת) appears in verses 15, 16, and 17. A dragnet is composed of wide netting that could be extremely long: 750 to 1,000 feet in length, 5 feet high on the ends, and 25 feet high in the center, according to Janny de Moor.[18] A dragnet like this is not necessary for the smaller Jordan River, but for the Tigris and Euphrates Rivers and for the Nile River, dragnets would be ideal active fishing tools to scour the water table from top to bottom. Galili, Zemer, and Rosen identify nets like these as "standing nets," which are "placed like a vertical wall, stabilized by floats on top and sinkers on the bottom."[19] A large net like this would require roughly fifteen to sixteen workers to set it out into the waters and gather it back together and harvest the catch. The goal was to scour the waters at every level to empty the waters of their fish.[20] With the imagery of fishing in verses 15–17, the prophet sets on display human ingenuity, rational design, communal cooperation, and human labor to highlight the massive yield that comes from technological advancement. And as a technological advance, fishing is a good thing for it brings the maximum amount food for the maximum amount of people for a minimum amount of labor.

But we must remember that in Habakkuk's imagery, Babylon's technology is not deployed for fishing. Fishing offers a literary vehicle to carry the hearer to the reality of warfare. Fishing becomes an ironic way to introduce the technology of *death* instead of the technology of *life*. As is evident, fishing is a technological advance, and the kinds of fishing demarcated here with nets and hooks employ greater and greater efficiencies to provide life-giving food for human populations. By presenting the literary vehicle of fishing with hooks and nets, Habakkuk 1:15–17 horrifically displays how efficient humans can be: both in fishing and in warfare. Habakkuk juxtaposes image against reality: fishing gives life to human beings, but in Babylon's hands the technology of fishing for nations brings death in an ever more efficient mode of implementation. Here are the parallels between the metaphor of fishing and the reality of warfare[21] (where the sign // stands for "parallel to"):

---

18. Janny de Moor, "In the Beginning There Was Fish: Fish in the Ancient Near East," in *Fish: Food from the Waters; Proceedings of the Oxford Symposium on Food and Cookery 1997*, ed. Harlan Walker (Totnes, UK: Prospect, 1998), 85–86.

19. Galili, Zemer, and Rosen, "Ancient Fishing Gear," 147.

20. De Moor, "In the Beginning There Was Fish," 85–86.

21. Thomas, *Habakkuk*, 95.

- Fishing // warfare
- Fishermen // Babylon
- Fish // nations and peoples
- Hooks, fishnet, dragnets (life-giving) // Babylonian war tech (death-dealing)

Noonan demurs to this analysis. She argues the parallels here do not map onto the argument I advanced in verses 15–17. Rather, she plausibly purports the

> symbolism of fishing in Habakkuk 1 seems to be pointing more to the exploitation of those weaker (i.e., fish exploited by the fishermen as smaller nations are exploited by Babylon). Understood in this way, technology benefits the one using it (fishermen//Babylon), but it is damaging to those upon whom it is used (fish//smaller nations).[22]

Noonan's perspective remains sensible, and she calls this reading more "direct" than the one I have advanced.[23] However, hers does not account for the concentration of technological language of fishing, which is striking in the span of three verses: "fishhook" (חכה, 1:15), "fishnet" (חרם, 1:15–16), and "dragnet" (מכמרת, 1:15, 16, 17). Moreover, she does not account for the absence of language indicating strength and weakness. One does see the language of Babylon's strength in Habakkuk 1:11, where Babylon's "strength" (כח) is not contrasted against a weaker or smaller nation; in verse 11 Babylon's strength is equated to "his god." If the argument is to distinguish stronger/bigger Babylon from smaller/weaker nations, then one must also explain (1) why the writer avoids this language altogether in verses 15–17, (2) opts for the fishing image in verse 14, and (3) concentrates the technological language of fishing in verses 15–17. Rather than drawing a distinction between big and little or weak and strong, I argue that the poet draws attention to the tools deployed and thereby creates space to reflect upon technology as a means of human ingenuity or destruction. As implements of technology, fishing horrifically represents ever more efficient means of capture and/or death; in so doing, the prophet critiques the technology of death in Babylon's war machine.

---

22. Jennifer E. Noonan, review of *Habakkuk*, by Heath A. Thomas, *JETS* 62/1 (2019):159–60.

23. Noonan, "Review of Heath A. Thomas, *Habakkuk*," 160.

ON CITIES: THE DOOM OF BABYLON IN HABAKKUK 2:12-14

Habakkuk presents another instance to reflect upon the goods or ills of technological advance in Habakkuk 2:12-14, the third and central woe oracle in the five woe oracles from Habakkuk 2:6-20. The five woe oracles are as follows:

1. "Woe to the one who heaps up what does not belong to him." (Hab 2:6)
2. "Woe to the one who makes an evil profit for his house." (Hab 2:9)
3. "Woe to the one building a city with bloodshed." (Hab 2:12)
4. "Woe to the one causing his friend to drink." (Hab 2:15)
5. "Woe to the one saying to the wood, 'Wake up!' " (Hab 2:19)

These five oracles represent distinctive critiques of the Babylonians and announce Babylon's ultimate demise.[24] The central woe oracle interests us here, as it presents Babylon as a city founded on "bloodshed" and funded by unjust gain.

Cities, especially capital cities as grand as Babylon, stand as technological marvels of the built environment. Cities transform existing country by innovating and creating to provide protection, communal space for trade and administration, and cultural development. But the notion of the city in the Old Testament, much less in the Prophets like Habakkuk, stands as a fraught reality. Rogerson argues that the built environment of a city in the Old Testament remains "ambiguous," saying,

> The city, as referred to in the Old Testament, thus became a powerful and necessarily ambiguous symbol. As an institution that summed up human nature in all its selfishness and destructive inhumanity, it was described as being founded by Cain, who murdered his brother Abel (Gen. 4:17). As an institution which, justly and rightly governed in obedience to God, could be a blessing to humanity, it became a symbol of hope for the nations of the world (Isa.2:2-4/Mic. 4:1-4).[25]

As centers of power, administrative prestige, finance, trade, politics, and religion, cities became necessary for the quotidian functioning of ancient

---

24. For further discussion, see Thomas, *Habakkuk*, 124-33.
25. J. W. Rogerson and John Vincent, *The City in Biblical Perspective* (London: Routledge, 2009), 4.

Israel, but those who write about them remain ambivalent about their place in human culture. In his own brief study on cities in the prophetic material, Robert Carroll affirms that a study on the *topos* of the city in the biblical material would necessitate a monograph-length effort, not least due to the myriad ways the biblical material conveys the meaning of the city.[26] Recent scholarship confirms the ambiguity of cities in the Minor Prophets, whether Israelite, Judahite, or the cities of other nations.[27] That is to say, cities can be configured as positive or negative; they can be places of peace or contention; cities can be pictured as refuges or as harbors of horrors.

Our text presents the horrors of the city, namely the city of Babylon as the capital of the Neo-Babylonian empire. Habakkuk 2:12–14 reads:

> Woe to the one building a city with bloodshed,
>> And establishing a city with injustice.
> Is it not from Yahweh of the Armies:
>> That peoples have worked without profit,
>> And nations weary themselves for nothing?
> For the earth will be filled,
>> To know the glory of Yahweh
>> Like the waters cover the sea.

In our text, the city in focus is constructed with "bloodshed"[28] and founded upon "injustice." In the prophet's woe, even the cultural and technological marvel of Babylon (as grand as it may be) is doomed from the start because the city is built upon the wrong foundation. But Babylon is not the only city built upon blood.

The language of Habakkuk 2:14 finds resonance with Micah 3:10, which condemns Jerusalem's leaders for "building Zion with blood and Jerusalem with injustice." These intertextual felicities are too significant to ignore. Micah conveys a bloody city ruled by the unjust leadership of Jerusalem,

---

26. Robert P. Carroll, "City of Chaos, City of Stone, City of Flesh: Urbanscapes in Prophetic Discourses," in *"Every City Shall be Forsaken": Urbanism and Prophecy in Ancient Israel and the Near East*, ed. Lester L. Grabbe and Robert D. Haak, JSOTSup 330 (Sheffield: Sheffield Academic, 2001), 45–61 (47).

27. Aaron Schart and Jutta Krispenz, ed., *Die Stadt im Zwölfprophetenbuch*, BZAW 428 (Berlin: de Gruyter, 2012).

28. Andersen believes the proper translation of דמים is not "bloodshed" but likely "murder" as it is the plural form of the noun. See Francis I. Andersen, *Habakkuk: A New Translation with Introduction and Commentary*, AB 25 (New York: Doubleday, 2001), 243.

while Habakkuk presents Babylon as a city stained with blood. The city built on bloodshed can be contrasted with an ideal city (not present in Habakkuk but previewed in Micah 4:1-7) in which God dwells. This city is founded with God's justice and righteousness and enjoys peace and joy in every segment of society. Any other city with any other foundation is set for the divine verdict.

Who speaks this woe of verses 12-14? This woe is unique because the speaker here, in fact, may not be the oppressed nation but rather the *house* that has been defrauded and abused by Babylon. In the second woe oracle of Habakkuk 2:9-11, verse 11 concludes: "For a stone from a wall will cry out, and a beam of woodwork will respond." This is a powerful use of personification, where an inanimate object is given voice and personality. No doubt, the poet personifies the beleaguered house to initiate a cry of violence against Babylon, and the "cry" and "response" is comprised in the third woe oracle. In other words, the speaker of the third woe may be, in fact, the *stone and beam* of the oppressed house of verses 9-11.[29] In this third woe oracle the oppressed city cries out against the city of bloodshed, Babylon herself.

Habakkuk 2:13 expands upon the injustice described in verse 12. The blood and injustice that permeate the city are matched with works designed to honor the city of bloodshed. The Hebrew phrase "nations weary themselves" in verse 13 connotes heavy toil under some sort of job. One such job may be public works projects. Achtemeier posits national self-glorification at the expense of the peoples is in view here:

> That government which thinks to glorify itself by its own achievements—by establishing a city or putting up public buildings or instituting new laws or providing services—and which does so by forced and unjust measures is making its subjects labor for that which cannot last.[30]

This labor is "for nothing," as verse 13b affirms. It is "without profit," in the sense that it benefits no one. Moreover, the nations and peoples do not produce anything that lasts. A built environment founded in the manner

---

29. For discussion of the verbs used in Habakkuk 2:11, see Samuel A. Meier, *Speaking of Speaking: Marking Direct Discourse in the Hebrew Bible*, VTSup 46 (Leiden: Brill, 1992), 167-82, 209-10. Meier notes that the direct discourse markers are ambiguous in Habakkuk.

30. Elizabeth E. Achtemeier, *Nahum—Malachi*, Interpretation: A Bible Commentary for Teaching and Preaching (Louisville: Westminster John Knox, 1986), 50.

of Babylon exploits its laborers and exhausts its gain. Such a city will be as ephemeral as a mirage. And its passing will come by divine judgment: "The sympathies of Habakkuk are entirely with these victims (1:17; 2:8, 10). The implied punishment would be the burning of the bloody city."[31]

JACQUES ELLUL, *TECHNIQUE*, AND CRITIQUE

In this third section of the essay, I relate the work of Jacques Ellul to the prophetic critique of Habakkuk 1:15-17 and the city of blood mentioned in Habakkuk's third woe oracle in Habakkuk 2:12-14. Ellul's work is strangely fitting for these texts even though, as far as I am aware, Ellul did not explore Habakkuk (he did several other biblical texts), nor has secondary scholarship explored the connections between Ellul and Habakkuk. The connections made here are not fully developed in an extensive Ellulian analysis of Babylon or Judah.

Instead, this section dialogically relates Ellul's insights on technology, the built environment of the city, and his biblical analysis in various works to our text of Habakkuk. This section draws upon two of Ellul's most significant contributions:

1. Ellul's concept of *technique* and its relevance to fishing and war in Habakkuk 1.
2. Ellul's concept of the built environment as the center for *technique* and its relevance to Babylon in Habakkuk 2.

From these insights, the text of Habakkuk provides an ancient critique on technology that may speak to the modern world.

Jacques Ellul was a sociologist in the past century, whose major contribution was the study of what he and others call *technique*. His eye turned to the modern world and envisaged a radical shift underway in the twentieth century. Namely, he saw something he identified as *technique* in the modern world, and *technique* dominated his society in a way unprecedented in any age that had gone before. For Ellul, *technique* is "the totality of methods rationally arrived at and having absolute efficiency ... in every field of human activity."[32] Technology and machines cannot be reduced to the broader concept of *technique* but should be understood as deployments of the reality

---

31. Andersen, *Habakkuk*, 242-43.

32. Jacques Ellul, *The Technological Society* (New York: Alfred Knopf, 1964), xxv; see also 73-74.

of *technique*. For Ellul, technology is any method or practice which humans rationally enact to maximize efficiency. So, specific deployments of technology or machines are extensions of *technique*.

Ellul argues that *technique* is one of the fundaments (if not *the* fundament) of human society. And *technique* has a history. From a sociological lens, Ellul charts the history of *technique* from the primitive world to the modern world. To be clear, our text in Habakkuk—which derives from the ancient Near East—fits into what Ellul calls a "primitive" period of *technique*. In this phase of the story of *technique*, humanity deployed technique in two primary areas: invention and magic.[33] Both were aimed at achieving efficiencies and results: "Technique is essentially Oriental: it was principally in the Near East that technique first developed, and it had very little in the way of scientific foundation. It was entirely directed toward practical application and was not concerned with general theories."[34] Ellul cites fishing, hunting, warfare, and invention as basic in primitive society.

Fishing and warfare, as we see them in Habakkuk 1:15–17, are deployments of *technique*. For the enterprise of fishing, efficiency means exercising the technology of hooks and nets. Dragging the rivers and seas with nets indicates an advanced level of technology beyond that of fishing with spears or harpoons precisely because of their increased efficiency, according to Janny de Moor.[35] Fishermen belonged to special guilds in Egypt and Mesopotamia, and de Moor provocatively asserts that fishing techniques were known technological advances prior to the invention of writing.[36] So fishing with implements (beyond one's bare hands) represents a great technological advance. This is more significant because fishing was not a major industry in Judah at the time of Habakkuk's prophecy, as we have seen. The prophet uses a technological advance from the Neo-Babylonian empire to make a point about the horror of the Neo-Babylonian war machine. In Habakkuk's image, Babylon's great failure is that their use of technology is death-dealing and does not accord with God's order of creation.

33. Ellul, *The Technological Society*, 23–28.
34. Ellul, *The Technological Society*, 27.
35. De Moor, "In the Beginning," 85–86.
36. De Moor, "In the Beginning," 85. See also the comprehensive analysis of Galili, Zemer, and Rosen, "Ancient Fishing Gear," 145–66.

THE USE AND ABUSE OF TECHNOLOGY

One of the great insights of Ellul's exploration on *technique* is that the Christian faith has *always* adjudicated the use of technology in terms of its justice and righteousness. Ellul states:

> Technical activity did not escape Christian moral judgment. The question, "Is it righteous?" was asked of every attempt to change modes of production or organization. That something might be useful or profitable to men did not make it right and just. It had to fit a precise conception of justice before God.[37]

I would take this point further and extend it backward to the prophetic witness of the Hebrew Bible. Habakkuk clearly does not embrace Babylon, precisely because their use of technology brings death and is unjust, at least by his reckoning. In this way, Habakkuk critiques technology that brings death instead of life.

It is fascinating, and no doubt intentional, that the prophet immediately links Babylon's misdirection of technology toward death with idolatry. The third woe oracle concludes with the futility of idolatry in verse 16: "Therefore he will sacrifice to his dragnet, and he will sacrifice to his fishnet." Upon closer inspection, Babylon's worship is not to their "nets" as much as what these fishing tools represent: the technology of war and the devastation it yields.

Habakkuk's critique of technology in his day becomes a resource for us to reflect upon technology, and its use, in the modern world. Technology can be productive or destructive. Habakkuk recognizes the benefits of technology even while using it to launch his critique, and this is why the discordance between fishing and fighting is so palpable in the image of Babylonians as fishermen. Habakkuk's image does not allow the interpreter to long for a return to a pristine, technologically free society. Fishing brings good, food, and life. But technology *misdirected* in destructive and sinful ways is surely death. The image of Babylonians as fishermen draws us to reflect upon how humans ought to deliberate (as much as we can) on the technologies we employ so we can direct them toward vitality and human flourishing. Without adequate reflection or adequate care, in the normal order of things, technology can go the way of Babylon.

---

37. Ellul, *The Technological Society*, 37.

It would be tempting to understand the prophet's critique as focusing upon war and the technological advances of war. Daniel Berrigan does just that as he explores the corrupt actions of Babylon in Habakkuk 1:12–14. He argues that the poet shifts his gaze to the *true* sin that marks Babylon: "uncontrollable crime, evil that is even rendered virtuous 'for reasons of the state' (crimes of war that is, liable as they are in principle to international law, but falling cunningly through the interstices of the net)—such crimes biblically understood, invariably imply—idolatry."[38] Berrigan sees in Habakkuk's complaint a critique of war (perhaps he allows a focus on the technology of war), and war remains the great evil.

Berrigan is right to highlight the emphasis upon war as an evil of the Neo-Babylonian imperial agenda, but there certainly is more here. The critique is sharper. Habakkuk critiques a deeper root as well: the *misdirection* of technology. Relating Habakkuk's emphasis upon the technology of war/ fishing to Ellul's thought, we see Babylon as embodying *technique* toward its own ends. Babylon's imperial war machine stands as horrifically efficient and effective in its production, but due to the oppression it creates, it is doomed to fail. Babylon's technological deployment perverted toward a goal without adequate theological, social, or ethical reflection stands as a call to the various deployments of technology today as well.

It is also notable how Ellul illumines the very concept of the city explored in Habakkuk 2. In his seminal work *The Meaning of the City*, Ellul addresses not the physicality of the city or city-life as it were. Rather, he explores what a city *represents* as an outworking of *technique*, a locus of human ingenuity and social progress. In *The Search for Ethics in a Technicist Society*, Ellul makes explicit the connection between the city and *technique*. He says:

> Technique is the complex and complete milieu in which human beings must live, and in relation to which they must define themselves. It is a universal mediator, producing a generalised mediation, totalizing and aspiring to totality. The concrete example of this is the city. The city is the place where technique excludes all forms of natural reality. Apart from the city, the only choices left are either the urbanization of rural areas, or "desertification" (nature then being submitted to a technical exploitation controlled by a very small number of people).

---

38. Daniel Berrigan, *Minor Prophets, Major Themes* (Eugene, OR: Wipf & Stock, 2009), 288.

This emphasizes again that technique is really the Milieu in which modern humanity is placed.[39]

In this quote, what is interesting is the way Ellul connects technique to the city. The built environment of the city culminates as the locus of technique and technique becomes the only form of life that is viable within the city.

The city is, for Ellul, the location of civilization and all that it represents, namely a revolution for self and sin. Rogerson's insight that the biblical material presents the city as "ambiguous" takes on a deeper significance in Ellul's thought. Ellul understands the story of the city originating in the primeval history (Gen 1–11), progressing through the primary history (Genesis-Kings), meandering through the Prophets, culminating in the larger biblical canon, and climaxing in the book of Revelation. Ellul links the "builders" of the city as the people of Cain, from Genesis 4 and Cain's movement eastward from Eden and building cities. His point is clear: *the built environment of the city is, in the biblical material, an instance of a fallen world*. He says:

> Cain takes possession of the world and uses it as he wishes, with the goal in mind that we have already indicated. Cain creates the art of craftsmanship. He carves stones and thereby makes them impure, unfit for use in an altar of God (Ex. 20:25). It is man's high-handed piracy of creation that makes creation incapable of giving glory to God. Cain bends all of creation to his will. … He forces creation to follow his destiny, his destiny of slavery and sin, and his revolt to escape from it. From his taking possession, from this revolution, the city is born.[40]

The story of the city is, for Ellul, a story of humanity's revolt against God only to be swallowed by their own machinations. Interesting for our analysis is the fact that Ellul traces the built environment of the city from Babel (Gen 11) to Babylon; and Babylon/Babel becomes the paradigmatic locus of humanity turned against God. Thus, city-building as an expression of technique—the apogee of technique—becomes a resource to reflect upon the

---

39. Jacques Ellul, "The Search for Ethics in a Technicist Society," *Journal of Research and Philosophy and Technology* 9 (1989): 23–36 (as elsewhere 23); originally published as "Recherche pour une Ethique dans une société technicienne," in *Éthique et Technique*, ed. Gilbert Hottois (Brussels: Éditions de l'Universite de Bruxelles, 1983), 7–20.
40. Jacques Ellul, *The Meaning of the City* (Grand Rapids: Eerdmans, 1970), 6–7.

world turned against God: "Let us build a tower so that we might be like God" (Gen 11:4). Ellul says: "So all that is said about Babylon can be applied to every other city, to today's cities even more than to any cities known by the seer [John]."[41] For Ellul, the city of Babylon is not neutral or even ambiguous. Rather, the city of Babylon, the zenith of *technique*, stands unredeemable, at least in human hands. There is no healing of its disease. Rather, he argues that the built environment of Babylon stands under God's curse and, therefore, is doomed. Babylon is doomed precisely because "into every aspect, therefore, of the city's construction has been built the tendency to exclude God."[42] It is only God's irruption in history, God's radical instantiation of new creation, that provides healing for the built environment of the city. For Ellul, Jesus is the founder of that city. For the Old Testament prophets, Zion is that city, and it is built by God (see Mic 4).

In light of Ellul's comments on the city, one takes a fresh look at Babylon in the third woe oracle in Habakkuk 2. This woe envisions Babylon as a depraved city of bloodshed whose deployment of *technique* has come to its logical end: it has created a city of violence, bloodshed, and futility. That ancient city, set in dialogue with Ellul, can be related to our cities. Despite the medical, social, scientific, and military advances in our age, for much of the world, the twentieth century was a time of bloodshed unprecedented in any age. The twenty-first century is on pace to match the previous age. The modern world embodies the city of Babylon in Ellul's thought.

Yet built environments of the city—in ancient or modern times—do not sit outside the control of God, as Habakkuk 2:14 reminds us. God's power still reigns supreme: "For the earth will be filled to know the glory of the LORD, like the waters cover the sea" (Hab 2:14). Habakkuk 2:14 contrasts the city of death, doomed to fail, with another city, a better one where death will be no more. This verse resonates with Isaiah 11:9, which depicts an eschatological context of restoration where there will be no more harm on the mountain-city of God. But for Habakkuk, the downfall of Babylon equates to God's glory being revealed in the earth. The fall of Babylon creates space, under the direction of God, where a new city will emerge—a city where evil will be set to rights. This verse provides the surety that divine vindication will take place.

---

41. Ellul, *Meaning of the City*, 50.
42. Ellul, *Meaning of the City*, 53.

CONCLUSION

In this brief essay I have offered a reflection on two texts in Habakkuk that are thought to be disparate: Habakkuk 1:15–17 and 2:12–14. These texts reflect upon Babylon, but I also drew upon what Jacques Ellul identifies as *technique*. It has been demonstrated that Habakkuk reflects upon the use and abuse of technology through a sophisticated reflection on fishing/city imagery and through the built environment of the city. Ellul's insights on technology and *technique* provide further avenues to explore the ancient Judahite rumination on the goods and ills, the use and abuse, of technology, both in their day and ours.

5

Luther's Lectures on Habakkuk as an Example of Participatory Exegesis

Thomas Renz

MARTIN LUTHER AS BIBLICAL SCHOLAR

It is sometimes thought that the determination of Martin Luther and other Reformers to free the interpretation of Holy Scripture from church authority and tradition started the process which unfolded as historical-critical research of the Bible.[1] This is debatable, given that historical-critical research was arguably shaped by the Enlightenment more than the Reformation.[2] Nevertheless, Luther was apparently the first to devote his academic lectures exclusively to biblical exegesis and, therefore, could be seen as making the first step toward establishing biblical studies as an independent discipline.[3] And yet today his exegesis garners more interest from historians and theologians than biblical scholars. The latter, by and large, do not expect there to be much to learn from exegesis that is half a millennium old. This has been true also for me. Having worked on Habakkuk for many years, I have only recently begun to ask whether there are things to be learned by

---

1. E.g., Hans-Joachim Kraus, *Geschichte der historisch-kritischen Erforschung des Alten Testaments* (Neukirchen-Vluyn: Neukirchener Verlag, 1988), 3.
2. See, e.g., Michael C. Legaspi, *The Death of Scripture and the Rise of Biblical Studies* (Oxford: Oxford University Press, 2010).
3. See Stefan Felber, " 'Hoc est in Christo ad literam factum': Realistische Schriftauslegung bei Martin Luther," in *Auslegung und Hermeneutik der Bibel in der Reformationszeit*, ed. Christine Christ-von Wedel and Sven Grosse, Historia Hermeneutica 14 (Berlin: de Gruyter, 2016): 69–110 (72).

engaging with Luther's exegesis of this prophetic writing. Martin Luther delivered lectures on Habakkuk from July 18th to August 2nd in 1525. They are known to us through student scripts in two versions.[4] Luther himself then published a German text in June 1526 for a wider readership.[5] He felt the need to make his explanation more widely known, because he believed that Habakkuk had not been clearly understood since the time of the apostles. Luther considered a knowledge of Hebrew essential for understanding the prophecy and claimed that the few in the past who had the requisite knowledge of Hebrew had not had the time and leisure to write on Habakkuk (LW 19:151).[6]

Luther was a reasonably competent Hebraist, but he did, of course, have to work with the knowledge and resources available five hundred years ago and much the same might be said about his knowledge of ancient history. In his sometimes scornful remarks about the Septuagint, e.g., on Habakkuk 1:5 (LW 19:110), Luther shows a readiness to break with church tradition, if need be,[7] but not the critical acumen to develop proper textual criticism. If biblical scholarship is philology only, then the progress made since Luther's days means that we may look at his commentary in much the same way he himself looked at medieval commentaries on Habakkuk. We would not expect to gain any new insights into Hebrew semantics or syntax from Martin Luther, nor into textual criticism or ancient history. But for Luther there is more to biblical interpretation than philological exegesis. Using Walter

---

4. *D. Martin Luthers Werke: Kritische Gesamtausgabe* (Weimar: Hermann Böhlau, 1883ff.). Vol. 13: *Praelectiones in prophetas minores 1524-1526*. The two different versions are found, e.g., at WA 13:424-48 (based on the Altenburg manuscript) and WA 13:395-423 (based on the Zwickau manuscript, with notes from a manuscript from Halle).

5. A Latin translation of the German work was available in August 1526. The German text is published, e.g., in WA 19:337-435. An English translation of WA 13:424-448 and WA 19:337-435 is found in *Lectures on the Minor Prophets II (Jonah, Habakkuk)*, vol. 19 of *Luther's Works*, ed. Hilton C. Oswald, trans. Charles D. Froehlich (from the Latin) and Martin H. Bertram (from the German) (Saint Louis: Concordia, 1974). My citations are from this American edition (LW 19), unless indicated otherwise.

6. Cf. WA 19:349-50. The 19th century editor, Joachim Karl Friedrich Knaake comments that Luther had probably no knowledge of the recent commentaries by Franz Lambert (1525) and Wolfgang Fabricius Capito (1526). We may add that he also shows no appreciation here for Jerome or Nicholas of Lyra.

7. Note that Jerome, who like Luther comments on the *hebraica veritas*, is nevertheless respectful of the Septuagint and uses it for exploring spiritual meanings. On Jerome's competence, see Michael Graves, *Jerome's Hebrew Philology: A Study Based on His Commentary on Jeremiah*, Vigiliae Christianae Supplements 90 (Leiden: Brill, 2007).

Moberly's working definition of theological interpretation, we may say that Luther reads "the Bible with a concern for the enduring truth of its witness to the nature of God and humanity, with a view to enabling the transformation of humanity into the likeness of God."[8] Luther engages with the subject of the text in ways that may still be of use today for readers who are concerned with ultimate truth. I call such an exegesis by interpreters who believe themselves to be participating in the realities to which the text bears witness "participatory exegesis."

PARTICIPATORY EXEGESIS

The term "participatory exegesis" is borrowed from the work of Matthew Levering,[9] one of a number of scholars who have recently been urging Christians to recover realist, Neo-Platonic metaphysics.[10] Levering argues that our interpretation of Scripture is shaped by our view of what "history" is, and he notes changes in the predominant metaphysics and hermeneutics away from realism beginning in the high Middle Ages. Early and medieval Christians, he argues, understood history as a process that participates in God's creative and redemptive presence as well as a set of linear moments. Later a nominalist metaphysics and a concept of history which considers it solely a set of linear moments distanced the interpreter from the realities of the text. In view of Levering's discussion, it may be controversial to speak of Luther as engaging in participatory exegesis. Luther was, after all, a nominalist, schooled by William of Ockham and Gabriel Biel,[11] and, as noted above, was rather dismissive of those who commented on Habakkuk before him. Yet I consider the term apt to contrast the kind of exegesis in which

---

8. Cited from R. W. L. Moberly, "What Is Theological Interpretation of Scripture?," *JTI* 3 (2009): 161–78 (163).

9. *Participatory Biblical Exegesis: A Theology of Biblical Interpretation* (Notre Dame: University of Notre Dame Press, 2008); "Principles of Exegesis: Toward a Participatory Biblical Exegesis," *Pro Ecclesia* 17 (2008): 35–51.

10. Cf. Francis Martin, "Revelation as Disclosure: Creation," in *Wisdom and Holiness, Science and Scholarship: Essays in Honor of Matthew L. Lamb*, ed. Michael Dauphinais and Matthew Levering (Naples, FL: Sapientia Press, 2007), 205–47; Hans Boersma, *Scripture as Real Presence: Sacramental Exegesis in the Early Church* (Grand Rapids: Baker Academic, 2017).

11. Heiko A. Oberman, *Man between God and the Devil* (New Haven: Yale University Press, 2006), 122. See also his *The Harvest of Medieval Theology: Gabriel Biel and Late Medieval Nominalism* (Grand Rapids: Baker Academic, 2000). References taken from Joshua Lim's essay "Post Tenebras Lux?: Nominalism and Luther's Reformation" on the Called to Communion blog, http://www.calledtocommunion.com/2014/01/post-tenebras-lux.

Luther, nevertheless, still engages with the ideal of a more detached exegesis within biblical scholarship shaped by the Enlightenment. If Luther's exegesis is in fact more medieval than modern in this respect, the question arises whether Levering is wrong to believe that a realist metaphysics is required to underpin this sort of exegesis or whether Luther was an inconsistent nominalist who engages in a form of exegesis that presumes a realist metaphysics.[12] I am not going to pursue this question. To answer it would require closer attention to the differences between Luther's exegesis and that of many of his predecessors, while I am here more interested in the differences between his exegesis and that of many of his successors— scholars who live on the other side of Lessing's "ugly broad ditch" which distances text and interpreter. Luther does not see history as getting in the way between him and the text but sees himself participating in the same history of God with his people and, in this sense, he engages in participatory exegesis.

The difference between this older and the more common contemporary approach can be compared to the one in social anthropology between a research strategy (emic) that relies on immersion in a culture, seeking the native viewpoint and describing motivations and results from within the culture analyzed, and a research strategy (etic) that relies on external criteria of significance, describing a culture from an outside observer's point of view, using external criteria to describe reasons and results of behavior and beliefs.[13] The objection that such a distinction cannot be validly transposed into biblical exegesis because we do not have access to native informers in the form of Babylonian or Persian period inhabitants of Judah and Jerusalem arguably assumes that the reality to which the biblical text belongs is "history" understood as a distant point in a line of events. Such an objection would, therefore, support Levering's claim that our view of history is very much a key point of contention. But I am appealing to the emic/etic distinction only as an analogy, which need not be exact to be of use. The distinction I have in mind can also be seen in literary studies generally. Regardless of any metaphysical questions involved, it seems clear

---

12. Felber does in fact speak of Luther's "Realistische Schriftauslegung," but he does not address the question of the relationship between metaphysics and exegesis.

13. In practice the emic and etic research strategies are not always easily separated, but the distinction is nevertheless heuristically useful. We find a similar blurring of lines in different approaches to biblical exegesis.

that a poem such as Sonnet X ("Death Be Not Proud") by John Donne can be examined in a detached way, analyzing its technical aspects and historical setting, paying attention to rhythm, lexical choices, imagery, etc., including the publication history and reception of the poem. Or "Death Be Not Proud" can be read, inhabited, and interpreted by someone who is suffering from a major, life-threatening illness or lives with someone who is succumbing to such an illness. I expect that most would grant that such a subjective experience of the themes of the poem can offer insights. Indeed, even if the illness of the interpreter were a figment of their imagination, this "false" experience could still yield insights. Furthermore, whether or not the interpreter believes in the resurrection, the poet did, and a full appreciation of the poem is arguably helped by imaginatively entering this thought-world for a while. Belief in the resurrection and an existential encounter with death do not necessarily make someone a superior interpreter of Donne's work; they certainly cannot substitute for the philological expertise required in addressing several questions about the text. But interpreters who are concerned with the subjects of the poem—such as death, resurrection, and faith—are likely to benefit from paying attention to readers who have immersed themselves in the poem as users, especially if these users also have decent technical skills. I want to argue that this is the case for Luther's engagement with Habakkuk. Luther had philological concerns, but he also came to the biblical text with a strong belief that he would encounter through the text of Habakkuk the very God he believed the prophet had encountered. In this essay I want to focus on a few examples that show Luther as a reader who engages in exegesis as a participant (someone who brings his knowledge of God and the world to bear), rather than an outside observer who seeks to bracket out questions of truth or who comes to the text with the belief that there is no god corresponding to the character Yahweh in the biblical text. I hope to show both the pitfalls and the opportunities of such an exegesis.

EXAMPLES FROM LUTHER'S LECTURES ON HABAKKUK

HABAKKUK THE PREACHER

What is going on in Habakkuk 1? Along with several contemporary exegetes, I read Habakkuk 1 as a single complaint to God that references an earlier divine oracle.[14] The complaint focuses on injustice within Judah and Jerusalem in the wake of Babylonian imperialism. Others believe that 1:2–4 are exclusively concerned with internal corruption to which the rise of the Babylonians provides a response. The chapter is then read as a dialogue between the prophet and God. An initial complaint about evil within Judah in 1:2–4 finds a reply in 1:5–11 which is followed in 1:12–17 by a further complaint, this time about the Babylonian invasion. In many ways this more common dialogical reading is also how Luther takes the chapter. He argues specifically against Jerome, who believes the violence spoken of in 1:2–4 is Babylonian.[15] Jerome even allows for the possibility that the prophet was active only after the destruction of the temple. Luther argues that "Habakkuk ... prophesied before the Babylonian captivity," announcing first to the two remaining tribes of Israel "that their destruction is coming" and then the destruction of the Babylonian king himself (LW 19:107).[16] He believes that the reason for Jerome's later date lies in his acceptance of the apocryphal story that has Habakkuk bring food to Daniel. But Jerome is, in fact, not committed to reading Bel and the Dragon as a historical account and does allow for the possibility that Habakkuk was written before the destruction of the temple. Even so, Jerome sees Habakkuk as responding— possibly in anticipation of future events—to the Babylonian conquest of Judah. Luther is convinced that this is wrong. He argues from the reference to seeing a מַשָּׂא in Habakkuk 1:1 that the punishment is future rather than present, threatened rather than actual (LW 19:157–58), and from the law-court language in 1:4 that the concern must be with Judean injustice because the Babylonians settled matters with weapons rather than laws (LW 19:109). I am not convinced that either of these points is as decisive as Luther thinks, but I agree with him that the prophet does not look upon his own nation as a victim only, and this is the relevant point here. What is intriguing is how Luther identifies the exact nature of the complaint.

---

14. For a detailed discussion see my NICOT commentary, *The Books of Nahum, Habakkuk, and Zephaniah* (Grand Rapids: Eerdmans, 2021), 235–39.

15. See Jerome, "Commentary on Habakkuk: Translated and Annotated by Thomas Scheck," in *Commentaries on the Twelve Prophets*, vol. 1, ed. Thomas Scheck (Downers Grove: IVP Academic, 2016), 185–243 (186).

16. In introducing chapter 2 in his Latin lectures, Luther comments, "Habakkuk's prophetic activity covered the periods before, during, and after the Babylonian captivity. Or, if someone prefers, in the prophetic manner he described as past or as now present things that were still in the future" (LW 19:119).

In Habakkuk 1:2 Luther hears the prophet's complaints as: "I do not stop shouting, preaching, and showing the people their wickedness" (LW 19:108) and in Habakkuk 1:3 he hears Habakkuk say, "What is this? Why have you sent me to preach? I do not improve them; they do not come to their senses, and so I am forced to see only miseries and calamities while I preach for nothing so long as they in blindness persist in their character. I see nothing but grief and disaster" (LW 19:108–9). The prophet "serves notice that he has preached very passionately and has taken great pains to correct the people but this has borne no fruit" and "that he was deeply concerned and worried about the people because of their future punishment and burden. He would like to save them and avert all of this" (LW 19:158). But "he is growing tired and weary of preaching" (LW 19:159).

In other words, the complaint is not simply about wickedness and injustice but about the failure of prophetic preaching to make a difference. If we suspect that Luther's own experience is shining through here, we are probably not mistaken. In fact, Luther states explicitly: "That is the experience of every godly preacher who is so eager to avert punishment from his people and to make them godly. When he sees that he is not progressing in this but that conditions are, as it were, growing worse, he almost despairs of his preaching" (LW 19:159).[17] Luther believes that Habakkuk's experience is both comforting and a challenge to preachers like him. But does his own experience lead him to overread the text? At first it certainly looks as if Luther was reading into the text something that simply is not there. Habakkuk explicitly laments God's lack of responsiveness to the prophet's prayers, not the people's lack of response to the prophet's preaching. There is no reference to the latter. But there may be more to Luther's argument than first meets the eye. Luther says he finds it everywhere in Scripture that "when God is about to punish a wicked nation, He sends his prophets ahead to smite them" (LW 19:108). If there is a prophecy of destruction, preaching against wickedness must have preceded it. It is inconceivable for Luther that a prophet would pray and complain to God about evil within the people of God without also having preached to the people about this. So, the "prophecy of destruction"

---

17. Luther preached regularly from 1512 until shortly before his death. Around 2,300 of his sermons are still available. During his thirty-four years of preaching in Wittenberg Luther averaged seventy sermons per year. In the year 1528 alone, he preached nearly two hundred times across Germany.

in 1:5-11 *must* have been preceded by "preaching against wickedness." In a sense, Claus Westermann's *Basic Forms of Prophetic Speech* makes a similar claim in stressing the relationship between rationale and announcement of punishment.[18] If 1:5-11 are understood as an announcement of punishment, it stands to reason that preaching preceded it. Indeed, not a few composition-critical proposals suggest that parts of Habakkuk 2 were originally sermons directed against Judah.[19] So the idea that the ineffectiveness of his preaching lies behind the prophet's complaint is worth considering, especially by those who read Habakkuk 1 as a dialogue.

But Luther takes it a step further. He stresses that while the verses give the impression of a prophet "quarrelling with God" and "chiding Him," what is really going on is that "he wishes to frighten the people and move them to repent" by rebuking them for their transgressions (LW 19:158). This also applies to 1:12-17. "The prophet pleads with God to confine Himself to the punishment and not let the Jewish people perish completely" (LW 19:178). But in doing so the prophet "reproves the sins of the blasphemers, rebuking them and comforting his own people," as the prayer reassures him and his people that there is only one true God against whom no other gods can accomplish anything (LW 19:177). Thus, by his own example of prayer the prophet publicly demonstrates "how faith lives amid trials and temptations [*Anfechtung*]" (LW 19:179). The prophet gives voice to "a faith engaged in struggle [*Kampfglauben*],"[20] as someone who himself was hurt and who experienced the weakness of being tempted to think that God is not just (LW 19:180). Luther finds other examples of such prayer in Jeremiah 12 and Psalm 73. While Luther does not altogether deny that the chapter can function as

---

18. This classic work of form criticism was first published in English in 1967 and again in 1991 (Cambridge: Lutterworth Press; Louisville: Westminster John Knox Press). The original *Grundformen prophetischer Rede* had been published in Munich by the Chr. Kaiser Verlag in 1960, 1964, and then 1978.

19. This was argued in particular by Eckhart Otto, "Die Stellung der Wehe-Worte in der Verkündigung des Propheten Habakuk," *ZAW* 89 (1977): 73-106. See also Walter Dietrich, *Nahum Habakkuk Zephaniah* (Stuttgart: Kohlhammer, 2016), 98-103, and Heinz-Josef Fabry, *Habakuk/Obadja* (Freiburg im Breisgau: Herder, 2018), 251-53, 261. In my view, it is rhetorically significant that the Babylonian empire is condemned in language that is applicable also to wrongdoing on other levels. For more, see *Nahum, Habakkuk, and Zephaniah*, 302-3.

20. The phrase is used several times. Bertram translates *Kampfglaube* as "struggling faith," which may convey the idea of faith growing weaker. Luther's *Kampfglaube* seems to be faith that is struggling in the sense of being actively engaged in combat. Note that already Jerome had referred to Habakkuk as engaging God in battle and struggle.

a prayer, he reads it as preaching. René Magritte's iconic 1929 painting "The Treachery of Images" ("Ceci n'est pas une pipe") comes to mind; the portrayal of a pipe is not a pipe. Habakkuk 1 may well have originated in prayer and depicts prayer, but the intended readership of the written text is not God; it is not a votive text. Nor is Habakkuk 1 explicitly given to others as a prayer to be used, unlike Habakkuk 3 which is given the "Psalter treatment," as it were, with the use of *Selah* and reference to the music director and instruments. Luther draws our attention to the fact that what looks like a prayer may fulfill a different function, including to rebuke evildoers and "to strengthen and console the people as well as himself" (LW 19:182).

It is noteworthy that while contemporary devotional readings of Habakkuk 1 tend to invite imitation of the prophet's prayer,[21] there is a strong tradition within early Christian exegesis, and perhaps Jewish exegesis,[22] to create some distance between the reader and the prayer. Habakkuk is described as impatient with God (e.g., Gregory of Nazianzus, Oration 2) and Jerome suggests the prophet "is expressing human impatience under his own persona" in a way that may be compared to the apostle Paul's "adopting for himself the various thoughts of men" in Romans 7:23.[23] In the same way Theodoret of Cyrus is convinced that Habakkuk presents the views of others, exposing the plight of those who are doubting before presenting a solution.[24] While Luther did not go down that route, he, too, does not read Habakkuk 1 as offering a model for prayer. Instead, he focuses on what readers are expected to learn from overhearing the prayer. It is interesting that most of the early editions of his German lectures came with a frontispiece depicting the prophet giving witness before king and people (i.e., preaching rather than praying).[25] It is presumably the same picture that was used in the 1545 edition of the Bible.

---

21. E.g., Martin Goldsmith, *Any Complaints? Blame God! God's Message for Today—Habakkuk the Prophet Speaks* (Milton Keynes: Authentic, 2008), who writes, "As Christians we are given a model which allows us to join the prophet in questioning what God is doing in our lives and in the world around us" (20).

22. James D. Nogalski, *The Book of the Twelve: Micah-Malachi*, Smith & Helwys Bible Commentary 18b (Macon: Smyth & Helwys, 2011), 646, claims that "in rabbinic tradition, at least two texts [*Tehillim* 90:385 and *Ta'anit* 23a] demonstrate some level of discomfort with the powerful confrontation of YHWH by the prophet."

23. Jerome, "Habakkuk," 195–96.

24. Theodoret of Cyrus, *Commentary on the Twelve Prophets*, vol. 3 of *Commentaries on the Prophets*, trans. Robert Charles Hill (Brookline, MA: Holy Cross Orthodox Press, 2006), 191–92.

25. See WA 19:337–39 for information on these first editions.

TextGrid Repository (2012), Martin Luther, Luther-Bibel 1545, Digitale Bibliothek, http://images.zeno.org/Literatur/I/big/lb21633a.jpg.

It looks suspiciously like Luther giving evidence before the Diet in Worms.[26] It also stands in marked contrast to the pictures used in German Bibles before Luther, e.g., the one used in black and white in the 1477 Zainer Bibel and in color in the 1480 Sorg Bibel which depict the prophet praying to Christ in the midst of violence and bloodshed (see on the following page).

26. "Die aus dem Bibeltext nicht zu entnehmende Szene erinnert an Luthers Auftreten vor dem Wormser Reichstag. Links neben dem König ein Geistlicher mit einer zusammengefalteten Urkunde, rechts und links im Vordergrund fürstliche Personen, links im Hintergrund berittene Lanzenreiter. In den Wolken Gott und Christus," http://www.zeno.org/Literatur/I/lb21633a.

Snippet of an image digitized by the MDZ of the Bayerische Staatsbibiothek, http://daten.digitale-sammlungen.de/bsb00026205/image_346.

The next example arguably shows how narrowly pursuing this perspective leads to a misreading of the text.

HABAKKUK THE WATCHMAN

A watchman is someone who stands on a sure foundation from where he can notice an enemy approach and so readies himself to defend the people. This is how Luther interprets Habakkuk 2:1. The sure foundation is God's word and the fight is against unbelief. Thus Luther sees Habakkuk 2:1 as a good example of how the prophet's faith (*Kampfglauben*) struggles not only for himself, holding on to faith in God in the face of Babylonian successes and excesses (in punishing Judah), but also against the unbelief of his people to comfort and strengthen them. In his lectures, Luther, unremarkably, interprets מַה־יְדַבֶּר־בִּי with reference to what God will reveal to the prophet. The critical phrase is the following, וּמָה אָשִׁיב עַל־תּוֹכַחְתִּי which he reads as: "And what I will answer him who chides me" (LW 19:191). Interpreting the suffix in תּוֹכַחְתִּי as indicating the target of the activity implied by the noun ("the complaint against me") rather than its source ("my complaint") is not uncommon. Unusually, however, Luther interprets the singular as generic and identifies not God but Habakkuk's opponents as the authorial voice of the complaint. In his Latin lectures he even used the plural,[27] translated by Froelich with "those complaining against me" (LW 19:120). He comments, "On this word depends the chief point and purpose of this whole chapter. For he is fighting, as I said, against the tongues of doubters who thought that the kingdom was now done for, since the city had been burned, the kingdom had been destroyed, and they themselves had been led into captivity. Therefore, they were accusing the prophets of lying, those prophets who had promised them that the kingdom would be safe, etc." (LW 19:120).

We may find this comment odd, given that Habakkuk did not come across in chapter 1 as a prophet who promised "that the kingdom would be safe." The German work clarifies what Luther had in mind. While many biblical scholars today think the eschatological hope of a faithful David ruling over a prosperous and peaceful Jerusalem is a later development, Luther is convinced "that all the prophets direct their prophecies primarily toward Christ" (LW 19:152), even if they also "pronounce many prophecies that pertained only to their own time and served only their time" and "interspersed prophecies regarding heathen kingdoms and principalities." Yet "all this has been done to train the Jewish people and to prepare them for the advent of Christ" (LW 19:153).[28] This (general, prophetic) vision did not preclude punishment and misfortune in the short term, but a disaster on the scale brought about by the Babylonians seemed to call the vision into question. "For how could God have initiated Christ's promised kingdom more foolishly and strangely than by having Jerusalem, where His kingdom was to be, destroyed by ungodly scorners and by His enemies and while He had His own people led away into exile?" (LW 19:190). How God's work is an affront to reason is a favorite theme of Luther's, and he points to Jeremiah 32 as "a true commentary on this" (LW 19:190), encapsulated in verses 24-25. "For that is what

27. Altenburg: *increpantes me*. Zwickau: *vobis calumniantibus et increpantibus*. Interestingly, the German translation of these Latin manuscripts in the Walch edition (Vorreden. - *Historische und philologische Schriften. - Auslegung des Alten Testaments* [Schluß.], vol. 14 of Dr. Martin Luthers *Sämmtliche Schriften*, rev ed., ed. Johann Georg Walch [St. Louis: Concordia, 1898], 1454, 1458, 1522, 1567-68) uses the singular in both instances.
28. He adds, "We in Christendom and in the New Testament must also do that, namely, teach the people to live right; and yet both our doctrine and our life are directed to the expectation of the Last Day and of eternal life" (LW 19:153).

Habakkuk is also doing here: he proclaims destruction and yet promises that all prophecies pertaining to the Christ will be fulfilled, contrary to and beyond all senses and reason" (LW 19:190, cf. his comments on pp. 124, 197).

This is why the prophet stands on guard against unbelief and impatience. In the German work Luther weighs up the possibility that מַה־יְדַבֶּר־בִּי anticipates God speaking but decides that this clause, too, refers to "the blasphemers ... who speak against [Habakkuk's] words and accuse him of lying" (LW 19:192) when he announces the devastation of the land at the hand of the Babylonians. Here Habakkuk, the faithful preacher against unbelief, altogether eclipses Habakkuk, the man who wrestles with God in prayer. The faithful preacher, however, does not announce punishment only. He also stresses "that this would not prevent or delay the Christ's advent. ... Thus our Habakkuk is a comforting prophet whose mission was to strengthen and to sustain the people, so that they would not despair of the Christ's coming, no matter how difficult the situation might appear to be" (LW 19:154–55, cf. 199). This brings us to our next example.

THE VISION IN HABAKKUK 2:4

The identity of the vision in Habakkuk 2:4 is a matter of much disagreement among modern commentators, but Luther sees no need to discuss various options. He is convinced that the vision is the one shared by all the prophets, the vision of the coming Christ. He notes the use of the term חָזוֹן in Daniel 9:24. Habakkuk was, of course, unable to write all that the prophets said about the coming kingdom on a single tablet. What the prophet is asked here, Luther believes, is to "inscribe something about the prophecy of the Christ on it, what one is to think regarding it, since the Jews are so timid, thinking that all is at an end" (LW 19:193).[29] This "something" is what immediately follows in verses 3–4. Because Luther reads כְּתוֹב חָזוֹן as "writing something *about* the vision," verse 3 can be considered to have been included on the tablet. In the

---

29. The misreading of לְמַעַן יָרוּץ קוֹרֵא בּוֹ as "so that he who runs past may read it" was probably introduced by Luther. It may have been facilitated by the use of *percurro* in the Vulgate, which was also used metaphorically for running over something in one's mind or scanning briefly (e.g., Cicero, de Orat. 1.50). See entry in Lewis, Charlton Thomas, and Short, Charles, *A Latin Dictionary* (United Kingdom: Nigel Gourlay, 2020). The Greek διώκω seems to me less open to this misunderstanding, as the object being pursued is surely more likely the content of the vision than the words on the tablet. See my "Reading and Running: Notes on the History of Translating the Final Clause of Hab 2:2," VT 69 (2019): 435–46.

light of Luther's conviction that the vision is about the coming Christ,[30] it is noteworthy that he interprets verse 3 as speaking about the vision which will not delay and for which we are to wait, rather than the Christ. The latter is an option that the Old Greek (OG) could have suggested, as it uses masculine forms, even though "vision" (ὅρασις) is a feminine noun in Greek.

Luther's understanding of the content of the vision has an impact on how he reads 2:4a. For Luther the end of the Babylonian empire is preliminary to, and therefore separate from, the actual hope the vision conveys. In fact, in the German work Luther introduces a chapter break between verses 4 and 5, thus clearly separating the announcement of the end of the Babylonian oppression in verses 5-20 from the remarks about the vision in verses 3-4.[31] While the received Hebrew text is arguably best understood as a reference to Babylonian greed,[32] the Greek and Latin versions of the text do not suggest this. The OG has the middle form of ὑποστέλλω, "to retreat"; Aquila uses νωχελεύομαι, "to be slothful." Luther finds in his Latin text *qui incredulus est*, "he who is unbelieving," and comments that it is a poor translation. עֻפְּלָה suggests to Luther a more active resistance, someone who stubbornly opposes the prophecy and refuses to hear it: "Such a person's soul will have no pleasure in that promise" (LW 19:123).[33] Luther interprets the contents of the tablet as a promise ("The vision will come true. ... It will not fail"), an exhortation ("If it seems slow, wait for it"), and a threat ("If anyone resists it, his soul will succeed in nothing"), concluding with "a masterly statement" urging belief in God's promise (LW 19:197), which he summarizes as follows: "The godly people are waiting for the Lord; therefore they live, therefore they are saved, therefore they receive what has been promised. They receive it by faith, because they give glory to the God of truth, because they hold the hand of the Lord" (LW 19:123). Clearly, a view about Israelite prophecy in general shapes the understanding of what is

---

30. Cf. "He who has been promised will come at the time when it will be fulfilled" (LW 19:123).

31. None of the Bibles printed before this time seem to have done this, nor was this chapter division adopted in German Bibles subsequently. It was, however, adopted in the 1552 Finnish and the 1584/1644 Icelandic Bibles.

32. I suggested "An Emendation of Hab 2:4a in the Light of Hab 1:5," *JHS* 13 (2013): art. 11 (*A Latin Dictionary*), which, if accepted, would make the first half of the verse refer to Yahweh.

33. Luther rejects the first-person suffix ("my soul") found in the OG and cited in Hebrews 10:38 as inappropriate. He adds, "Although the author of the Epistle of the Hebrews has erred in his wording, still he has captured the real meaning of the prophet quite clearly and suitably etc." (LW 19:123).

specifically going on in Habakkuk. The reason why such an understanding of Habakkuk 2:2–4 is not usually discussed as a possibility among contemporary scholars has to do with the different understanding of Israelite prophecy within the guild today.

THE TARGET OF THE THREATS IN HABAKKUK 2:5–20

Luther concludes his discussion of Habakkuk 2:3–4 in 1525 with "This is the first and most important part in this prophet, where he promises that the Christ is going to come and that the promises which have been made to the fathers are going to be fulfilled. The second part now follows, in which he describes the destruction of the kingdom of the Chaldeans, although it was a very powerful, very wealthy, and famous kingdom" (LW 19:124). As indicated above, in 1526 Luther marks the break with a chapter division. He summarizes as follows:

> In the first chapter the prophet threatened the people of Israel and proclaimed destruction. There he complained bitterly about the destroyer, the king of Babylon. In the second chapter [2:1–4] he again consoled them by words and external signs [the tablet] with the advent of the Christ and of His kingdom. And now in the third chapter [2:5–20] he utters many threatening words and verses against the king of Babylon and his empire. All of this is done to keep the Jews from despairing, as if their captivity were to last forever, and to console them with the news that their enemy will, in turn, be destroyed, and that they will be delivered and attain far more glory, as indeed he will encourage them in the fourth chapter [Hab 3] by pointing to the past miracles of God. (LW 19:199)

Commenting on verse 5 Luther paints a striking image of a drunkard who becomes so helpless that even children can mock and laugh at him (LW 19:200, cf. 202), thus smoothing the way for verse 6. The image of the drunkard who throws up also anticipates the payback announced in subsequent verses. Luther observed that the king of Babylon "was obliged to spew forth again so disgracefully what he had guzzled down. For he had to surrender all the countries and peoples, and he himself had to perish too" (LW 19:200).

Within contemporary scholarship, the question is raised whether the condemnations in chapter 2 really had an imperial force as its original target or whether the chapter reflects condemnation of behavior within Judah. Luther is, instead, concerned to note parallels with the authorities of his own time whose weaknesses are being exposed: "That is what is also happening to the pope and his ilk today. Now everybody who formerly did not dare to mumble or mutter sings, rhymes, laughs, jeers, and mocks." "And also today, where princes and bishops oppose the Gospel most vehemently there it must take root and flourish most. And then people will taunt and say: 'What has become of those who would not tolerate it? They are reposing in their graves, the worms are consuming them, and the Word of God still remains and abides in their dominion'" (LW 19:203). Throughout his commentary on this chapter Luther keeps in mind that Habakkuk describes in advance "what happens when a tyrant is securely established and is then suddenly overtaken by misfortune" (LW 19:205). "For if Babylon was unable to survive, how will the Turk, how will our emperor, kings and princes survive, who could hardly qualify as citizens in Babylon?" (LW 19:209). Luther suggests that "this brings consolation to all who are persecuted, taken captive, and plagued by tyrants. For if He was able to deliver the Jews from Babylon, which contained such arrogant, mighty, and evil tyrants, why should He not be able to deliver from far lesser tyrants?" (LW 19:209).

It is noteworthy that Luther, while observing common patterns, did not moralize about evil in general, but retains a focus on God bringing down the mighty. This happens not only in Habakkuk 2 where the target is the Babylonian empire, but also in chapter 1, where Luther thinks Judean society is in view. He comments on 1:3, "All of his preaching is addressed to the lords and judges" (LW 19:161). On the one hand, Luther expounds the verse broadly: "Everyone was bent on his own welfare, defrauding his neighbor, cheating him, grasping, robbing, and stealing wherever possible" (LW 19:160). On the other hand, he suggests the phrase שֹׁד וְחָמָס in 1:3 refers to the destruction and devastation that typically happens "in cities and countries that are without law and order and when the rich and the tyrants do as they wish," not respecting the law (LW 19:160, cf. "care not how much blood it costs" on p. 206). Noting it was the upper class that was deported to Babylon, Luther claims this is, in fact, the pattern throughout history: "that God always deposes one king through another, one lord through another, and that he leaves the people and country intact, unless it is His purpose to destroy country and people, as was the case with Sodom and Gomorrah and the like" (LW 19:162).

Luther does not spell out the implication that deposing rulers is the responsibility of God acting through other rulers, not of the people seeking to rid themselves of oppressors. It is what he believes, and why he spoke strongly against the peasants' revolt; but his emphasis here lies elsewhere. Luther allows that "the sword" (governing authority) is necessary but stresses that like all God's gifts it is constantly abused; "Swords and government always remain in the world, but the persons sitting on thrones must continue to topple and tumble as they deserve" (LW 19:162–63). "Might before right" is "the world's true color" for as long as the devil is "the prince of the world" (LW 19:163). "And yet God does not permit this to go unpunished. As the world does not cease sinning, God does not cease punishing" (LW 19:163).

Similarly, in 1:4 Luther saw behavior that he thought quite typical of jurists and judges who are not concerned with good causes that make no money but who bend the law in the ways that are most profitable to them (LW 19:163–65; cf. Mic 7:3). It is when he comes to 1:11 ("their heart will be exalted and they will continue and sin") that Luther observes a lack of moderation characterized by those who took part in the rebellion as much as those who suppressed the revolt (LW 19:174), although again Luther puts the emphasis on condemning the authorities.[34] "Because God granted [our bishops and princes] victory over the peasants and at the same time has permitted them to torture and persecute many innocent Christians, they are convinced that their cause is just and right and pleasing to God. They are defiant and insolent and 'suppose that they are rendering God a service' (John 16:2)" (LW 19:176). "However, they will come to an ugly end" (LW 19:177).

As noted above, recent discussion of the target of the condemnations in chapter 2 has been more concerned with whether inner-Judean injustice is addressed or Babylonian imperialism. It seems to me that the chapter seeks to apply a general truth about the deconstruction of evil, first of all, to the specific case of Babylonian oppression but with implications for what it means to be "righteous" and desist from evil. This explains both why the material would have been suitable to condemn corruption within Judah

---

34. Note that Luther's comments on 2:9 express his belief that the insurrectionists were successful in laying waste to firm castles and houses because God, "the true Builder and Protector," had forsaken the greedy rich (LW 19:210), and see his observation on 2:12, "I do believe that avarice is avenged, now that such fortresses turn about and do as much with snapping as enemies with weapons" (LW 19:214).

and why it can readily be applied to later situations, as Luther does. But in taking account of the nonspecific, and therefore inclusive, character of the condemnations, Luther reminds us not to lose sight of an important dynamic of the chapter: God's humiliation of the mighty.

THE WOLVES IN HABAKKUK 1:8

The next example concerns a well-known and long-standing philological issue in 1:8 and illustrates that even decisions on philological matters are affected by one's prior knowledge and experience of the world.[35] In the 1525 Latin text we read:

> There is a difference of opinion among the linguists whether it ought to be translated "evening wolves" or "wolves of the desert." Jerome translated "evening wolves," influenced by this line of reasoning: Since evening wolves have suffered hunger throughout the day, they attack a flock more viciously than other wolves do, and they do not leave until they have filled themselves. Who does not see that such an interpretation is weak? Therefore I prefer to adopt the other interpretation, so I translate "wolves of the desert," that is, wolves that are fierce and untamed. (LW 19:112–13)

But the 1526 German text has:

> The Hebrew letters admit either. … I believe that these are evening wolves. I think that this means to say that wolves, which are rapacious, ravenous, murderous beasts by nature, are far more so in the evening because they have not roamed about during the day and their hunger looks to the evening. Therefore the term "evening wolves" is practically synonymous with "hungry wolves" who have not eaten for a long time. (LW 19:170)

---

35. See my "The Colour Red and the Lion King: Two Studies in Nahum," in *Sprache lieben— Gottes Wort verstehen: Festschrift für Heinrich von Siebenthal*, ed. Walter Hilbrands, BWM 17 (Gießen: Brunnen, 2011), 179–201, in which I note that many commentators interpret Nahum based on their understanding of the behavior of African lions in open fields, while Nahum more likely assumes an understanding of the behavior of Asiatic lions in the thickets of the Jordan Valley. See also David Clines, "Misapprehensions, Ancient and Modern, about Lions (Nahum 2.13)," in *Poets, Prophets, and Texts in Play: Studies in Biblical Poetry and Prophecy in Honour of Francis Landy*, ed. Ehud Ben Zvi et al. (London: T&T Clark, 2015): 58–76.

Luther's dislike for Jerome leads one to expect that he will decide for "wolves of the desert" as soon as he mentions that Jerome opts for "evening wolves," even if a little piece of rhetoric ("Who does not see that such an interpretation is weak?") here substitutes for actual argument—a strategy not entirely unknown among contemporary scholars. What made Luther change his mind so that only a year later he agreed with Jerome, albeit without saying so? We should first note that in 1525 Luther reads "wolves of the desert" as "wolves that are fierce and untamed." He thereby seems to allow for the existence of tamed wolves from which "wolves of the desert" are to be distinguished. In 1526, however, he describes wolves as "rapacious, ravenous, murderous beasts by nature," apparently not allowing for the possibility of wolves being tamed. It is unlikely that Luther read a zoological treatise in the meantime. The question whether wolves can be tamed today is of course irrelevant if we ask how the phrase might have been heard in ancient Judah; the question is whether domesticated wolves were known or thought to exist in ancient Judah. But Luther does not appeal to new historical-zoological insight. What was new was his awareness of the brutal suppression of one of the great revolts of European history which had started in the spring of 1525 with as many as three hundred thousand peasants rising up against their masters. It was arguably the fierce response of the authorities to the peasants' uprising, leaving tens of thousands dead, that convinced Luther that there are no tame wolves after all (see his more detailed comments on p. 174). He concluded his exegesis of verse 7 with the observation that "it is not without meaning that noblemen commonly show a lion, a bear, wolves, and other wild beasts in their coat of arms. This reflects their nature" (LW 19:170). Because for him the translation "wolves of Arabia" refers to a distinction between wild and tame wolves and he now believes all wolves/rulers to be ferocious, it is no longer a tenable translation. זאבי ערב therefore must mark out the wolves as *especially* ferocious due to not having eaten for a while, just as Jerome had claimed. In changing his interpretation, Luther reverts to a traditional interpretation of the text, albeit by accident rather than design. He does, however, offer what appears to be a genuinely novel reading of Habakkuk 2 further on in his 1526 interpretation. This is our next example.

THE SEQUENCE OF WOES IN HABAKKUK 2

Luther seems to assume that "the taunts against the Babylonian tyrant" in Habakkuk 2 "will be current in the countryside" because he distinguishes the first four taunts from the fifth, which he supposes "is added by Habakkuk himself" (LW 19:204). He believes the sequence of the first four taunts reflects "the way and order of the world: first it strives for money and goods; then it begins to build; then joy and pleasure are sought; and finally might and honor" (LW 19:204, cf. 207). This had not yet been explored in his Latin lectures. The condemnation of greed in the first taunt is obvious. The second does indeed focus on building one's house. It is the interpretation of the third and fourth that are colored differently by observing this sequence. The third taunt could be understood in terms of building a *society* on injustice, not least as we take note, as does Luther, of the parallel in Micah 3:10. But the Babylonian reputation for magnificent gardens and buildings prompts Luther to detect a desire for joy and pleasure here, which is not obvious in the text itself. Consequently, when he comes to verse 13, he observes that "tyrants employ the people's labor for their own pleasure" (LW 19:215), building pretty and costly buildings at the expense of the many, both those who are taxed heavily and slaves. This fits with the emphasis on the condemnation specifically of a tyrant rather than a society as a whole. Habakkuk 2:15 on its own might lead one to focus on the tyrant's shaming of others, but as he interprets the fourth taunt Luther draws on Daniel 2–3 as evidence for the Babylonian king's desire to be honored above others and cites the German proverb *Gut macht Mut* ("Wealth inspires courage"). He thereby suggests that shaming others is usually a way of magnifying oneself and brings into relief what verse 16 implies: an imperial desire to be sated with glory. We see here historical knowledge and pastoral or psychological insight converge in reading between the lines in a way that I find insightful. The historical-archaeological evidence, about which we know more than Luther, and the historical veracity of Daniel 2–3 are arguably less important than the Babylonian reputation in the mind of Habakkuk's readers. Luther assumes a reader that is engaged with a certain story about Babylon and aware of general human traits that come to be of relevance here.

THE CHARACTERIZATION OF THE PRAYER IN HABAKKUK 3

Luther ends his discussion of 2:20 with the words:

May that suffice on Habakkuk's prophecies. ... And now he adds a prayer in the form of a song,[36] in order to console and strengthen the weak in faith still more. He collects and gathers many of the ancient wonderful deeds of God, which he showed His people in times past and by which He often delivered them miraculously. They must bear these in mind and not doubt that their God, who often delivered them mightily in the past, will also deliver them now from Babylon. For it is most heartening to faith to recall miracles of the past. (LW 19:225-26)

This gives us a neat summary of how Luther reads Habakkuk 3. This final example explores Luther's understanding of the title in 3:1. Pre-modern commentators, ancient and modern, Jewish and Christian, by and large understood the phrase עַל שִׁגְיֹנוֹת in Habakkuk 3 to refer to the content of the prayer. The standard OG rendering μετὰ ᾠδῆς ("with song") is a prominent exception to this, although, for example, Aquila, Symmachus, and the Quinta edition read ἐπὶ ἀγνοημάτων.[37] Today עַל שִׁגְיֹנוֹת is nearly universally understood as a musical term or related to Akkadian *šigû* (often rendered "lament"), neither of which is in fact as convincing upon further research as it looks at first and the older tradition of seeing in עַל שִׁגְיֹנוֹת a reference to the content of the prayer rather than its genre or musical category may well be correct.[38]

Luther explains שִׁגְיֹנוֹת with the Latin *ignorantia et ignorantiae* (cf. Vulgate *pro ignorationibus*), lack of knowledge (of something), or *inconscientia*, lack of awareness (of something). He adopts the same explanation for שִׁגָּיוֹן in the heading of Psalm 7 with which David claims that "his conscience knew nothing" of the accusation Shimei made (2 Sam. 16:7ff, see v. 4 [ET 3]). "In the absence of a better German term, we must translate this with *Unschuld* ('innocence').[39] However, this is too strong a term. ... For a person may not feel any evil in his conscience and yet not be innocent, as Paul declares in

---

36. Strangely, in his Latin lectures, Luther insisted that this prayer was not a song (LW 19:133), maybe because he rejected the OG rendering of עַל שִׁגְיֹנוֹת. See below for more.

37. Theodotian has ὑπὲρ τῶν ἑκουσιασμῶν (perhaps ὑπὲρ τῶν ἀκουσιασμῶν is meant, the reading suggested by Louis Cappel and given by Joseph Ziegler in the *Duodecim Prophetae*, vol. 13 in *Göttingen Septuagint*, 3rd ed. (Göttingen: Vandenhoeck & Ruprecht, 1984). The Washington papyrus has ὑπὲρ τῶν ἀγνοιῶν. For fuller discussion, including of Jewish medieval exegesis, see Dominic Barthélemy, *Ezekiel, Daniel, les 12 prophetes*, vol. 3 in *Critique textuelle de l'Ancien Testament* (Göttingen: Vandenhoeck & Ruprecht, 1992): 857-60.

38. See my *Nahum, Habakkuk, and Zephaniah*, 334-41.

39. In the Latin lectures, not yet having come up with *inconscientia*, Luther used *innocentia* as the proper equivalent here to *ignorantia* (see W2, 14:795, 819).

1 Cor. 4:4: 'I am not aware of anything against myself, but I am not thereby acquitted. It is the Lord who judges me'" (LW 19:227). Moving from the abstract noun to a concrete noun, he renders it as "a prayer ... for the innocent," by which he means those who like Daniel and his companions were led away into exile in spite of having a clear conscience. "Habakkuk wants to pray for the godly, who were led away to Babylon together with the ungodly" (LW 19:227). In his Latin lectures he elaborated: "[Habakkuk] prays that the Lord would be willing to bring them back, since indeed their conscience is ignorant of the sin for which others had deserved captivity. In this way he is complaining that the guilty and the innocent are being afflicted equally, as often happens in wars" (LW 19:134). Luther cannot offer us philological insight superior to ours, but he works very well with what he has, not least with the conviction that there is an overall coherence to the prayer and its place within Habakkuk. It is true that Habakkuk 3 no longer distinguishes between the innocent (righteous) and the wicked (guilty) within the people of God as Habakkuk 1 had done. Even if we may not be altogether convinced by Luther's translation, his claim that the prayer is prayed with "the innocent" in mind fits well with what follows. Luther both recognizes the limits of our knowledge and confidently offers an interpretation that coheres with the immediate context and Christian theology.[40]

CONCLUDING OBSERVATIONS

Luther felt the need to publish on Habakkuk because he believed that Habakkuk had not been clearly understood since the time of the apostles. As far as understanding the details of the text is concerned, the progress made as a result of the *ad fontes* movement during the Renaissance gave Luther reason for gratitude and reason not to think too highly of his predecessors. In turn, the progress made in Hebrew studies and related disciplines in the last five hundred years may give us reason to pay little attention to Luther, and especially so if we do not share his basic convictions. But linguistic and historical knowledge is not all that is required to understand a text well. An understanding of the text's subject matter is also critical, and in this respect, we are not necessarily more advanced than Luther. Many

---

40. "This seems to me to be the meaning, and I cannot understand it in any other way. In this way the prayer agrees very well with the preceding prophecy. Although I have myself as the only authority for this interpretation, still I do not think that I am mistaken" (LW 19:134).

contemporary commentaries walk a well-trodden path, so one advantage in reading Luther or other pre-modern interpreters is that they do not necessarily walk on the same paths.[41] In addition, there are two or three areas in which reading pre-modern commentaries may challenge us.

First, scholars like myself who work on the biblical text not simply as a historian or literary critic, but with an eye to its relevance today, reflect on parallels in our world and what pastors usually call "application" but we do so as a second step. For Luther, the exegesis and the application are more integrated. I reckon this is because he believes that understanding "the way of the world" informs one's understanding of the biblical text and not only the other way around. In more recent times Nicholas Lash made a similar point in his powerful essay "What Might Martyrdom Mean?" where he critiques the distinction between exegesis understood as the historical task of analyzing what a biblical text meant and exposition understood as the theological task of exploring what it means today.[42]

Second, just as there is a tendency for Christians and other interpreters of the biblical text to move from exegesis to application, there is a tendency to move from considering God as a character in the text to questions of theology. "There can be little doubt that the disentangling of biblical study from dogmatic theology in the 18th and 19th centuries brought enormous gain and insight, not least because ecclesial perspectives were so often used to prejudge or short-circuit the disciplines of philological and historical work."[43] But if ecclesial dogmatism presents a risk for not seeing the text as it is, anti-ecclesial prejudice may pose a similar risk today. It may be worth asking again whether bracketing theological questions in the first instance is a self-limitation that must lead to an underreading or even misreading of the text. Given that I bring to bear what I know about producing "the color red" or the "behavior of lions" when translating Nahum,[44] why should I side-step what I know about God when interpreting Habakkuk? We are rightly nervous about this intermingling of concerns, but while we have

---

41. The same could be true of paying attention to "global" readers and untrained, "lay" Bible readers. What Luther brings to the table is genuine learning formed within a different culture from ours.

42. Originally published in 1981 and reprinted in *Theology on the Way to Emmaus* (London: SCM, 1986): 75–92.

43. Moberly, "What Is Theological Interpretation?," 175.

44. See Renz, "The Colour Red and the Lion King," in *Sprache lieben*.

seen that it can trip up Luther, it can also shed new light on texts and our fear that refusing to bracket out theological commitments inevitably means that one's exegesis is "controlled and determined by prior theological commitment" to a tradition is not realized in an interpreter like Luther.[45]

Third, the style of Luther's commentary is markedly different from contemporary commentaries. There are, for example, the ways in which key metaphors serve as a backbone for the discussion, such as the image of the drunkard in Habakkuk 2, or the thought that the rays which make known God are his works in Habakkuk 3. The latter leads Luther to write in his commentary on 3:9, "That was also a ray when from the rocks He provided streams in the wilderness so that both man and beast could drink thereof (Num. 20:2ff.)" (LW 19:233). This both strengthens the coherence of the work and conveys the impression that the earlier word (in this case, 3:4) has been accepted and now informs one's understanding of other words. Even more prominent is the way in which Luther explains verses by re-phrasing them rather than analyzing them only in the third person. One of many examples that could be given is his thoughts on 2:13:

> It is as though he were saying, "Oh, you are erecting something very
> costly here! But what a great fire will arise from the building on which
> so many people are laboring at present! How many fine, empty plots
> of land there will be where so many people are working themselves
> weary now! Your plan will be completely reversed. It will not mate-
> rialize as you wish. You want it to adorn and embellish the city; but it
> will mar and disfigure it. Where you are now laying out pleasure-gar-
> dens, burnt-out and desolate areas will be found. But this will not be
> perpetrated by your subjects; there will be no rebellion. No, by the
> Lord Sabaoth. To be sure, He will find people to do this, namely, the
> Persians and the Medes." (LW 19:216)

We may object that this is the language of a preacher, not an exegete. But insofar as exegesis is drawing out the meaning of a text (and its subject matter), I wonder whether this language, whose source lies in Luther's participatory approach, does not have an advantage over a more clinical description.

---

45. R. W. L. Moberly, "Biblical Criticism and Religious Belief," *JTI* 2 (2008): 71–100 (83), summarizing the fear expressed in John Barton, *The Nature of Biblical Criticism* (Louisville: Westminster John Knox, 2007).

6

Perspectives on Theodicy in Habakkuk and Malachi vis-à-vis Job

S. D. (Fanie) Snyman

INTRODUCTION

The Bible, especially the Old Testament, addresses the issue of human suffering. The technical term used for this inquiry is "theodicy." It is not easy to give a precise definition of what the term means. Theodicy is used to explain the relation between God and evil. It derives from the Greek words for "god" (θεός) and "justice" (δίκη) and aims at explaining why God—the loving, almighty, and good God—can allow evil in this world. In popular language it is seen as the question of why bad things happen to good people. Theodicy can also be seen as the question of why the righteous suffer. Attempting to define theodicy from an Old Testament perspective, James Crenshaw states, "We may thus define theodicy loosely as the attempt to pronounce a verdict of 'Not Guilty' over God for whatever seems to destroy the order of society and the universe."[1] Theodicy remains an intriguing question in the field of theology in general and in the Old Testament in particular. Old and New Testament scholars still study the many questions raised by the issue of theodicy as is illustrated by the book Anthony Tambasco edited.[2] In the first chapter of the book Tambasco says, "Theodicy is a constant concern of the

---

1. J. L. Crenshaw, ed., *Theodicy in the Old Testament*, IRT 4 (London: SPCK, 1983), 1.
2. A. J. Tambasco, ed., *The Bible on Suffering: Social and Political Implications* (New York: Paulist, 2002).

entire Bible."[3] Theodicy is a problem also discussed in the fields of dogmatics[4] and philosophy.[5]

The problem of theodicy is addressed in the Old Testament, especially in the book of Job, the Psalter (especially Pss 49 and 73), and the book of Habakkuk. The book of Habakkuk begins with the question "How long, O LORD, must I call for help, but you do not listen? Or cry out to you, 'Violence!' but you do not save? Why do you make me look at injustice? Why do you tolerate wrong?" (1:2–3).[6] The book of Malachi is not normally considered when the problem of theodicy is discussed in the Old Testament; but in Malachi 2:17 the prophet voices the concern of the people when they asked, "Where is the God of justice?" According to R. Kessler the question put in Malachi 2:17 is about the righteousness of God, or a theodicy question.[7] In Malachi 3:13–14 the issue is raised again: "What did we gain by carrying out his requirements and going about like mourners before the LORD Almighty? But now we call the arrogant blessed. Certainly, the evildoers prosper, and even those who challenge God escape." In light of this evidence, this contribution investigates briefly the answers the books of Habakkuk, Malachi, and Job respectively provide on the question of theodicy.[8] Since Job is the book par excellence in dealing with the problem of theodicy, some attention must be paid first to its contribution to the issue before the books of Habakkuk and Malachi can be investigated. Second, the aim is to establish what similarities and differences there are between these three books in addressing the issue of theodicy. The method followed is a probe that offers a theological interpretation of the three books, focusing on the theme of theodicy through a close reading of the text.

---

3. A. J. Tambasco, "Introduction: The Bible and Human Suffering," in *The Bible on Suffering*, 3–15 (12).
4. E.g., A. van de Beek, *Waarom? Over lijden, schuld en God* (Nijkerk: G. F. Callenbach, 1984); D. L. Migliore, *Faith Seeking Understanding: An Introduction to Christian Theology* (Grand Rapids: Eerdmans, 2014), 132–35.
5. M. T. Eggemeier, "Levinas and Ricoeur on the Possibility of God after the End of Theodicy," *Philosophy & Theology* 24, no. 1 (2012): 23–48.
6. Scripture quotations use the NIV Third South African edition 1985 unless otherwise noted.
7. R. Kessler, *Maleachi*, HThKAT (Freiburg: Herder, 2011), 227.
8. It is interesting to note that A. Meinhold, *Maleachi*, BKAT XIV/8 (Neukirchen-Vluyn: Neukirchener, 2006), 362, also relates Job, Habakkuk, and Malachi in his discussion of Malachi 3:14.

THEODICY IN THE BOOK OF JOB

It is widely agreed that the book of Job is Israel's most ambitious counter-testimony concerning the crisis of theodicy.[9] In Job 21:7 the "why" question is pertinently asked: "Why do the wicked live on, growing old and increasing in power?" Job is the prototype of an upright, decent, righteous human being suffering for no apparent reason, and the "why" question is posed with brutal honesty. Why do (righteous) people have to suffer? Why do good people have to suffer? Where is God in human suffering?[10]

The book of Job is a vast book, and any summary will fail to do justice to it, but in general the story of Job is well-known. He is by all accounts living the life of a righteous man and his wealth and good fortune are ample proof of this (1:1–5). Job enjoys the rich blessings of God in abundance. The reader of the book (but not Job) is then allowed to have a glimpse of a scene in heaven. God and the *satan*[11] are in dialogue, with the *satan* challenging God: Job serves God only for the benefit of the good life God blessed him with. Do ordinary human beings worship God out of self-interest and expect to be rewarded because of their righteous lives? That is the question at stake.[12] Will Job still serve God when everything is taken away from him? With this scene in heaven, the crucial issue of theodicy has been introduced and will be debated for the rest of the book.[13] God accepted this challenge from the *satan*, and even though Job lost everything he had, he still trusted God and remained markedly loyal to him. His unshakable faith in God is exemplified in two crucial verses at the beginning of the book: "Naked I came from my mother's womb and naked I shall depart. The LORD gave and the LORD has taken away; may the name of the LORD be praised" (1:21), and in Job 2:10 he says, "'Shall we accept good from God and not trouble?' In all this Job did not sin in what he said." As A. van Selms put it, there are really people on earth who do not serve God for the sake of any material or spiritual advantage

---

9. W. Brueggemann, *Theology of the Old Testament: Testimony, Dispute, Advocacy* (Minneapolis: Fortress, 1997), 386.

10. H. Ausloos and I. Bossuyt, "Job in Bijbel en cultuur," in *Job tussen leven en lijden*, ed. H. Ausloos and I. Bossuyt (Leuven: Acco, 2010), 7–12.

11. As the noun here has the article (הַשָּׂטָן), it is treated as a common noun.

12. N. Habel, *The Book of Job: A Commentary*, Old Testament Library (London: SCM, 1985), 61.

13. N. Whybray, *Job* (Sheffield: Sheffield Academic Press, 1998), 15.

but for his sake.[14] The test put to Job was also as much a test for Yahweh. Should Job fail the test, this would mean that no true, disinterested fear of God exists in the world, and if this is the case, then Yahweh's entire plan for humanity will be worthless.[15]

In chapter 2, three friends of Job (Eliphaz, Bildad, and Zophar) enter the scene. The purpose of their visit is to console their friend Job in his dire situation. Job then, contrary to his previous behavior of quietly accepting his fate, curses the day he was born (3:1). Their contribution to the mystery of Job's suffering despite his blameless life is to claim that in some way he must have sinned and, consequently, Job is wrong in claiming his innocence (22:5-10). The logic is clear: since God is by his very nature the one who acts righteously,[16] Job's suffering must be the result of sin and moral evil on his side. Job reacts to this accusation by insisting he is innocent ("I am blameless," 9:21), even to the point where he is willing to enter into a lawsuit with God. Contrary to his friends, who never address God, Job's complaints are directed at God in a very personal way. Elihu, a fourth friend, also enters the discussion (Job 32) by stating that suffering should be seen as a divine reprimand to human beings, to turn them from their wrong ways and so repent. Thus, suffering has a pedagogical function.[17] This kind of reasoning is equally unacceptable to Job.

In Job 38, there is a new turn of events; God enters the scene where he speaks to Job in two speeches (38:1-40:2; 40:6-41:34). Right from the beginning of God's speeches he makes it clear that instead of Job questioning God, God will question Job, and Job will have to answer to God. Job expects God to answer his questions on suffering, but God is not primarily interested in Job's suffering. In fact, Yahweh never refers to Job and the suffering he endured, nor does he speak about human beings in general. Instead of answering questions, God poses even more of them. The questions God asks are about the greatness of creation. Indeed, creation is a mystery; and although there is a certain order detected by human beings, creation, both in terms of what humans can observe and that which cannot be seen with

14. A. van Selms, *Job: A Practical Commentary*, Text and Interpretation (Grand Rapids: Eerdmans, 1985), 16.

15. Whybray, *Job*, 15.

16. Habel, *Job*, 61.

17. H. Ausloos and V. Kabergs, "De schreeuw van Job, Als lijden Gods orde verstoort," in Ausloos and Bossuyt, *Job*, 46.

the naked eye, is incomprehensible. To add to the problem, there is also a chaotic element in creation signified by two mythical monsters, Behemoth and Leviathan. There is a flipside to the neat order of creation: the powers of chaos threaten the orderly creation. The natural order of creation does not allow one to conclude that the wicked will be punished and the innocent immune to suffering;[18] therefore, the principle of retributive justice does not function as a mechanical law of the cosmos.[19] In the larger scheme of the entire creation human beings are insignificant.[20] Job responds to God by admitting that this is indeed the case: "I am unworthy—how can I reply to you? I put my hand over my mouth. I spoke once, but I have no answer— twice, but I will say no more" (40:4-5). Finally, Job submits to Yahweh's overwhelming majesty and power. In Job 42:1-6, Job admits that he spoke of things he did not understand—things too wonderful for him to compre- hend. In the past he has heard about God "but now my eyes have seen you" (42:6). Job encounters God in a completely new way, so much so that he can speak of an inner vision he had of God and that made all the difference. In the epilogue (42:7-17), Job is restored while the way in which his friends spoke of God is pointed out as the wrong way to speak about God. Job is commended by God because he had the audacity to argue against God.

The repeated conclusion scholars came to is that the problem of theo- dicy is not solved in the book of Job. Whybray opines that the book offers no solution to the problem of human suffering.[21] Rendtorff states: "God's answer is not an answer to the questions that Job has posed."[22] God does not solve the problem of theodicy.[23] This is also the conclusion Ausloos and Kabergs come to: "The book of Job is not so much an answer to the problem of suffering itself."[24] In the end Job realizes the answer to the "why" ques- tion does not exist.

---

18. Habel, *Job*, 65.

19. Habel, *Job*, 66.

20. Whybray, *Job*, 24.

21. Whybray, *Job*, 26.

22. R. Rendtorff, *The Canonical Hebrew Bible: A Theology of the Old Testament*, Tools for Biblical Study 7 (Leiden: Deo, 2005), 357.

23. B. K. Waltke, *An Old Testament Theology: An Exegetical, Canonical, and Thematic Approach* (Grand Rapids: Zondervan, 2007), 943.

24. Ausloos and Kabergs, "De schreeuw van Job," in, *Job*, ed. Ausloos and Bossuyt, 58 (my trans- lation); the Dutch reads, "Het boek Job wil niet zozeer een antwoord bieden op de lijdenprob- lematiek zelf."

If the questions Job posed are not answered, what then is the book's contribution to the problem of theodicy?

The first observation one must make is that the book of Job tells us that there is no one and final answer to the problem of suffering. The friends of Job surely do not have the answer. The questions Job put to God are also not answered. It is interesting that Job is never informed about the wager between God and the *satan*. The real reason for the suffering Job endures is not disclosed to him, and therefore a direct answer to the suffering of Job is not given. The way in which God created and organized the universe remains a majestic mystery impossible for mortals to comprehend. One the one hand, Job's friends do not have the wisdom to come up with the right answer to the "why" question. But, on the other hand, neither Job nor God has the answers either. Job questions the answer given by his friends and God does the same when he bombards Job with questions that Job is incapable of answering. God's way of answering Job's questions is to pose more questions to him. In a strange way, this odd answer is good enough for Job. He realizes he is powerless against God and that he has spoken without proper understanding (42:1–4). Job's protest to God makes room for resting in God. Job is content that he will never understand or be able to explain the mysteries of creation, let alone understand and explain the creator of the incomprehensible creation. Job came to this point as a result of what he experienced as a personal encounter with God. Job was afflicted, and yes, God may act in just that way.[25]

Second, it is remarkable that Job, despite his accusations against God, still clung to God. God has won his wager against the *satan*. Job has proven that a person can serve God without seeking his own advantage, even up to the point where it seems as if God turns against him.[26] God, from his side, in no way critiques Job for his questions or even his anger against God. It seems as if God understands Job's anguish and, in the end, it was Job and not his friends who spoke the truth about God and his actions in the world.

Third, Job came to the realization that he is part of a far more comprehensive narrative, and that it is simply impossible for him to come to grips or even remotely understand the larger picture God has in mind. In Job's words: "Surely I spoke of things I do not understand, things too wonderful for me to know" (42:3).

---

25. Habel, *Job*, 67.
26. Van Selms, *Job*, 19.

Human wisdom is inadequate to explain the riddles of life and the mystery of divine governance.[27]

THEODICY IN THE BOOK OF HABAKKUK

Habakkuk is a prophetic book, but also treats the question of theodicy (a topic usually found in wisdom texts such as the book of Job and Psa 73). The book of Habakkuk may be seen as a dialogue between the prophet and Yahweh. The book starts off the dialogue with the "why" question coming from the prophet and addressed to Yahweh: "Why do you tolerate wrong?" (1:2–4). In this sense Habakkuk is driven by a large unresolved question—the question of the suffering of the righteous.[28] In recent research scholars have become more and more conscious of the fact that Habakkuk treats a topic that otherwise is generally found in wisdom texts: the problem of the suffering of the righteous and theodicy.[29] The real issue raised by the prophet is not only the occurrence of violence and destruction but his observation that Yahweh does not act upon this serious situation. The emphasis is not on who committed the violence but rather on why Yahweh is apparently absent and therefore ignorant of the plight of especially the righteous people living in the land. Bratcher formulates Habakkuk's problem as follows: "Why does God, who is the author of justice, not act justly by punishing the wicked and restoring the proper order for the righteous?"[30] The prophet received a strange answer to his "why" question. The question Habakkuk has posed is not answered; it is amplified and complicated. The violence Habakkuk complains about will not go away; instead it will increase and even worsen when the Babylonians march to take power. The coming Babylonians are described in fearsome detail: "They are a ruthless and impetuous people" (1:6), "they fly like a vulture swooping to devour; they all come bent on violence" (1:8–9), "they laugh at all fortified cities" and capture them (1:10), they are "guilty men, whose own strength is their god" (1:11). To a certain extent, an answer is given to the questions Habakkuk posed. The answer is that God is in control. His control may be seen in the way in which the Babylonians will rise as the next world superpower, thereby conquering the Assyrians once and for all. The question, however, remains: if God is in control, how is it possible that the evil forces of the world continue as if they are in control?[31] Furthermore, in what way does it help if God claims to be in control of world events but little of that can be seen?

The answer Habakkuk receives does not satisfy him, and in a second complaint he reminds Yahweh who he is: "Your eyes are too pure to look on evil; you cannot tolerate wrong" (1:13). It is all the more incomprehensible that Yahweh would be silent while the wicked swallow up those more righteous than themselves (1:13) and treat people in the most undignified way one can imagine.

In Habakkuk 2:2–4 Yahweh gives his second reply to Habakkuk's complaint. Yahweh commissions his prophet to create a huge poster so that people may read his answer to Habakkuk's questions.[32] The second reply is then given in verse 4 and consists of two parts. Time and space do not allow us to get into the details of this difficult verse. In the first part Habakkuk (and his audience) is reassured that violence and injustices committed in society will be dealt with. According to James Nogalski,[33] the prophet is convinced that the answer to the problem of injustice is essentially to wait and trust that Yahweh knows best. In the second part of the answer, Habakkuk must tell his people to keep faith and trust Yahweh. To keep faith means to keep believing in the God of justice even where there is little evidence of his justice to be seen. To keep faith means to continue to do what is right simply because it is right to do so even with no promise of reward.[34] Andersen concludes along these lines: "The way things are in this world does not match a God who is supposed to be good, strong, compassionate, wise, just. ... The two realities of God and the world do not seem to fit. Biblical faith holds on tenaciously to both realities. The world is real and the God who created it is also real. This is what Habakkuk believes and he manages somehow to survive by faith."[35]

---

31. Bratcher, *Theological Message*, 67.

32. A. S. van der Woude, *Habakuk Zefanja*, De Prediking van het Oude Testament (Nijkerk: G. F. Callenbach, 1978), 34.

33. J. D. Nogalski, *The Book of the Twelve: Micah–Malachi*, Smyth & Helwys Commentary (Macon, GA: Smyth & Helwys, 2011), 667–68.

34. Bratcher, *Theological Message*, 322.

35. F. I. Andersen, *Habakkuk: A New Translation with Introduction and Commentary*, AB 25 (New York: Doubleday, 2001), 11.

THEODICY IN THE BOOK OF MALACHI

The book of Malachi is not always considered one of the contributors to the problem of theodicy in the Old Testament. Yet, the question of theodicy is addressed in two units within it.

In Malachi 2:17 the question voiced by the people and taken up by the prophet is about the apparent absence of the God who is known for his justice, but according to the observation of the people the opposite is true: "'Everyone doing evil is good in the eyes of Yahweh. It is in them that he de-lights' or 'where is the God of justice?'"[36] God as the god of justice serves as the starting point for the issue raised. Elsewhere in the prophetic literature it is a given that Yahweh is a god of justice. In Isaiah 30:18 it is explicitly said that God is a god of justice. In Jeremiah 9:24 Yahweh himself states: "I am the LORD, who exercises kindness, justice and righteousness on earth, for in these I delight." And in Deuteronomy 1:17 it is said that justice belongs to God. In the books of Amos (5:14) and Micah (3:2) the people are admonished by God to "seek good, not evil." If this is God, where is he now to show his justice? If God does nothing, then the question may be asked if he is God at all.[37] The first and obvious answer is that Yahweh will come in the future to execute justice. The announcement of Yahweh's coming can be seen as the theme of this unit.[38] The answer to this complaint by the people is, however, a surprising one. When asking questions about the just actions of God, they are informed that God will first come to the temple to investigate the quality of the sacrifices brought.[39] First and foremost, Yahweh will execute jus-tice to be served in the temple. Once this has happened, sacrifices brought will once again be pleasing to Yahweh as was the case in former times. It is important to note that prior to the coming of Yahweh to the temple is the coming of a messenger to prepare the way before Yahweh. The idea of a way-preparer is a unique contribution to the issue of Yahweh executing his justice. What is also a unique contribution to the problem of theodicy is the cultic dimension of Yahweh's justice highlighted by the prophet. Second,

---

36. S. D. Snyman, "Where Is the God of Justice? Listening and Hearing the Word of God in Malachi 2:17–3:7a," in *Reading and Listening: Meeting One God in Many Texts*, ed. J. Dekker and G. Kwakkel, Amsterdamse Cahiers voor exegese van de Bijbel en zijn tradities Supplement Series (Bergambacht: Uitgeverij 2VM, 2018), 120.

37. Kessler, *Maleachi*, 227.

38. Kessler, *Maleachi*, 244–55.

39. Snyman, "God of Justice," 122.

Yahweh's justice will be experienced in his judgment of human relationships. Social injustices particularly mentioned are sorcery, adultery, perjury, oppression of laborers, widows, and orphans, and finally thrusting aside the aliens in society. Two of these transgressions are also prohibited in the Decalogue (Exod 20:14, 16; Deut 5:18, 20) while the other transgressions are dealt with in the legal parts of the Torah (Exod 22:18, 22:21–24; Deut 18:12; 24:14–15, 17–22; 26:12–13; Lev 6:3, 5; 19:12). The people are assured of Yahweh's coming in the future, and therefore they must be prepared for his coming both cultically as well as ethically on the level of social justice.

The theodicy question posed in Malachi 2:17 is answered in two ways. The people are reassured that the God of justice will come, and the people are also informed that the coming of Yahweh to execute justice will include the sacrificial practices performed at the temple. The God of justice will also execute judgment on the level of human relationships. Righteousness within the religious sphere is also connected to righteousness in the sphere of human relationships. Added to the transgressions on the level of human relationships is the disregard for Yahweh that is shown in an attitude of not fearing Yahweh. Human relationships are brought into the realm of the people's relationship with Yahweh. To fear Yahweh does not only mean to honor him and to serve him in the right way; it means to treat fellow human beings in the right way.[40] The God of justice is perceived to be absent and inactive where his people are doing justice an injustice. God's justice is seen where his people are doing justice in society. Because God is concerned about justice in society, he will come to judge his people, not to destroy but to restore justice in and by the people who asked for the God of justice. The people then got it wrong. Everyone doing evil is not good in the eyes of Yahweh, and he does not delight in those who do evil instead of good.

In Malachi 3:13–21 the question of theodicy is addressed again. Kessler[41] notes a link between Malachi 2:17–3:5 and 3:13–21,[42] and similarly, so does Noetzel.[43] The theodicy question of the present is cast into the future. Kessler[44] speaks in this regard of a perspective in the future that is opened

---

40. S. D. Snyman, *Malachi*, HCOT (Leuven: Peeters, 2015), 141.

41. Kessler, *Maleachi*, 272.

42. My translation. The German reads, "Ein erster Blick auf Mal 3,13–21 zeigt schnell dass die Perikope Ähnlichkeiten mit dem IV. Diskussionswort 2,17–3,5 hat."

43. J. Noetzel, *Maleachi, ein Hermeneut*, BZAW 467 (Berlin: de Gruyter, 2015), 237.

44. Kessler, *Maleachi*, 298.

up in the last unit of the book. Noetzel agrees, saying, "In the VI Disputation, the solution to this discrepancy has been put in an eschatological frame."[45] The future will bring a change in the current situation. Hope then is the driving force. The distinction made within the people of God is also interesting. Not all the people claiming to belong to the people of God will be vindicated. Only a portion of them within the people of God will experience the change for the better. Another characteristic is that the righteous people are not treated as a group. The redemption of the righteous will be experienced by individuals. The Day of Yahweh will be directed not against a particular people but against individuals.[46] The future will reveal "the difference between a righteous person and a wicked one, between the one who serves God and the one who does not serve him" (3:18)[47]. In this case Malachi differs from the conclusion of the book of Isaiah (65:1-16) or from Zechariah 12-14, where the focus is more on the fate of the people of God as a whole rather than the individual.[48]

SYNTHESIS

What are the similarities and the differences between the answers Job, Habakkuk, and Malachi provide us on the issue of theodicy? We will compare the three different contributions to the issue of theodicy and examine some similarities and also differences in their respective treatments of the issue.

SIMILARITIES

The most striking similarity is that the question of theodicy is not really answered in any of these books. In the book of Job, the main character is never informed about what was really behind all the suffering he had to endure. In the book of Habakkuk, the prophet found the initial answer of Yahweh to his questions simply incomprehensible. In the book of Malachi an unspecified Day of Yahweh is foreseen when the righteous will experience healing and joy in place of their current suffering. The question initially

45. Noetzel, *Maleachi*, 237 (my translation). The German reads, "Im VI. Diskussionwort wird die Auflösung dieser Diskrepanz eschatologisch in Aussicht gestellt."
46. Noetzel, *Maleachi*, 238.
47. Author's translation.
48. Kessler, *Maleachi*, 299.

asked, "Where is the God of justice?" is not answered. These books, along with the rest of the Old Testament, give different responses to the problem of theodicy.

People ask difficult questions, and in none of these cases are those who ask questions judged. God is not angry or dissatisfied with Job for asking questions. In the book of Habakkuk, the prophet is also allowed to ask his questions, and even when he is not satisfied with the first answer to his questions, Yahweh does not reprimand him for that. It is the same in the book of Malachi. The people are allowed to question the justice of God, and neither the prophet nor Yahweh challenges the skeptical questions asked by the people.

In the book of Job, Job clung to God even in the most difficult of times. In Habakkuk the people are encouraged to keep faith in God. Both Job and Habakkuk are not satisfied with the answers given to the problem of unjust suffering. Job kept on asking questions, and Habakkuk did the same after Yahweh gave his first answer to the prophet. When doubt is expressed in the book of Malachi, the people are reminded of a book of remembrance "concerning those who feared the LORD and honored his name" (3:16). That there will be faithful believers is taken for granted and the aim is to strengthen their faith.

In the prophetic books, the emphasis is to keep on doing what is right even in the harshest of situations. In Habakkuk the people are encouraged to live by faith, and to live by faith means to live the life of a righteous person by doing what is right. In Malachi the emphasis is on the need to live life according to the ethical standards expected from the people of God; otherwise Yahweh will come to testify against "the sorcerers, adulterers and perjurers, against those who defraud labourers of their wages, who oppress the widows and the fatherless, and deprive aliens of justice, but do not fear me" (3:5). The difference between the books is that whereas Habakkuk speaks in general of doing what is right, Malachi gives more direct indications of what is ethically expected of believers.

In both the books of Habakkuk and Malachi the evildoers and wicked people will suffer punishment. In the book of Habakkuk, the prophet and his audience are assured that those who afflict the righteous will be judged (2:1-20). In the book of Malachi, the evildoers and arrogant people will be like stubble on the day that will burn like a fire so that they will be like ashes under the feet of the righteous ones (3:18-4:3).

DIFFERENCES

It is important to note the difference in literary genre between the three books. Job is part of the wisdom literature, while both Habakkuk and Malachi form part of the *corpus propheticum*, making use of literary genres typical of what is found in prophetic books. In the case of Job, the book is a protest against the current wisdom personified in the speeches by the friends of Job and Job's critique of their point of view. In the cases of Habakkuk and Malachi, the prophecies arose from particular historical circumstances. In the book of Habakkuk, the lack of justice in light of the prevailing violence in the community of Judah was the reason for the prophet's questions of Yahweh's apparent inactivity. In the book of Malachi, the people questioned the justice of Yahweh at a time when there was little hope for Judah on the international political scene.

Closely connected to the use of different literary genres is the difference in time and historical circumstances. Habakkuk is normally dated prior to the Babylonian rule in 605 BCE. Malachi is dated sometime during the fifth century BCE (460–450 BCE), while Job is probably one of the younger books in the Old Testament.

It is only in Job where the reaction to the one suffering is given. In Job 42:1–6, Job succumbed to Yahweh's response to his initial complaints. In Habakkuk and Malachi, the prophets delivered their respective prophetic messages; but we are not informed how the listeners responded to the message they received from the prophet. However, it should be noted that the book of Habakkuk closes on a personal note from Habakkuk. After a description of a mighty theophany of Yahweh, Habakkuk responds very much in the same way as Job: overwhelmed by the majesty of God with his heart beating, his lips quivering, and his legs trembling (Hab 3:16). In Malachi 2:17–3:7a, no response from the people is reported. In Malachi 3:16, the people reacted not to the eschatological message of the prophet but rather to the accusation the prophet leveled against the people. The answer Yahweh gives starts in Malachi 3:17 with no response from the people to the message of the prophet.

In the case of Job, the question plays itself out on a personal level; it is all about an individual that suffered in ways that are simply incomprehensible. In Habakkuk the question of theodicy is asked more on the level of world political events and the role the people of God will play within them. In

Malachi the focus is on the fate of the individual believer within the community of Israel in a time of distress. This difference between an emphasis on the individual, as in the case of Job, vis-à-vis an emphasis on the broader scope of world events, as in the case of the prophetic books, may be ascribed to the difference in literary genre. Wisdom literature focuses more on the individual in society, whereas the scope of the prophets in earlier times is more on world political events. In recent research, scholars point to wisdom influences in the book of Malachi that would explain the emphasis on the fate of the individual believer.[49]

In Malachi the emphasis on the ritual practices is noteworthy, while it is as good as absent in Job and Habakkuk. Also unique to Malachi is the idea of a way-preparer prior to the actual coming of Yahweh himself to restore justice. The idea of a written book of remembrance is also a unique contribution from Malachi with the aim of comforting people in times of suffering and doubt.

In the book of Habakkuk, the people are encouraged to wait patiently on Yahweh's action in the future and to keep faith and trust Yahweh in their present situation of suffering violence and injustices. In the book of Malachi there is also a shift toward the future. In the future, Yahweh will bring a change in the situation when there will be a clear distinction between those who serve Yahweh and those who do not. Hope should then be the driving force to comfort the people in their present distress. In the book of Job, the crisis is resolved not in the distant future but within the lifetime of Job.

CONCLUSION

To claim that the Old Testament does not provide an answer to the theodicy problem is perhaps a bit of an overstatement. It is safer to say that the Old Testament does not provide the answers the people expected to hear. The Old Testament does not provide its readers and believers with a single, clear-cut answer to the question of theodicy. Different situations ask for different answers to the problem. In the book of Job, the main emphasis is on the incomprehensibility of the way in which God directs events. Human beings are incapable of understanding God's ways of dealing with the

---

49. K. W. Weyde, *Prophecy and Teaching: Prophetic Authority, Form Problems, and the Use of Traditions in the Book of Malachi*, BZAW 288 (Berlin: de Gruyter, 2000).

world and the fate of individual believers. In the case of Habakkuk there
is also an emphasis on the incomprehensibility of God's way of controlling
world events, but the main emphasis is the encouragement to the people to
keep faithful because "the righteous will live by his faith" (2:4). In the case
of Malachi, the emphasis is on the future that will bring a decisive turn of
events with a complete reversal of the situation. While the evildoers prosper now (Mal 3:15) they will be like stubble on the day that is coming and
will burn like a furnace (4:1). While those who fear Yahweh are of the opinion that it is futile to serve Yahweh (3:14), they will, on the Day of Yahweh,
leap like calves released from the stall (4:2).

The question of unjust human suffering will remain an issue to be discussed in theology, in the field of Old Testament studies, and in other subjects as well. Within the Old Testament it seems that the question is not
fully resolved with a single answer. Different answers were given over time
to this intriguing question. There is no single explanation of the issue of
human suffering, but the variety of answers may aid us in a deeper understanding of this extremely complex phenomenon.

7

The New Covenant in the Book of the Twelve

Anthony R. Petterson

INTRODUCTION: THEMATIC STUDIES
OF THE NEW COVENANT

In thematic studies of the new covenant in the Old Testament, the Book of the Twelve is often not seen to contribute very much.* For instance, Peter Gentry and Stephen Wellum state: "Explicit references to the new covenant are rare in the Twelve (Minor) Prophets."[1] While I agree that the new covenant per se is not a major theme in the Book of the Twelve, scholars working in more detail on aspects of the Twelve (particularly those writing commentaries) identify the presence of new covenant concepts more frequently than thematic studies suggest. In this essay, I identify passages in the Book of the Twelve that contain new covenant concepts (from Hosea, Joel, Micah, Haggai, Zechariah, and Malachi) and discuss their significance.

---

*This article was originally presented as a biblical theology plenary lecture at the Tyndale Fellowship Conference, 2019.

1. Peter J. Gentry and Stephen J. Wellum, *Kingdom through Covenant: A Biblical-Theological Understanding of the Covenants* (Wheaton: Crossway, 2012), 530. It is curious what they mean by "explicit references" since the only time the phrase "new covenant" appears in the Old Testament is in Jeremiah 31:31. See also Pierre Buis, "La Nouvelle Alliance," *VT* 18 (1968): 1–15; Walter C. Kaiser Jr., "The Old Promise and the New Covenant: Jeremiah 31:31–34," *JETS* (1972): 11–23; David K. Fredrickson, *Is Isaiah's "Servant Covenant" the New Covenant? An Exegetical Study* (Lewiston: Edwin Mellen, 2014).

NEW COVENANT CONCEPTS

Since Jeremiah 31:31–34 is the only passage where the phrase "new covenant" occurs, it must be taken as the starting point for identifying the component themes. Determining a list of elements beyond this passage is somewhat arbitrary.[2] Further elements could be added by identifying other passages that contain some of the themes of Jeremiah 31:31–34 and determining what else is present. For instance, the "everlasting covenant" in Ezekiel 37, like Jeremiah 31, includes the reunion of the northern and southern kingdoms (Ezek 37:15–22, 31; cf. Jer 31:31), return to the land (Ezek 37:21; cf. Jer 31:16), removal of sin and cleansing (Ezek 37:23; cf. Jer 31:34), and obedience to the law (Ezek 37:24; cf. Jer 31:33).[3] In addition, Ezekiel 37 speaks of a new David (Ezek 37:24–25) and a new sanctuary (37:26–28).[4] Having identified additional elements, we could then identify other passages based on these concepts, and the process could continue almost ad infinitum. At some point a decision needs to be made as to what constitutes the essential elements of the new covenant. For the purpose of this study, I will be concerned with identifying the following elements of Jeremiah 31:31–34, captured succinctly by Bruce Ware, with a couple of modifications:[5]

1. A *new mode* of implementation, namely, a divine initiative to internalize the law ("I will put my law in their minds").[6] This contrasts with the old covenant directive to put it there themselves (cf. Deut 6:6; 11:18).[7]

---

2. E.g., Fredrickson, *New Covenant*, 190, argues that all models for determining new covenant passages "all incorporate some amount of unacknowledged arbitrariness or extra-biblical premises into their construction."

3. Scripture quotations are from the NIV2011 unless stated otherwise.

4. These elements are also present in Jeremiah 33:15–18, but not in direct association with the new covenant.

5. Bruce A. Ware, "The New Covenant and the People(s) of God," in *Dispensationalism, Israel and the Church*, ed. Craig A. Blaising and Darrell L. Bock (Grand Rapids: Zondervan, 1992), 68–97, (75). The modifications include the addition of a divine initiative in point 1 and the addition of the full and final abolition of sin in point 3.

6. Compare Jeremiah 32:39; Ezekiel 11:19–20; 36:26–27.

7. Willem A. VanGemeren, "A Response," in Blaising and Bock, *Dispensationalism, Israel and the Church*, 331–46 (338), rightly points out that the internalization of the law is not new. However, the divine initiative to put it there is.

2. A *new result*, namely, faithfulness to God ("they will all know me").[8]

3. A *new basis*, namely, full and final forgiveness ("for I will forgive their wickedness") with sin fully and finally abolished ("and will remember their sins no more").[9]

4. A *new scope* of inclusion, namely, covenant faithfulness characteristic of all covenant participants ("from the least of them to the greatest").[10]

Gerhard von Rad observes a great similarity between Jeremiah's new covenant and the theology of Deuteronomy.[11] Even though the terminology differs, both look toward God changing the human heart to enable obedience.[12] In the rhetoric of Moses's speech in Deuteronomy, the blessings and curses in chapters 28–30 function as incentives and disincentives to obedience. Yet, it becomes clear that Moses anticipates that Israel will fail to keep the covenant in the land and the covenant curses will fall.[13] This is first implied by the number of curses way outnumbering the blessings, and it becomes explicit in Deuteronomy 30:1 when Moses says that the curses *will* come on the people and they *will* be driven from the land. Deuteronomy

8. Joshua N. Moon, *Jeremiah's New Covenant: An Augustinian Reading*, Journal of Theological Interpretation Supplements 3 (Winona Lake, IN: Eisenbrauns, 2011), 239–40: "This knowledge of Yhwh, once again, concerns the fidelity of the people to Yhwh." Compare Jeremiah 2:8; 9:3, 23–24; 22:15–16. The idea that a person will no longer teach their neighbor does not necessarily mean that there will no longer be any teaching under the new covenant, but that there is no *need* for instruction and exhortation to covenant faithfulness. Jack R. Lundbom, *Jeremiah 21–36: A New Translation with Introduction and Commentary*, AB 21b (New York: Doubleday, 2004), 470, aptly states, "Jeremiah envisions a day when people the likes of himself will be out of a job."
9. Bernhard W. Anderson, "The New Covenant and the Old," in *The Old Testament and Christian Faith*, ed. Bernhard W. Anderson (London: SCM, 1964), 225–42 (235), "The foundation of the enduring covenant will be divine forgiveness."
10. Cf. Scott J. Hafemann, "The Covenant Relationship," in *Central Themes in Biblical Theology: Mapping Unity in Diversity*, ed. Scott J. Hafemann and Paul R. House (Nottingham: Apollos, 2007), 20–65 (14).
11. Gerhard von Rad, *The Message of the Prophets* (London: SCM, 1968), 235. More recently, see Paul A. Barker, *The Triumph of Grace in Deuteronomy* (Carlisle: Paternoster, 2004), 181, "Deuteronomy 30 shares much the same theological position as the promise of the new covenant in Jeremiah 31."
12. von Rad, *Prophets*, 236.
13. The problem with the old covenant was Israel's infidelity, something which broke the covenant from the beginning (Jer 11:1–13). In Jeremiah, the new covenant is a key aspect of God's salvation of his people after the judgment of exile.

30:2–6 then promises a new action of God predicated on Israel's failure. What Israel cannot do under the old covenant, God will do under the new. He will do the work on their heart that will make love and obedience possible. As Gordon McConville states:

> The answer to Israel's infidelity lies in God himself. He will somehow enable his people ultimately to do what they cannot do in their strength, namely, to obey him out of the conviction and devotion of their own hearts.[14]

God changing his people's hearts so that they might obey him lies at the heart of Jeremiah's new covenant. Since this idea goes back to Deuteronomy, it is reasonable to expect to see it in the earlier books of the Twelve. Consequently, in identifying new covenant concepts in the Twelve, I will not simply be searching for traces of the language of Jeremiah 31:31–34, since many of the books are set before Jeremiah. I am more concerned about identifying the four concepts above, which may be expressed differently.

NEW COVENANT CONCEPTS IN HOSEA

The prophet Hosea's marriage to Gomer portrays the brokenness of Israel's covenant relationship with the Lord (the marriage metaphor is present in Jeremiah 31:32: "They broke my covenant, though I was a husband to them").[15] Gomer's sexual promiscuity is a powerful metaphor for Israel's covenant infidelity expressed chiefly in its idolatry and alliances with non-Israelite nations. Yet the ultimate point of Hosea's marriage to Gomer is that God will persist in his relationship with Israel, despite Israel's unfaithfulness. This is conveyed by changing the names of Gomer's children and by Hosea's final action of taking Gomer back as his wife. New covenant concepts are seen in both.

---

14. J. Gordon McConville, *Grace in the End: A Study in Deuteronomic Theology* (Grand Rapids: Zondervan, 1993), 137. See also J. Gary Millar, *Now Choose Life: Theology and Ethics in Deuteronomy*, NSBT 6 (Leicester: Inter-Varsity Press, 1998), 180; Barker, *The Triumph of Grace in Deuteronomy*, 181; Jack R. Lundbom, *Deuteronomy: A Commentary* (Grand Rapids: Eerdmans, 2013), 818.

15. Barbara A. Bozak, *Life "Anew": A Literary-Theological Study of Jer. 30–31*, Analecta Biblica 122 (Rome: Editrice Pontificio Instituto Biblico, 1991), 120, "Thus in the context of this poetic cycle *b'l*, while certainly meaning 'lord,' can also mean 'husband,' a lordship in intimacy and authority rather than power, accenting not a punitive but caring authority."

In relation to the children's names in chapter 1, Jezreel and Lo-ruhamah ("No-love") convey God's punishment of Israel.[16] Yet there is a startling turn at the end of verse 6, where God declares, "But I will completely forgive them" (author's translation).[17] The Hebrew is often reconstrued to say the opposite: "that I should at all forgive them."[18] However, the juxtaposition of punishment with forgiveness is essential to God's character (see Exod 20:5–6; 34:6–7). Furthermore, the theme of God's salvation continues into verse 7, and the stark contrast of wrath and love is seen verses 9–10, as well as throughout the book.[19] The wider context of the book also envisions the reunification of Israel and Judah (Hos 1:11; 3:5; see also Jer 3:5; Ezek 37:15–23; Zech 10:6), so God not forgiving Israel makes little sense. Elsewhere Judah also suffers God's wrath before being saved (Hos 5:14–15; 6:11; 10:11). While forgiveness is not said here to be full and final (as in Jer 31), it is essential to repairing the covenant relationship.

The name of Gomer's third child after her marriage to Hosea ("Not-my-people") has clear covenantal associations. The covenant formula (with variations), "I will take you as my own people, and I will be your God" (Exod 6:7), recurs throughout the Old Testament (e.g., Gen 17:7–8; Lev 26:12; Deut 29:13; 2 Sam 7:24; Jer 31:33; Zech 8:8).[20] Hosea 1, therefore, speaks of the punishment and rejection of God's people for their unfaithfulness, with the dissolution of the covenant relationship ("Not-my-people"), but also promises its restoration: "Say of your brothers, 'My people,' and of your sisters, 'My loved one'" (Hos 2:1 [MT 2:3]). The announcement of the reversal of the children's names occurs at the end of chapter 2, of which Paul Williamson

16. Jezreel means "God sows" or "God scatters [seed]"—a positive agricultural image as it anticipates a crop. The name also sounds like "Israel," to whom the message is directed. While the name has a positive meaning, it had negative associations for an Israelite in Hosea's day. In 845 BCE, Jehu killed Jezebel and violently assassinated those who remained of the house of Ahab at Jezreel (see 2 Kgs 9:10, 36–37; 10:11).

17. Following Duane A. Garrett, *Hosea, Joel*, NAC 19a (Nashville: Broadman & Holman, 1997), 60–61.

18. See the discussion in Eric J. Tully, *Hosea: A Handbook on the Hebrew Text*, BHHB (Waco, TX: Baylor University Press, 2018), 27–28.

19. David B. Wyrtzen, "The Theological Center of the Book of Hosea," *BSac* 141 (1984): 315–29 (316–19), demonstrates five judgment-salvation cycles: Cycle 1 (1:2–2:1); Cycle 2 (2:2–23); Cycle 3 (3:1–5); Cycle 4 (4:4–11:11); Cycle 5 (11:12–14:8).

20. See Rolf Rendtorff, *The Covenant Formula: An Exegetical and Theological Investigation*, OTS (Edinburgh: T&T Clark, 1998).

says, "The three symbolic names of Hosea's children are turned around in this restoration oracle to speak of the new covenant (2:23)."[21]

In Hosea 1, God's forgiveness lies at the heart of the restoration of the covenant relationship (1:6–7). Associated with it is the reunion of the nation (1:11) and a future Davidic king (1:11; 3:5). These ideas are present in the wider context of Jeremiah (31:6; 33:15–16).

God's plan to restore his covenant relationship with unfaithful Israel is played out in Hosea's relationship with Gomer in Hosea 2. Hosea's statement, "For she is not my wife, and I am not her husband" (2:2 [MT 2:4]), may be a statement of divorce or simply a description of the brokenness of the marriage relationship.[22] In either case, Gomer's adultery and promiscuity has ended the relationship. Yet as the chapter develops, it becomes clear that after due punishment, Hosea (representing God) intends to restore it. Many see a reference to the new covenant in Hosea 2:18 [MT 2:20]:[23]

> In that day I will make a covenant for them with the beasts of the field,
> the birds in the sky and the creatures that move along the ground.
> Bow and sword and battle I will abolish from the land, so that all may
> lie down in safety.

Paul Williamson is correct to observe that the covenant directly in view here is not the new covenant, but a covenant with all the creatures of the earth for the benefit of the people.[24] Yet as he acknowledges, the new covenant is in view in the wider context, particularly toward the end of chapter 2. When God promises to "betroth you to me forever" (2:19 [MT 2:21]), what seems to be in view is a permanent reestablishment of the relationship so that the people "know the LORD" (ESV) (Hos 2:20 [MT 2:22]; cf. Jer 31:34).[25] Accompanying this will be restoration to the land and agricultural abundance (Hos 2:21–22 [MT 2:23–24]), which are features associated with the new covenant in Jeremiah (31:5, 8–9, 12, 16, 23) and behind this, Deuteronomy (30:4, 9). Hosea makes it clear that this is God's work when he says that he

---

21. Paul R. Williamson, *Sealed with an Oath: Covenant in God's Unfolding Purpose*, NSBT 23 (Nottingham: Apollos, 2007), 178.

22. See the recent discussion in Joshua N. Moon, *Hosea*, ApOTC 21 (London: Apollos, 2018), 51–52.

23. E.g., Kaiser Jr., "Old Promise," 14; Douglas K. Stuart, *Hosea-Jonah*, WBC 31 (Waco, TX: Word, 1987); Gentry and Wellum, *Kingdom*, 530.

24. Williamson, *Sealed*, 177.

25. Williamson, *Sealed*, 177: "The situation portrayed here appears in any case to be unassailable and irreversible."

will "allure her" and "speak to her heart" (author's translation) so that she will rightly respond (Hos 2:14). Hans Walter Wolff is enthusiastic about the new covenant concepts here:

> But what is essentially new in comparison with the old covenant is that Yahweh provides everything for its establishment and its endurance, including mercy for the guilty (v. 25; cf. v. 21) [ET v. 23; cf. v. 19] and healing for their guilt (v. 19) [ET v. 17]. This is, therefore, not the restoration of the old covenant. ... Here is the announcement of a marriage that establishes a new, final communion between God and his people (cf. Mk 2:18–22). Jeremiah 31:31–34 adds little more to this than the appropriate catchword "new covenant." The basic outline of this theme is Hosean.[26]

It seems that both Hosea and Jeremiah were influenced by Deuteronomy (or some form thereof).[27] Eduardo Eli demonstrates this in relation to Hosea 14.[28] He notes that the sins for which Israel is indicted in verse 3 (MT v. 4) reflect the stipulations of Deuteronomy—trusting in foreign powers (Deut 17:16a), in horses (Deut 17:16; cf. Isa 30:16; 31:3; 36:8), and idolatry ("what our own hands have made"; cf. Isa 2:8; Mic 5:13). The compassion of the Lord to the fatherless (or "orphan") is also found throughout Deuteronomy.[29] Furthermore, the agricultural blessings promised to Israel in Hosea 14:6–8 (MT 14:7–9) evoke key words from Deuteronomy 30:3, 5, 9; 32:39. After calling on the people to "return to the LORD" and appealing to God to "forgive all our sins" (Hos 14:2 [MT 14:3]), God promises to "heal their waywardness and love them freely" (14:4 [MT 14:5]). The logic reflects that of Deuteronomy 30 where after exile the people return to the Lord (Deut 30:2) and God changes

---

26. Hans W. Wolff, *Hosea* (Augsburg: Fortress, 1974), 55. More recently, Moon, *Hosea*, 67: "Hosea is describing the same rhetorical world as the 'new covenant' in Jeremiah." For similar comments, see Walter Brueggemann, *Tradition in Crisis: A Study in Hosea* (Richmond: John Knox, 1968), 116–17; Wyrtzen, "Hosea," 315, 323; McConville, *Grace*, 137; Garrett, *Hosea, Joel*, 88; Stephen G. Dempster, "Geography and Genealogy, Dominion and Dynasty: A Theology of the Hebrew Bible," in *Biblical Theology: Retrospect and Prospect*, ed. Scott J. Hafemann (Downers Grove, IL: IVP, 2002), 66–82 (79); Michael Horton, *God of Promise: Introducing Covenant Theology* (Grand Rapids: Baker Books, 2006), 49; Victor H. Matthews, *The Hebrew Prophets and Their Social World: An Introduction*, 2nd ed. (Grand Rapids: Baker Academic, 2012), 92.

27. Brueggemann, *Tradition*, 117, argues that Hosea 2 reflects Deuteronomy 30:15–20.

28. Eduardo F. Eli, "The Presence of the Covenant Motif in Hosea: An Intertextual Approach for the Last Oracle in the Book," *JBQ* 45 (2017): 34–42 (39).

29. Deuteronomy 10:18; 14:29; 16:11, 14; 24:17, 19–21; 26:12–13; 27:19.

their hearts so that they might love him and live (30:6).[30] The promise to "heal their waywardness" can also be translated as "heal them from their turning," which emphasizes God's work to turn them from their spiritual depravity and apostasy.[31] Tom Schreiner claims: "The promise of healing matches the new covenant in Jeremiah and the covenant of peace in Ezekiel."[32]

In summary, Hosea demonstrates three of the four core elements of Jeremiah's new covenant. The new mode is reflected in 2:14 (MT 2:16) where God says he will allure Israel and speak to her heart, and in 14:4 (MT 14:5) where he promises to heal her from her turning. The new result is that Israel will know the Lord (2:20 [MT 2:22]). The new basis is complete forgiveness (1:6–7).

NEW COVENANT CONCEPTS IN JOEL

While the word "covenant" does not occur in Joel, the book presumes the national covenant. James Nogalski argues that the problems identified by Joel are a result of Judah breaking its terms.[33] Drawing on the work of Douglas Stuart, Nogalski shows how the threats and promises in Joel mirror the covenant curses and blessings of Deuteronomy 27–32.[34] He comments: "A scenario like that described in Joel 1—where drought, locusts, enemy attack, and heat combine simultaneously—portrays the current situation as the actualization of the curse that signifies disobedience to the covenant stipulations."[35]

Nogalski observes that what he calls the "new covenant promises" in Deuteronomy 30:4–10 are all motifs found in Joel 2:18–27.[36] These new cov-

---

30. See also Stuart, *Hosea–Jonah*, 214–15.

31. There is a similar expression in Jeremiah 3:22, where there is a play on the word "turn": "turn sons of turning; I will cure your turning."

32. T. R. Schreiner, *The King in His Beauty: A Biblical Theology of the Old and New Testaments* (Grand Rapids: Baker Academic, 2013), 410. Also Michael B. Shepherd, *A Commentary on the Book of the Twelve* (Grand Rapids: Kregel, 2018), 111.

33. James D. Nogalski, "Presumptions of 'Covenant' in Joel," in *Covenant in the Persian Period: From Genesis to Chronicles*, ed. Richard J. Bautch and Gary N. Knoppers (Winona Lake, IN: Eisenbrauns, 2015), 211–28 (217).

34. Stuart, *Hosea–Jonah*, 232. (Note especially: Deut 28:49–50; cf. Joel 1:6–7; Deut 28:51; cf. Joel 1:5, 9–10, 20; Deut 28:37; see also 29:24; cf. Joel 2:17; Deut 28:22, 24; cf. Joel 1:10–12, 17, 19–20; Deut 28:38, 42; cf. Joel 1:4; 2:25).

35. Nogalski, "Presumptions," 219.

36. Many of these are also secondary elements in Jeremiah (31:8, 16).

enant promises include return from exile (Deut 30:4), removal of enemies (30:7), and the return of prosperity (children, livestock, agriculture) (30:9). While these are not the core elements of the new covenant in Jeremiah 31:31–34, they certainly accompany it (e.g., Jer 31:8–11, 23–25). Like Deuteronomy 30:2, Joel indicates that restoration depends on repentance (Joel 2:12–13; cf. Jer 31:19). Joel's call to repent also includes a double reference to the heart: "Return to me with all your heart. ... Rend your heart and not your garments" (2:12–13). While Joel does not speak of God transforming the people's hearts, he later speaks of God pouring out his Spirit on all people so that they have the experience of the prophets. Here the scope of inclusion reflects Jeremiah 31 (Joel 2:28–29 [MT 3:1–2]): "And afterward, I will pour out my Spirit on all people. Your sons and daughters will prophesy, your old men will dream dreams, your young men will see visions. Even on my servants, both men and women, I will pour out my Spirit in those days."

Leslie Allen states: "It is comparable with Jeremiah's great prophecy of the New Covenant in which an intimate knowledge of the Law and of Yahweh is promised to all the people, 'from the least of them to the greatest.' "[37] The linking of the work of the Spirit and the internalizing of the law in Ezekiel (see Ezek 11:19–20; 36:26–28; 37:14) also leads many to see new covenant themes here.[38] While not present in Jeremiah, the agency of God's Spirit is prominent in Ezekiel.[39]

However, there are differences between Joel and Jeremiah. Jeremiah speaks of the universal knowledge of God, while Joel speaks of all the people being prophets. Yet these may not be that far apart. Integral to the prophetic role was calling the people to covenant faithfulness. Moses himself expresses the hope that all the people would be prophets with the Spirit upon them (Num 11:29), and Joel may be reflecting this ideal.[40] Certainly the wider context of Joel, which contains ancillary elements of the new covenant found in Deuteronomy and Jeremiah, supports seeing new covenant themes here, especially its universal scope.

37. Leslie C. Allen, *The Books of Joel, Obadiah, Jonah and Micah*, NICOT (Grand Rapids: Eerdmans, 1976), 99.

38. E.g., Fredrickson, *New Covenant*, 200; Paul R. House, *Old Testament Theology* (Downers Grove: InterVarsity Press, 1998): 356.

39. Ware, "New Covenant," 77.

40. Shepherd, *Commentary*, 132, calls this "the new covenant ideal."

NEW COVENANT CONCEPTS IN MICAH

The book of Micah consists of three cycles of judgment and salvation prophecies (Mic 1:2–2:13; 3:1–5:15; 6:1–7:20). Like Joel, the word "covenant" does not appear in the book, but the whole presentation presumes the national covenant and hints at the new covenant with its portrayal of divine forgiveness that restores relationship.

Because of the sins of Samaria and Jerusalem, God envisages the destruction of Israel with the people swept from the land. The lament in 7:1–6 represents the low point of the book, portraying community anarchy and family treachery. Yet Micah expresses hope that the Lord will hear him and save him (7:7).

Micah then speaks on behalf of the remnant of Jerusalem and expresses the hope that after bearing the Lord's wrath at the hands of the nations for his sin, he will be restored by the Lord (7:8–9). This restoration is pictured relationally ("He will bring me out into the light; I will see his righteousness"; 7:9) and geographically as a return to Jerusalem/Zion (7:11–12). Central to the future restoration is God's forgiveness of their sins, promised in terms that echo the character creed of Exodus 34:6–7 in Micah 7:18–19: "Who is a God like you, who pardons sin and forgives the transgression of the remnant of his inheritance? You do not stay angry forever but delight to show mercy. You will again have compassion on us; you will tread our sins underfoot and hurl all our iniquities into the depths of the sea."

God's character is the basis for hope.[41] Significantly, in Exodus God's character is revealed to Moses after the golden calf incident, which broke the covenant and is the basis for its renewal. In addition, Micah's reference to the promises pledged to Jacob and Abraham gives the future restoration a covenantal flavor (Mic 7:20). Shepherd notes the connection between divine forgiveness and Jeremiah's new covenant here: "Forgiveness of iniquity and sin will take place in the new covenant relationship (Jer. 31:31–34) for the remnant of his inheritance."[42] Micah's description of forgiveness indicates it is full and final: "… tread our sins underfoot and hurl all our iniquities into the depths of the sea" (7:19).

---

41. See Joel Barker, "From Where Does My Hope Come? Theodicy and the Character of YHWH in Allusions to Exodus 34:6–7 in the Book of the Twelve," *JETS* 61 (2018): 697–715 (712).
42. Shepherd, *Commentary*, 283.

Micah knows that God's people are unable to save themselves. Kenneth Cuffey comments in relation to 7:1-6: "The people of God are completely unable to please God. Their spiritual realm has been totally ruined and thus the entire scope of life and relationships as well."[43] While Micah does not speak of God changing the hearts of his people, nor of a new scope of inclusion, he does underscore the new basis of the new covenant as God's full and final forgiveness that restores relationship so that those who are restored "will see his righteousness" (7:9).

NEW COVENANT CONCEPTS IN HAGGAI

Haggai is the first book in the Twelve explicitly set in the postexilic period. Haggai calls on the returnees to build the temple and to obey the national covenant.[44] Expectations are high because the people have returned to the land. There are new covenant echoes in the reported response of the people to Haggai's preaching in 1:12-14:

> And Zerubbabel son of Shealtiel, Joshua son of Jehozadak, the high priest, and all the remnant of the people obeyed the voice of the LORD their God, that is [they obeyed] in accordance with the words of Haggai the prophet, because the LORD their God had sent him. And the people feared the LORD.
>
> And Haggai, the messenger of the LORD with a message of the LORD, said to the people, "I am with you, declares the LORD."
>
> And the LORD stirred up the spirit of Zerubbabel son of Shealtiel, the governor of Judah, and the spirit of Joshua son of Jehozadak, the high priest, and the spirit of all the remnant of the people, and they came and they did work in the house of the LORD of hosts their God. (author's translation)

---

43. Kenneth H. Cuffey, *The Literary Coherence of the Book of Micah: Remnant, Restoration, and Promise*, LHBOTS 611 (New York: Bloomsbury T&T Clark, 2015), 249.

44. Earlier prophets envisaged that the temple would play a key role in the restoration (e.g., Isa 2:2-3; 44:28; Ezek 40-48; Joel 3:18; Mic 4:1-2). Therefore, when the people returned to the land, rebuilding the temple should have been their priority. It would indicate their return to the Lord.

While not as intimate as the phrase "my people," Haggai calls those who have returned to the land "the people" (1:12 [x2], 13, 14),[45] which is a vast improvement on 1:2 where God speaks of them as "this people," depicting relational distance on account of their disobedience in not building the temple.[46]

Most remarkable in relation to the theme of the new covenant (and the Prophets in general) is that the people are reported as obeying the Lord (emphasized in the Hebrew by the verb's prominence at the beginning of verse 12—"and they obeyed") and fearing him. Some scholars propose a two-stage response where the people first "heard" (rather than "obeyed") and are "afraid" (rather than "fear"). The Lord then announces he is with them (1:13). This then results in true obedience (1:13).[47] Yet the actions in verses 12–14 are better understood as coinciding—the people's response is first reported and then God's action which enabled it.[48]

The "spirit" (רוּחַ; 1:14 [3x]) here refers to "the impulse that governs a person's life and controls his or her behaviour."[49] In other words, it refers to a person's "will" or "disposition." God moved the wills of the leaders and the people so that they obeyed the word of God proclaimed by Haggai and came to work in the temple (cf. Isa 41:2, 25; 45:13; Jer 50:9; Ezra 1:1, 5; 2 Chr 36:22). God's work in the life of his people so that they might obey his word and fear him reflects the new mode of the new covenant and suggests that it may be being realized in Haggai's day. Throughout Jeremiah God's people consistently are said to disobey and be unable to change by themselves.[50] It is only in the new covenant that God enables their obedience. Similarly, the word "obey" (שָׁמַע) is also found in Deuteronomy 30:2 (cf. Deut 4:30),

---

45. See further, Tim Meadowcroft, Haggai, Readings: A New Biblical Commentary (Sheffield: Sheffield Phoenix, 2006), 140; Carol L. Meyers and Eric M. Meyers, Haggai, Zechariah 1–8: A New Translation with Introduction and Commentary (New York: Doubleday, 1987), 45.

46. R. A. Taylor, "Haggai," in Haggai, Malachi, NAC 21a (Nashville: Broadman & Holman, 2004), 21–201 (138–39).

47. See Michael H. Floyd, Minor Prophets: Part 2, FOTL 22 (Grand Rapids: Eerdmans, 2000), 269; Elie Assis, "To Build or Not to Build: A Dispute between Haggai and His People (Hag 1)," ZAW 119 (2007b): 514–27 (522–27).

48. Mark J. Boda, Haggai, Zechariah, NIVAC (Grand Rapids: Zondervan, 2004), 106.

49. Robin Routledge, Old Testament Theology: A Thematic Approach (Nottingham: Apollos, 2008), 144.

50. E.g., Jeremiah 3:13, 25; 7:24, 26–28; 9:13; 11:8; 17:23; 22:21; 25:3–4, 7–8; 29:19; 32:23; 34:17; 35:14–17; 36:31; 37:2; 40:3; 42:21; 43:4; 44:5, 23. See John Kessler, "Tradition, Continuity and Covenant in the Book of Haggai: An Alternative Voice from Early Persian Yehud," in Tradition in Transition: Haggai and Zechariah 1–8 in the Trajectory of Hebrew Theology, ed. Mark J. Boda and Michael H. Floyd, LHBOTS 475 (New York: T&T Clark, 2008), 1–39 (20).

where Moses envisages a time after exile when the people return to the Lord and obey his word as a result of God circumcising their hearts.

Mark Boda contends that Haggai "reflects the vision of the new covenant seen in Jeremiah (Jer. 31–33), in which God not only writes the law on the hearts of the people (31:33) but even moves their affections (32:40)."[51] In addition, Boda observes that the themes of the Davidic line, the sanctuary, and the remnant, which are associated with the new covenant in Ezekiel 37:15–28, are key themes of Haggai.[52]

God's promise "I am with you" (Hag 2:4; cf. 1:12) is an important aspect of the national covenant (Exod 25:8; 29:45–46; 33:14, 16; cf. Isa 41:10; 43:5; Jer 30:11). It is also a promise associated with Solomon's construction of the temple (1 Chr 22:18) and hence relevant for its reconstruction.[53] The link between the promise "I am with you" and the presence of God's Spirit (Hag 2:5) may suggest that the new covenant has arrived, since the Spirit both moves the people to obedience and empowers them for their work on the temple (see Zech 4:6). Yet it is interesting that Haggai says "my Spirit remains," which implies that God's presence by his Spirit is not completely new.[54]

In summary, Haggai reflects the new mode and the new result of the new covenant with God working by his Spirit so that the people obey his word. Yet Haggai is silent about the new basis and the new scope of inclusion.

NEW COVENANT CONCEPTS IN ZECHARIAH

Zechariah begins on the same note of expectation as Haggai. After recalling God's anger with the preexilic generations (the ancestors), Zechariah issues God's call to "return to me," with the promise that "I will return to you" (Zech 1:3). The end of the introduction reports that "they repented" (1:6b).[55]

---

51. Boda, *Haggai, Zechariah*, 108.

52. Boda, *Haggai, Zechariah*, 110.

53. See Meadowcroft, *Haggai*, 141 (cf. Ezek 37:27).

54. James M. Hamilton Jr., *God's Indwelling Presence: The Holy Spirit in the Old and New Testaments* (Nashville: Broadman & Holman, 2006), convincingly argues that while the Spirit empowers believers in the Old Testament and dwells among them in the temple, there is "no clear statement that all old covenant believers were individually indwelt by the Holy Spirit" (p. 55). The dwelling of the Spirit within believers occurs after Jesus's glorification (John 14:17, 23).

55. "Return" and "repent" translate the same word: שׁוב. William L. Holladay, *The Root Šûbh in the Old Testament* (Leiden: Brill, 1958), 116–57, provides a thorough study of its "covenantal usage."

In the flow of Zechariah's argument, "they" must refer to Zechariah's contemporaries (rather than the ancestors), since God's judgment overtook the ancestors and they are no more (1:5-6a).[56] Their repentance coheres with the account of the people's obedience in Haggai and, against the backdrop of Deuteronomy 30:1-6, may suggest that God has circumcised his people's hearts.

Similarly, in chapter 4, Zechariah has a vision of a gold menorah that has a continual supply of oil to its seven lamps from two olive trees via various pipes and a bowl. While it is difficult to be certain about aspects of the interpretation of this vision (the prophet struggles himself to understand), it seems that the main message is that the temple will be rebuilt: "Not by might nor by power, but by my Spirit" (4:6). The close association of God's Spirit with the new covenant and obedience in earlier Prophets suggests the Spirit is at work in the hearts of the people so that they obey the words of the prophets and complete the temple.

At the same time, there are indications in Zechariah that not all the hearts of the people are transformed and sin continues. In the same vision, there are some in the community who "despise the day of small things" (4:10). The scope of the knowledge of God and his ways is not universal. Elsewhere in Zechariah, the sixth vision indicates there are some who trouble the community by stealing and swearing falsely and that there is a failure of justice since they are wrongly acquitted of their crimes (5:3-4).[57] The seventh vision of a flying ephah portrays iniquity, wickedness, and idolatry persisting in the land and indicates their removal lies in the future (5:6-7). In the narrative about a delegation from Bethel who come to Jerusalem to inquire about the need to continue to fast (Zech 7-8), it is evident that at least some in the community do not have the Torah written on their hearts since Zechariah sees the need to reiterate some of its key requirements, contrary to Jeremiah 31:34 (Zech 7:8-10; 8:16-17, 19). In the two oracles that complete the book, God's people are warned against idolatry (10:2) and later God promises to remove idolatry, false prophets, and the resulting uncleanness from the land (13:2-6). David Baker rightly comments: "After the exile and restoration, it might have seemed that the covenant had been renewed

---

56. See Mark J. Boda, *The Book of Zechariah*, NICOT (Grand Rapids: Eerdmans, 2015), 84-85.

57. See further, Anthony R. Petterson, "The Flying Scroll That Will Not Acquit the Guilty: Exodus 34.7 in Zechariah 5.3," *JSOT* 38 (2014): 347-61.

and the people of God reinstated to their former position. Yet *Zechariah* still looks to the future for the realization of such hopes."[58]

The use of the covenant formula in Zechariah also shows that the restoration of relationship is future. Zechariah 8:7–8 reads:

> So says the LORD of hosts, "Look, I will save my people from the land where the sun rises to the land where it sets. I will bring them and they will dwell in the midst of Jerusalem, and they will be my people and I will be their God, in truth and in righteousness." (author's translation)

The use of the third person ("they" and "their") in the covenant formula, rather than the second person ("you"), speaks of a future generation.[59] The covenant formula is also echoed in 2:11 [MT 2:15]: "Many nations will be joined with the LORD in that day and will become my people." Here Zechariah widens the scope of the covenant people to include the nations. This goes beyond Jeremiah but is consistent with Isaiah (e.g., Isa 56:3–8).[60]

Zechariah 9–14 is largely oriented to the future. Here the word "covenant" occurs twice (9:11; 11:10). In Zechariah 9, God promises to save the residents of Zion in the future through his king (9:9), setting them free from the waterless pit (an image of exile) "because of the blood of my covenant with you" (9:11). The Sinai covenant was ratified with blood (see Exod 24:8) and this is the basis for God's future deliverance.

In Zechariah 11, the national covenant is portrayed as broken when the prophet is called to play the role of a shepherd to represent the way the people have rejected the Lord as their shepherd. He takes a staff called "Favor" and breaks it, "revoking the covenant I had made with all the nations [lit. peoples]" (11:10). This covenant is best understood as the national covenant,

---

58. David L. Baker, "Covenant: An Old Testament Study," in *The God of Covenant: Biblical, Theological, and Contemporary Perspectives*, ed. Jamie A. Grant and Alistair I. Wilson (Leicester: Apollos, 2005), 21–53 (46).

59. Earlier prophets spoke of the new covenant being established with a future generation and often used the covenant formula with the third-person plural ("their God" rather than "your God") to reflect this (e.g., Jer 24:7; 31:1; 31:31; 32:38; Ezek 11:20; 14:11; 34:24; 37:23, 27) but not always (e.g., Jer 30:22; Ezek 36:28). Similarly, when the people are addressed directly in the present, it is usually "God for you" (e.g., Jer 7:23; 11:4) but not always (e.g., 2 Sam 7:24). A list of occurrences of the covenant formula is found in Rendtorff, *Covenant Formula*, 93–94.

60. See further, Christopher J. H. Wright, "Covenant: God's Mission through God's People," in Grant and Wilson, *The God of Covenant: Biblical, Theological, and Contemporary Perspectives*, 54–78 (76–78).

and the symbolic action explains why the nation has suffered punishment and exile.[61]

In terms of new covenant concepts, the call to obey the Torah is a key feature of Zechariah 1-8 (especially chs. 7-8). However, while the people are initially said to repent, and God promises that his Spirit will enable them to rebuild the temple, nothing is explicitly said about God putting the law in their minds and writing it on their hearts.[62] Nor does Zechariah speak of the new result ("they will all know me").[63] However, the new basis of the new covenant, namely cleansing and the abolition of sin, is present throughout the book. Zechariah 3 is a vision of the cleansing of the high priest Joshua that foreshadows a greater cleansing when the Lord brings his servant, the Shoot (the future Davidic king); God promises, "I will remove the sin of this land in a single day" (Zech 3:9).[64] Significantly, the sacrificial system is not presented as the means by which sin is ultimately removed as it was under the old covenant. Instead, Zechariah 12-14 shows that it is through the death of a future Davidic king that ultimate cleansing comes.[65] Zechariah prophesies another attack on Jerusalem in which a future Davidic king is pierced by his own people (12:10-11).[66] Through this a fountain is opened to cleanse the community from sin and uncleanness (Zech 13:1; cf. 3:9). Associated with this is God changing the disposition of his people such that they mourn and grieve for the one that they pierced. It is unclear whether "a spirit" refers to the disposition God gives his people or is a reference to God's Spirit that brings about this change of disposition.[67] Either way, God's work reflects

---

61. Anthony R. Petterson, *Haggai, Zechariah & Malachi*, ApOTC 25 (Nottingham: Apollos, 2015), 248.

62. Christopher J. Thomson, "The Removal of Sin in the Book of Zechariah" (PhD diss., University of Cambridge, 2013), 146, argues that the Lord's removal of sin and the provision of a new heart to resist it (see Ezek 36:25-27) may lie in the background of the seventh vision (Zech 5:5-11).

63. Zechariah 8:4-8, which envisages the elderly and the youth enjoying life in the streets of Jerusalem, conveys the ideas of peace and prosperity rather than universal knowledge of God.

64. Kenneth L. Barker, "The Scope and Center of Old and New Testament Theology and Hope," in Blaising and Bock, *Dispensationalism, Israel and the Church*, 293-328 (321), sees new covenant themes here.

65. See the "Excursus," in Petterson, *Haggai, Zechariah & Malachi*, 280-84.

66. This account draws on the death of King Josiah (see 2 Chr 35:23-25). See Antti Laato, *Josiah and David Redivivus: The Historical Josiah and the Messianic Expectations of Exilic and Postexilic Times*, ConBOT 33 (Stockholm: Almqvist & Wiksell, 1992), 293.

67. See further, Petterson, *Haggai, Zechariah & Malachi*, 263.

the new mode of the new covenant as several scholars observe.[68] It also reflects the new scope, with all the members of the clans caught up in the grief (12:12–14).[69]

Similarly, Zechariah 13:7–9 is a short oracle that envisages another exilic experience in which the shepherd of God's people is struck and the nation is refined in fire like silver and gold, with those who emerge enjoying a restored covenant relationship with God. The oracle finishes with a variation on the covenant formula: "I will say, 'he is my people,' and he will say, 'The Lord is my God'" (13:9; author's translation). The pronouns are unusual but seem to use the singular with a collective sense.[70] The use of the third person ("he") rather than the second person ("you") looks to a future generation, as does the wider context of the oracle where these activities are set "on that day" (cf. 13:1, 2, 4; 14:1).

While the book of Zechariah, like Haggai, contains indications of new covenant activity in the early postexilic period (particularly at the beginning of the book), it soon becomes clear that the experience of exile and return to the land has not changed the hearts of all the people. In the end, the book looks toward the future for the full realization of the new covenant, particularly the full and final abolition of sin accompanying the work of the Messiah (3:8–9; 12:10–13:1, 7–9).

NEW COVENANT CONCEPTS IN MALACHI

The theme of covenant is fundamental to the book of Malachi.[71] The word "covenant" occurs six times, referring to the covenant of Levi (2:4, 5, 8), the covenant of the fathers (i.e., the national covenant) (2:10), the covenant of marriage (2:14), and the messenger of the covenant (3:1). Several scholars

---

68. Barker, "Scope," 303; Fredrickson, New Covenant, 200; Boda, The Book of Zechariah, 715.

69. Carol L. Meyers and Eric M. Meyers, Zechariah 9–14: A New Translation with Introduction and Commentary (New York: Doubleday, 1993), 346, note that women were often associated with mourning rituals in the ancient Near East, and mentioning them may reflect the extent of the mourning. Julia M. O'Brien, Nahum, Habakkuk, Zephaniah, Haggai, Zechariah, Malachi (Nashville: Abingdon, 2004), 266, notes a literary connection to Jeremiah 44:9, which underscores that the women were "equally responsible for the need for mourning."

70. The unusual pronouns do not justify the claim of Rendtorff, Covenant Formula, 37 (cf. 78), that Zechariah 8:8 is "the sole example of the covenant formula in the prophetic books outside Jeremiah and Ezekiel."

71. Steven L. McKenzie and Howard N. Wallace, "Covenant Themes in Malachi," CBQ 45 (1983): 549–63; Jonathan Gibson, Covenant Continuity and Fidelity: A Study of Inner-Biblical Allusion and Exegesis in Malachi, LHBOTS 625 (London: T&T Clark, 2016), 1.

argue that "the messenger of the covenant" in 3:1 is the Lord, and the covenant in view is the new covenant.[72] However, a close analysis of Malachi's rhetoric shows that the messenger of the covenant is a different figure from the Lord and that the covenant is the national covenant.[73] Malachi is responding ironically to the people's two complaints in 2:17. Their first complaint is "Everyone doing evil is good in the eyes of the Lord and he *delights in them*" (author's translation). The second complaint is: "*Where is the God of justice?*" Malachi responds to their second complaint first: "I will indeed send my messenger and he will clear a way before me. Then suddenly the Lord *whom you are seeking* will come into his temple" (author's translation). In other words, the God they are "seeking" will come. Malachi then responds to their first complaint: "The messenger of the covenant which you are *delighting in* is indeed coming" (author's translation). This could mean that they are delighting in the messenger of the covenant, or more likely that they are delighting in the covenant which the messenger will prosecute when he comes.[74] Malachi is deeply ironic here. The complaints of the people might be expressing a concern for justice and the judgment of the evildoer, but it is clear from their reported behavior in the rest of the book that they are not really concerned with covenant faithfulness at all. Hence the "covenant" is not the new covenant, but the national covenant,[75] and "the messenger of the covenant" is best identified as the Elijah figure (see 4:4–6 [MT 3:23–24]), who represents the Lord and calls the people to obedience to the law of Moses.[76]

Like Haggai and Zechariah, Malachi indicates that some in the postexilic community feared the Lord and esteemed his name (Mal 3:16). God promises that on the future day of judgment they will be his "treasured possession" and he will have compassion on them as a father has compassion

72. Gibson, *Covenant*, 163–65; Andrew E. Hill, *Malachi: A New Translation with Introduction and Commentary*, AB 25d (New Haven: Yale University Press, 1998), 270.

73. I have argued this much more fully in Anthony R. Petterson, "The Identity of the 'Messenger of the Covenant' in Mal 3:1—Lexical and Rhetorical Analyses," *BBR* 29 (2019): 277–93.

74. For this latter interpretation, see William J. Dumbrell, "Malachi and the Ezra-Nehemiah Reforms," *RTR* 35 (1976): 42–52 (48).

75. So too, Pamela J. Scalise, "To Fear or Not to Fear: Questions of Reward and Punishment in Malachi 2:17–4:3," *RevExp* 84 (1987): 409–18 (410); Pieter A. Verhoef, *The Books of Haggai and Malachi*, NICOT (Grand Rapids: Eerdmans, 1987), 289; Floyd, *Minor Prophets*, 620.

76. Note David L. Petersen, *Zechariah 9–14 and Malachi: A Commentary*, OTL (London: SCM, 1995), 210: "The figure is surely a prophetic one, since it was common in the postexilic period to think about prophets as messengers (e.g. 2 Chron. 36:15–16)."

on his son (3:17). The phrase "treasured possession" elsewhere highlights Israel's unique covenant relationship and the special affection that God has for them, along with their call to holy obedience (Exod 19:5; Deut 7:6; 14:2; 26:18; Ps 135:4).[77] Here it refers to a remnant who fulfills Israel's calling by fearing, honoring, and serving the Lord. The kinship imagery (literally "just as a man has compassion on his son") suits the covenant relationship between the Lord and his people (cf. Mal 1:6; Exod 4:22-23). Significantly, this is something that will be realized in the future. Most English translations render the verb שׁוּב in 3:18 as an auxiliary ("again"). However, Jason LeCureux suggests it could look back to the imperative in 3:7: "Return to me, and I will return to you."[78] In this case, Malachi responds to those who say the righteous gain nothing from serving the Lord and the evildoers prosper (3:14-15) by saying that those who return to the Lord will see the distinction between the righteous and the wicked on the day when God comes to judge (cf. 4:1-3 [MT 3:19-21]). The language of "return" also brings Deuteronomy 30:2 to mind and suggests amid the covenant unfaithfulness in Malachi's day that the new covenant fulfillment lies in the future.

The final verse in the book (4:6 [MT 3:24]) is enigmatic but may have new covenant associations. God promises to send the prophet Elijah before the great and dreadful day of the Lord comes: "And he will turn the heart of fathers to sons and the heart of sons to their fathers, lest I come and I strike the land [with] complete destruction" (author's translation). This alludes in the first instance to God's promise in 3:1 to send the messenger of the covenant who will prepare for God's coming. Here the messenger is identified as Elijah who will "turn" (שׁוּב) the hearts of God's people so that they might avoid destruction on the judgment day. Significantly this promise comes after the call to "remember the law of my servant Moses" (4:4 [MT 3:22]). Moses is the towering figure in the Torah and the mediator of the national covenant. Elijah called the people back to covenant obedience at a time of national unfaithfulness.

Perhaps the most common interpretation of this verse is that Elijah will bring intergenerational reconciliation and renewed social order, where

---

77. Joel S. Kaminsky, *Yet I Loved Jacob: Reclaiming the Biblical Concept of Election* (Nashville: Abingdon, 2007), 85.

78. Jason T. LeCureux, *The Thematic Unity of the Book of the Twelve*, HBM 41 (Sheffield: Sheffield Phoenix, 2012), 222.

the breakdown was possibly the result of the divorces and mixed mar-
riages mentioned in 2:10–16.[79] Yet several scholars argue that it refers to
a future restoration of the people's covenant relationship with the Lord.[80]
For instance, Beth Glazier-McDonald contends that the phrase might be
better translated " 'to turn the hearts of the fathers together with that of
the children' to Yahweh (implied)."[81] She notes God's promise to give his
people a new heart that they might live according to his laws (Ezek 11:19;
36:26). While her translation is strained, the reasoning behind it seems val-
id. Indeed, Hill reasons similarly when he notes that when the word "turn"
(שׁוּב) is used in the Old Testament it means repentance and implies turning
toward God (cf. Mal 3:7).[82] Even if Glazier-McDonald's translation is rejected, it seems correct to hear in the language of "turn the hearts" the new
mode of implementation under the new covenant, all the more since this
turning is not something done by the people but is "an act of God, who will
send his prophet 'Elijah' to perform it."[83] The kinship language of "fathers"
and "sons" also brings Israel's covenant relationship with the Lord to mind
(cf. 1:6; 3:17).[84] Gibson also notes that the pronoun on "their fathers" seems
to project this restoration into the future, especially since earlier Malachi
refers to "our fathers" (2:10) and "your fathers" (3:7).[85]

   The dominant note of Malachi is covenant failure, even after the people have returned to the land and rebuilt the temple. Yet Malachi underscores the message of Haggai and Zechariah that the full realization of the
new covenant lies in the future and the presence of a remnant who fears
the Lord and honors his name anticipates in some ways the new covenant,
where these things will be experienced on a larger scale.

---

79. Noted by Verhoef, *Haggai and Malachi*, 342.
80. Verhoef, *Haggai and Malachi*, 342–43.
81. Beth Glazier-McDonald, *Malachi: The Divine Messenger*, SBLDS 98 (Atlanta: Scholars Press, 1987), 256.
82. Andrew E. Hill, *Haggai, Zechariah and Malachi*, TOTC 28 (Downers Grove: InterVarsity Press, 2012), 366. See also Holladay, *The Root Šûbh*, 141.
83. Verhoef, *Haggai and Malachi*, 343.
84. Elie Assis, "Moses, Elijah and the Messianic Hope: A New Reading of Malachi 3,22–24," *ZAW* 123 (2011): 207–20 (212–13).
85. Gibson, *Covenant*, 254–55.

SUMMARY: NEW COVENANT THEMES
IN THE BOOK OF THE TWELVE

While the phrase "new covenant" never appears in the Book of the Twelve, the concepts that it entails certainly do, and the Book of the Twelve contributes more to the theme of the new covenant than many thematic studies indicate. In terms of the *new mode*, namely God's initiative to change the hearts of his people, this is seen in Hosea by his representation of God's relationship with Israel as God pursued the relationship despite their breaking the terms of the covenant. God is the one who promises to "allure her" and "speak to her heart" (Hos 2:14 [MT 2:16]); to "betroth you to me forever" (2:19 [MT 2:21]). God is the one who "will heal them from their turning" (14:4 [MT 14:5]). In Haggai, God moved the wills of the people so that they obeyed his word, built the temple, and feared him (Hag 1:12–14). God's Spirit is said to be present among the people to empower them for obedience (2:4–5). In Zechariah the people repent at the preaching of the prophet (Zech 1:6), and God's Spirit will empower them to rebuild the temple (4:6). God will also change the disposition of his people so that they look to him and mourn, grieve, and weep for the one they have pierced (12:10–14). At the end of Malachi, God will send the prophet Elijah, who will turn the hearts of the people so that they avoid God's judgment.

The *new result* of faithfulness to God is seen in Hosea where Gomer/Israel is said to "know the LORD" (Hos 2:20 [MT 2:22]) and respond in covenant obedience (2:15 [MT 2:17]). This covenant obedience is seen to some extent in Haggai and Zechariah (e.g., Hag 1:12, 14; Zech 1:6; 4:6). Yet by the end of Zechariah, it is clearly something that will be realized in the future. The use of the covenant formula also looks for its realization in a future generation (Zech 8:7–8; 13:9).

The *new basis* of full and final forgiveness is seen in Hosea, where God promises he will completely forgive (1:6) with the result that "not my people" become "children of the living God" (1:10; cf. 2:1, 23 [MT 2:3, 25]). Micah underscores the basis of the new covenant as God's full and final forgiveness, restoring their relationship with God (7:18–19). In Zechariah, the concept of full and final forgiveness is present throughout the book. A key contribution of Zechariah is that it is not the sacrificial system through which forgiveness comes, but the death of the future Davidic king, which opens a fountain for cleansing from sin and uncleanness (3:8–9; 13:1).

The *new scope* of inclusion is seen in Joel where God promises to pour out his Spirit on all people (2:28-29), and in Zechariah where God moves his people (probably also by his Spirit) so that all the clans and their wives mourn (12:10-14). Zechariah 2:11 [MT 2:15] also broadens the scope of the covenant people to include the nations.

All of these concepts are crucial in the New Testament claims about Jesus as the mediator of the new covenant. Through his death, resurrection, and ascension, Jesus has instigated the new covenant's new mode by his Spirit, renewing the hearts of his people (e.g., Rom 2:15; 5:5; 2 Cor 1:21-22; 3:3, 6; Gal 4:6; Titus 3:4-7), with the new result of knowing God (e.g., 2 Cor 4:6; Gal 4:9; Eph 1:17-23; Col 1:9-14; 1 Thess 1:2-9), on a new basis of full and final forgiveness (e.g., Heb 8:12; 9:15; 10:15-18), and a new scope of inclusion (e.g., Acts 15:7-9; Gal 3:28; Eph 2:11-22; Rev 7:9).

8

Filled, Empowered, Dwelling, Trembling, and Fleeing: Mapping God's Spirit and Presence in the Book of the Twelve

Beth M. Stovell

INTRODUCTION

Scholars have often questioned the relationship between divine presence and divine spirit in the Hebrew Bible. While scholars have examined the depictions of divine spirit and divine presence in the Book of the Twelve separately, such study has rarely examined how these two concepts are linked linguistically or explored how these linguistic links impact the rhetoric of the Book of the Twelve as a corpus.

This chapter will explore how the conceptions of divine presence and divine spirit are linguistically linked for specific rhetorical purposes in the Book of the Twelve. Using the conceptual metaphor theories of Gilles Fauconnier and Mark Turner alongside linguistic theories on lexical cohesion, this chapter will explore the frequent collocations and conceptual domains associated with God's presence and God's Spirit in Hosea, Amos, Micah, Jonah, Nahum, and Zechariah. It will then examine how metaphors associated with God's presence are conceptually linked to metaphors associated with God's Spirit in Jonah, Micah, and Zechariah.

This chapter will suggest that these depictions frequently highlight expectations for renewal and transformation for specific rhetorical purposes and will demonstrate how these themes interweave with the larger shared themes within the Book of the Twelve.

CONCEPTUAL BLENDING THEORY[1]

Conceptual blending theory[2] has several central features. Fauconnier and Turner describe their theory in terms of network. They are concerned with "the on-line, dynamical cognitive work people do to construct meaning for local purpose of thought and action."[3] According to Fauconnier and Turner, conceptual blending is the central process by which this cognitive work of meaning construction occurs. A key element of conceptual blending is "mental spaces." Mental spaces are "small conceptual packets constructed as we think and talk, for purposes of local understanding and action."[4] These mental spaces contain partial elements from conceptual domains and from the given context.[5] In conceptual blending theory, mental spaces make up the input structures, generic structures, and blending structures in the network. "Generic space" is the mental space that describes the connection drawn between the two input spaces allowing them to blend with one another. The "blended space" is the result of the connections created between the two input spaces. To put it another way, this new mental space called "blended space" contains the results of "blending" the two inputs, while

---

1. I have articulated a similar description of conceptual blending theory in several of my works including Beth M. Stovell, "Who's King? Whose Temple? Divine Presence, Kingship, and Contested Space in John 1, 12, and 19," in *Johannine Prologue*, eds. Stanley E. Porter and Andrew Pitts, Johannine Studies (Leiden: Brill, forthcoming) and Beth M. Stovell, "Son of God as Anointed One? Johannine Davidic Christology and Second Temple Messianism," in *Reading the Gospel of John's Christology as a Form of Jewish Messianism: Royal, Prophetic, and Divine Messiahs*, ed. Gabriele Boccaccini and Benjamin E. Reynolds (Leiden: Brill, 2018), 149–77.

2. At times, Fauconnier and Turner simply call this theory "conceptual blending" and at other times the "network model of conceptual integration." See Gilles Fauconnier and Mark Turner, "Mental Spaces: Conceptual Integration Networks," in *Cognitive Linguistics*, ed. Dirk Geeraerts, Cognitive Linguistics Research 34 (Berlin: de Gruyter, 2006), 303–71 (312); Gilles Fauconnier and Mark Turner, *The Way We Think: Conceptual Blending and the Mind's Hidden Complexities* (New York: Basic Books, 2002).

3. Fauconnier and Turner, "Mental Spaces," 312.

4. Fauconnier and Turner, "Mental Spaces," 307–8.

5. Fauconnier and Turner, "Mental Spaces," 331. For a more detailed discussion of the definition, use, and influence of "mental spaces," see Mark Fauconnier and Eve Sweetser, *Spaces, Worlds, and Grammar: Cognitive Theory of Language and Culture* (Chicago: University of Chicago Press, 1996); Mark Fauconnier, *Mental Spaces: Aspects of Meaning Construction in Natural Language* (Cambridge: MIT Press, 1985); Mark Fauconnier, *Mappings in Thought and Language* (Cambridge: Cambridge University Press, 1997).

the mental space called "generic space" contains the means for this blending. An example would be the terms "Son of God," "Father," and "King of Israel" in John 1:14, 18, and 49. Because "Son of God" was associated with Davidic kingship and with the father-son familial metaphor in the Hebrew Scriptures, it allows for conceptual blending between "Father" and "King of Israel" through the generic space of kingship.[6]

THE CONCEPTUAL DOMAINS OF GOD'S SPIRIT AND PRESENCE IN THE TWELVE[7]

Scholars have frequently noted how the depictions of God's Spirit and presence in the Twelve are influenced by such depictions in the Psalter and the Pentateuch.[8] While this study will not focus on such intertextual links (as I have done such work elsewhere),[9] it will note some of these links as we examine the conceptual domains in the Twelve.

BEFORE GOD'S PRESENCE: TREMBLING, DWELLING, FLEEING, AND RESTORING

Nahum 1:5: Trembling before the Lord's Presence
Nahum 1 provides us with a set of conceptual entailments frequently used of God's presence in the Pentateuch but configured in a new context. The direct mention of God's presence is through the use of a shortened version of the phrase "before/the face of the Lord"; in Nahum 1:5 the word used for this larger phrase is *mifanah* ("from his face/before him"). The metaphor here is that the earth trembles before the Lord's presence. This personification is picturing the earth as trembling like a person because the Lord's presence is so frightful, yet it also picks up the conception of earthquake

---

6. See my extended discussion of this topic in Beth M. Stovell, *Mapping Metaphorical Discourse in the Fourth Gospel: John's Eternal King*, Linguistic Biblical Studies (Leiden: Brill, 2012), 135–80.

7. This research extends my previous work on God's Spirit and presence in Haggai and Joel in Stovell, "Metaphors of Presence: Divine Presence and Divine Spirit in the Book of the Twelve," in *Performance, Voicing, and Metaphor in Poetic Prophesy*, ed. Carol Dempsey, Elizabeth R. Hayes, and Beth M. Stovell, LHBOTS (New York: T&T Clark Bloomsbury, forthcoming). Elements of this chapter are also reworked from my paper, Beth M. Stovell, "Divine Presence in the Hebrew Bible" (presented at Interfaith Seminar, University of Wales Trinity Saint David, Lampeter, Wales, July 11, 2018).

8. See, e.g., Mark Boda's exploration of the use of Psalm 33 in Zechariah 4 around the depiction of God's Spirit in *The Book of Zechariah*, NICOT (Grand Rapids: Eerdmans, 2016), 289.

9. See Stovell, "Metaphors of Presence" and Stovell, "Divine Presence in the Hebrew Bible."

tremors. But the depiction of the Lord's presence is not confined to this sentence. Nahum 1 is replete with conceptual language to describe divine presence. Nahum 1:3 evokes Moses's encounter with God on Mount Sinai in Exodus 34 where the Lord reveals his character as "slow to anger" (Exod 34:6), yet in his own reconfiguration, Nahum focuses on the second half of this divine revelation in Exodus 34:7, God's continuing wrath, leaving out the language of steadfast love, faithfulness, and forgiveness, before launching into the promise that the Lord will not leave the guilty unpunished.[10] Nahum 1:4 brings in further language associated with divine presence. This time the language is in the context of theophany and of God's journey with the people in the wilderness in Exodus and Numbers. The language of whirlwind and clouds both point to these exodus experiences (see Exod 14:19–21), while the language of storm connects with the divine presence depicted in the Psalms (Ps 50:3). Similarly, the language of God making the sea dry up points to God's power via Moses at the crossing of the Red Sea (Exod 14:22). The quaking of the mountains in Nahum 1:5 also connects to God's revelation of his presence to the people at Mount Sinai in Exodus 19:18. Thus, in Nahum 1, the depiction of God's presence is primarily in terms of judgment against the guilty and the fearfulness and power evoked in experiences of God's presence.

Haggai 2: God's Presence Abiding with the People

Evidence for the conception of God's presence in Haggai 2:1–9 comes by several means. First, the statement by the Lord of Hosts, "I am with you," in both Haggai 1:13 and 2:4 points to the spatial proximity as well as relational proximity of the Lord of Hosts to Zerubbabel, Joshua, and the people.[11] This conception of God's presence harkens back to "my Presence will go with you" in Exodus 33:14. In both Haggai 1:13 and Exodus 33:14, the promise of God's presence becomes the motivation for movement and action. These elements of spatial and relational proximity relate to the larger concepts of spatial and relational deixis discussed in Exodus above. It appears that Zerubbabel, Joshua, and the people all need the courage given to them by the presence of the Lord with them.

---

10. For more on Exodus 34 and other parts of Exodus in Nahum 1, see Duane Christensen, *Nahum: A New Translation with Introduction and Commentary*, AYB (New Haven: Yale University Press, 2009), 219–22.

11. Scripture quotations use the New International Version (NIV) unless otherwise noted.

Besides this spatial and relational deixis, temporal deixis links the earlier development of the former temple to this new temple's construction through the promise within the story of the people's exit from Egypt. The language "once again" (Hag 2:6) and the differentiation between "former" and "latter" (2:3 and 2:9),[12] as well as the language of what the Lord will do among the people all point to temporal shifts in three directions: to the past (e.g., the former glory of the temple, the former experiences of the exodus event);[13] to the present (e.g., the experience of the current temple under construction as nothing); and to the future (e.g., when God will take part in the actions of shaking and filling that will cause the temple to surpass its former glory.) In each of these temporal contexts, the divine presence is essential. The Lord was present with the people in the past during the exodus event, the Lord is present now ("I am with you" and "my spirit abides with you"), and the Lord will be present with the people by filling the temple as the Lord did in prior times. This temporal deixis functions alongside spatial deixis in creating higher levels of relational deixis: because the Lord is present in the past, the present, and the future, because the Lord is near to the people, the Lord can also speak in terms of "my" and "with you" to proclaim his relational closeness.

Besides God's direct statement, "I am with you," as a picture of God's presence, an awareness of the semantic domains associated with divine presence yield other aspects of divine presence in this passage that create lexical cohesion. As noted above, in the exodus account the tabernacle was associated with divine presence and the tabernacle was described as God's house. In Haggai 2:7 and 9 the temple is described using this term "house" (*beth*). The commonness of this usage does not necessarily point to the exodus account, but in light of the direct reference to the exodus event in verse 5, the likelihood of this connection is heightened. Three times in this passage we have another lexeme commonly associated with divine presence in the exodus account: "glory" (*kabod*) (2:3, 7, 9). Throughout the exodus account, the glory of the Lord accompanies the people, and Moses

---

12. Taylor demonstrates the complexities associated with these uses of "former" and "latter" in verse 3 and elsewhere. See Richard Taylor and E. Ray Clendenen, *Haggai, Malachi*, NAC (Nashville: B&H, 2004), 167.

13. As Taylor points out, verse 5 contains "deictic force" in covenanting "with you." See Taylor and Clendenen, *Haggai, Malachi*, 157.

encounters this glory in his theophanic experiences. In Haggai 2, Haggai expresses the Lord's longing for the former glory of his house to be restored.

Haggai 2:7 demonstrates that this glory is not something intrinsic in the temple building itself, but something that occurs because of the Lord's actions. Specifically, Haggai 2:7 states that the Lord "will fill this house with glory [splendor]." As noted above the language of "filling" is associated both with divine presence as the glory of the Lord fills the tabernacle (Exod 40:34) and with divine Spirit as the Lord fills a person with his Spirit (Exod 31:3).[14] The *piel waw* consecutive form first-person singular of *malah* found in Exodus 31:3 is adapted to a *piel* perfect first-person masculine singular form in Haggai 2 due to context of the verb usage. Description of this hope for "glory" creates a framework that links verse 3 to verse 9, framing the rest of the passage in verses 3–9. Whereas verse 3 asks a question regarding the former glory, which now appears as nothing to the people, verse 9 provides an answer: the people will see the glory and it will exceed the former glory and, in this place, God will give peace.[15] What begins in lament thus ends in triumphant hope. In this way, a longing for God's glory, his *kabod*, a key aspect of God's presence in the exodus account, becomes the external frame for the entire discourse of God's words through Haggai in verses 3–9. Thus, God's presence is depicted as a memory of God's actions in the past in the tabernacle/temple in verse 3 and a hope for God's return and renewal of his presence in an even greater way in verse 9. The lexical cohesion of "glory" to "glory" in verse 3 and verse 9 becomes a means to make a rhetorical and theological point: God's glory will be greater than his first glory in the

---

14. John R. Levison points to the links between God's Spirit and God's presence in Haggai as an essential part of the development of the notion of God's Spirit after the exile. See Levison, *The Holy Spirit before Christianity* (Waco, TX: Baylor University Press, 2019).

15. This notion of God's presence as the means toward peace may echo the promise in Exodus 33:14 that God's presence will be with Moses and give him rest. However, as the linguistic structures and the lexemes used in these passages differ, such a relationship can only be speculative. Eugene Merrill appears to suggest such a connection in a broader way via a "theology of presence" that he sees running throughout the Old Testament and into the New. He sees this theology of presence as critical to the depictions of presence in Haggai and Zechariah. See Eugene Merrill, *Haggai, Zechariah, Malachi: An Exegetical Commentary* (Garland, TX: Biblical Studies, 2003), 113. Sweeney argues that this promise of the temple as a place of peace "builds upon the tradition of Jerusalem as the city of peace and the Temple as the source of peace for the city and the world," pointing to the etymology of the name "Jerusalem" itself as evidence. See Marvin Alan Sweeney, *The Twelve Prophets*, Berit Olam: Studies in Hebrew Narrative and Poetry (Collegeville, MN: Liturgical, 2000), 549.

new temple and the people will move from the current nothingness they see to a renewal of God's presence in his greater glory in the temple to come, if they will only work with God on this project.

Michael Floyd argues that the language of the exodus in this passage is used to dispel the fear of those who support the temple project:

> In order to maintain their morale, they are urged to see themselves as participants in a recapitulation of the great world-transforming process, through which Yahweh brought his people out of slavery in Egypt, gave them land, and made them a nation. ... The restoration of the temple thus signals that Yahweh's people have once again been liberated from captivity ... and that they have once again resumed their place in the land.[16]

In order to restore the people to their morale, the rhetorical purpose of these metaphors must match their theological purpose: the people must see who their God is and who they are in relation to God so that they may work toward the goals that God has laid out for them. Furthermore, the allusions to the exodus event provide a key link between faithfulness to God's covenant and the experience of God's presence. Throughout the exodus account, the availability of God's presence is linked to the participation of the people in God's covenant. Sinai is an event of both Torah and presence. God's promise of "I am with you" is linked via "the covenant" to "my Spirit abides among you." This points rhetorically and theologically to the necessity of obedience to the covenant as the linchpin, joining God's presence with the Israelites to God's Spirit among them. The triple imperative structure of "take courage, take courage, take courage" in verse 4 is echoed by a double *hiphil* plus *piel* structure in first-person singular in verses 6–7. If the people "take courage" and follow God's covenant by working for God in the construction of the temple, they will in turn see what God will do.

Jonah 1–2: Fleeing from God's Presence
In comparison to other depictions of God's presence in the Book of the Twelve, Jonah's depiction is unique, in that it is primarily focused on fleeing rather than coming into the Lord's presence or being given hope based on

---

16. Michael H. Floyd, *Minor Prophets: Part 2*, FOTL (Grand Rapids: Eerdmans, 2000), 286.

the Lord's presence as in Haggai 2. In Jonah 1, after the word of the Lord comes to Jonah, he actively sets out to "flee" (barach) from the presence of the Lord. This phrase is used only one other time in the Hebrew Bible in Psalm 139:7. In Psalm 139:7, the emphasis is on the inability to flee from God's presence, equated using parallelism to going away from God's Spirit. The echo between Psalm 139 and Jonah 1 appears intentionally as one of the ironic points in Jonah 1–2; despite Jonah's attempts to flee from God's presence, he is incapable of doing so.[17] James Limburg puts it this way: "Jonah's story illustrates the truth of the psalm. Whether in the depths of the sea, in the belly of the fish, or in the suburbs of Nineveh, Jonah never succeeded in running away from God."[18]

In Jonah 1, twice a phrase is used that combines "from" and "before the face of/the presence of" with "Yahweh" (miliphneh adonai). While liph-neh can simply mean "before someone or something," when joined with "Yahweh" it frequently refers to the presence of God and is accompanied by other semantic entailments associated with divine presence such as glory, light, and so on.[19] For example, in Exodus and elsewhere in the Pentateuch this phrase is used to depict God's presence meeting his people.[20] Haggai also uses the language "before me" when the Lord is speaking as indicative of the Lord's presence.[21]

Notably as Jonah tries to flee the Lord's presence in repeated style, his actions bring him down and down. The doubling of "from the presence of the LORD" is met with the repeated use of "go down" (yarad) in 1:3, 5, and

---

17. Timmer links this idea of Jonah fleeing from God's presence to Psalm 139. See Daniel C. Timmer, *A Gracious and Compassionate God: Mission, Salvation and Spirituality in the Book of Jonah* (Downers Grove, IL: InterVarsity Press, 2011), 67.

18. James Limburg, *Hosea-Micah*, IBC (Louisville: Westminster John Knox, 2011), 141.

19. Timmer provides examples of this, indicating that "this phrase can indicate God's presence generally (Gen. 19:13, Jon. 1:2; very rarely negatively, as in Lam. 4:16) in a theophany (Gen. 19:27), as a personal accompaniment (Exod. 33:16), as the object of prayer (1 Kgs 13:6), or in the cult (Leviticus passim, Deut. 16:16)" and points to scholarly interaction with this topic in H. F. van Rooy, "פנים, " *NIDOTTE* 3:637–39 and Horacio Simian-Yofre, *Metodología Del Antiguo Testamento Biblioteca Estudios Bíblicos*, vol. 106 (Salamanca: Ediciones Sígueme, 2001). See Timmer, *A Gracious and Compassionate God*, 67 n. 27.

20. For more on exodus imagery in relation to the Twelve, see Stovell, "Metaphors of Presence." Zechariah uses similar language for being before the angel of the Lord, which could link the conception of the angel of the presence in Numbers and elsewhere. See Mignon Jacobs, *The Books of Haggai and Malachi*, NICOT (Grand Rapids: Eerdmans, 2017), 83, who draws links between Zechariah, Numbers, and Haggai.

21. See the discussion on Haggai above.

2:6. Limburg notes how this emphasizes Jonah's descent: "Notice the way in which the verb 'go down' traces the descent of Jonah: he went down to Joppa (1:3), he went down into the ship (1:3), went down into the hold (1:5), and finally went down to the bottom of the mountains (2:6)."[22] Jonah is not only fleeing from the presence of the Lord, he is doing so by descending deeper and deeper, even into the depths of the world. The notions of divine presence are significant when placed along other descriptions of divine presence. Whereas divine presence is often depicted in an omnipresent fashion or commonly in the heavens or coming down from the heavens, Jonah's fleeing moves in the opposite direction of where he intends to find God's presence. Yet, as Psalm 139 demonstrates, going to the depths does not necessarily mean that Jonah will escape from God's presence. In fact, it is in the depths where Jonah prays and experiences God's presence in Jonah 2.[23]

Zechariah 2: God's Presence as City Walls

Zechariah 2 shows a striking resemblance to the themes of divine presence in Deuteronomy and in Ezekiel[24] where the divine presence itself becomes the sacred space and thereby becomes a form of protection for the people (e.g., in the case of Deuteronomy the divine presence is depicted in battle for the people). Zechariah 2 depicts a vision of the divine presence wherein the city itself is given protection and provision via the divine presence in its midst. The language of fire and glory used to depict divine presence in the Pentateuch returns here in Zech 2:9 (v. 5 ET). As Peter Craigie explains,

> Vision and oracles combined to affirm that the transformation of the future city of Jerusalem would be a consequence of the divine presence in its midst. In the vision [in Zechariah 2], the wall of fire without and the divine glory within would replace the required ramparts of a secure city. In the oracle, twice it is declared: "I will dwell in the midst of you" (verses 10, 11). Thus, to a populace busy restoring the

---

22. See James Limburg, *Jonah: A Commentary*, OTL (Louisville: Westminster John Knox, 1993), 27.

23. Amos 9:2–4 provides a similar parallel within the Twelve in which none can escape God's hand.

24. See my discussion of this in more detail in Stovell, "Divine Presence in the Hebrew Bible." For more on Ezekiel's and Deuteronomy's depictions of divine presence, see John Kutsko, *Between Heaven and Earth: Divine Presence and Absence in the Book of Ezekiel*, Biblical and Judaic Studies (Winona Lake, IN: Eisenbrauns, 2000) and Ian Wilson, *Out of the Midst of the Fire: Divine Presence in Deuteronomy*, SBL Dissertation Series (Atlanta: Scholars Press, 1995).

physical structures of the city of Jerusalem, the prophet reminds them of certain absolute basics. Restored walls are no good without the surrounding "wall of fire" (verse 5). A restored temple, whatever its splendor, would be of no significance unless the Lord were in the city. But walls and temple, insofar as they symbolized reliance on divine protection and divine presence, were important features of the city.[25]

If the temple is the heart of the city of Jerusalem by rank of importance, then what we see here is an extension of the notion that God's presence dwells as fire within the constraints of the temple. Instead, the divine presence in the form of fire moves beyond the confines of the temple to the outskirts of the city—itself becoming its protective barrier.

God's Voice and Name as Vehicles of God's Presence in the Twelve

Of the variety of collocations with the Lord's presence found in the Pentateuch, several are also picked up in the Twelve, including the Lord's name and voice. Scholars such as Ian Wilson have noted that Deuteronomy often blends aspects of the divine name with divine presence,[26] and this seems to be the case in sections of the Twelve as well. Scholars have also noted that the exodus depiction of theophany in Exodus 19–21 includes several references to God's voice as a manifestation of God's presence with Moses.[27] Thus, as the Twelve uses aspects of Exodus and Deuteronomy we see conceptions of divine presence and God's name and voice.

One such example of God's voice as emphasized alongside God's presence is found in Joel. Joel's depiction of God also links his place in Zion as king with his depiction as a lion roaring, which emphasizes God's voice to the people.[28] Like the repeated use of trumpet calls in Zion, this aural reference has the rhetorical force of drawing the reader to hear in new ways, but it additionally focuses on the quality and power of God speaking to the

25. See Peter Craigie, *Hosea, Joel, Amos, Obadiah, Jonah*, vol. 1 of *The Twelve Prophets* (Louisville: Westminster John Knox, 1984), 172.

26. Wilson would not use the language of "blending" for this, as this is cognitive linguistic language. But he does link God's name with God's presence as a key theme in Deuteronomy. See Wilson, *Out of the Midst of the Fire*.

27. See discussions of God's voice as part of theophanies in Mark G. Boyer, *Divine Presence: Elements of Biblical Theophanies* (Eugene, OR: Wipf & Stock, 2017), xx–xxi, 26–29.

28. See in Joel 3:17 ET/4:17 MT links between God's holy mountain and his dwelling in Zion, and God as lion roars in Zion, which in turn relate to the blowing of the trumpet in Zion (2:1, 15) via the noises coming from Zion.

people, which is strong enough to shake the heavens and the earth (3:16 ET/4:16 MT). The power of God's voice and the experience of God's revelation are then in part conditioned by a memory of God's Spirit and presence with the people in their exodus journey. This revelation brings salvation and extends to all people (2:28, 29 ET/3:1–2 MT). Joel's depiction of God is in this way pneumamorphic in its depiction of the Spirit proceeding from the Father who is ruler and king of all creation, such that his voice shakes creation from top to bottom and his spirit poured out impacts all people.[29]

Micah 4–5 provides a picture of the association between God's presence and his name. Micah 4 uses the language of the mountain of God as a sacred place for his presence during "the last days" (4:1). This mountain of the Lord will be raised as the highest mountain and people will come to it in droves. As they come to the mountain of the Lord, they will choose to turn their weapons into gardening tools, to no longer make war, and they will walk "in the name of the LORD" (Mic 4:5). The "name of the Lord" takes on many of the key characteristics often associated with God's presence in Micah 4–5. The name of the Lord becomes a pathway for the people associated with the mountain where God's presence dwells (4:2), and the name of the Lord brings peace and restoration as the people walk in it forever (4:5). This picture of God's name is associated with God as the great king and as divine warrior in the remaining section of Micah 4. In Micah 5, the name of the Lord is associated with the Lord's shepherding rule, his majesty, and his strength (5:4 ET/5:3 MT), and this shepherding and his name allow the people to live securely as his greatness is known around the world. Narratively Micah 4 following Micah 3 also sheds light on another aspect of God's name and God's presence. Whereas Micah 3 shows us the depths of Israel's injustice and only the prophet, endowed with God's Spirit can speak the words of God to the people to overturn their ways, Micah 4 points to the need for God's name and his presence as the means toward restoration of a people who have been destroyed by their own injustice.

---

29. Some scholars have described this passage as having egalitarian tendencies. For example, Bruce Birch notes Joel's egalitarian spirit and its impact on Paul and Acts. See Bruce C. Birch, *Hosea, Joel, and Amos*, Westminster Bible Companion (Louisville: Westminster John Knox, 1997), 3. For further discussion of the outpouring on all people, see Erika Moore, "Joel's Promise of the Spirit," in *Presence, Power and Promise*, ed. David G. Firth and Paul D. Wegner (Downers Grove, IL: IVP Academic, 2011), 245–56 (251–55).

MANIFESTATIONS OF GOD'S SPIRIT IN THE TWELVE

The Spirit of God is conceptualized in diverse but overlapping ways within the Twelve. Close analysis of such usage in Joel, Micah, Haggai, and Zechariah provides additional insight into the conceptual framing and lexical cohesive links used to bring together images of God's Spirit.

JOEL: GOD'S SPIRIT AND AGRICULTURAL AND CELESTIAL METAPHORS[30]

Throughout Joel 2-3 ET/2-4 MT, relational deixis is used with the repeated phrases "your God" (2:13, 14, 23, 26, 27; 3:17 ET/4:17 MT) and "my Spirit" (speaking of God's Spirit, repeated twice in Joel 2:28-29 ET/3:1-2 MT), "my people" and "my heritage" (2:26-27; 3:2 ET/4:2 MT) and the use of "your" to speak of the Lord's people and heritage (2:17). This use of pronominal suffixes points to the relationship between God and his people, Israel. Noticeably these forms of relational deixis intensify after the temporal deixis of Joel 2:12.[31]

Besides pronominal suffixes, the repeated reference to God as "I" emphasizes the singular identity of God and his description of his identity. In both Joel 2:27 and 3:17, 21 ET/4:17, 21 MT, the identity of God and his actions for the nation of Israel are linked to God being "in their midst" and dwelling in Zion. The language of being in the midst of Israel is similar to Haggai 2, where God says, "I am with you," and "my Spirit remains among you." Yet uniquely in Joel, this concept of God in their midst and dwelling in Zion is also an aspect of their knowledge. By these actions, this knowledge of Yahweh will be given.[32] Similar to Haggai 2, the presence of God provides courage to the people (and to the land itself in Joel) described in the repetition of "do not fear" in Joel 2:21-22, similar to "take courage" in Haggai 2:4 and "do not fear" in Haggai 2:5.

As God's presence comes, another set of semantic domains are frequently joined with one another: celestial and agricultural domains. The celestial

---

30. This section is dependent on my previous work on the use of Exodus in Joel and Haggai in relation to divine Spirit and presence. See Stovell, "Metaphors of Presence."

31. Finley argues that this section depends on the character of God for the people's response. See Thomas J. Finley, *Joel, Amos, Obadiah: An Exegetical Commentary* (Richardson, TX: Biblical Studies, 2003), 51.

32. Hays and Longman note this focus on knowledge and presence in Joel 2. See J. Daniel Hays and Tremper Longman III, *Message of the Prophets: A Survey of the Prophetic and Apocalyptic Books of the Old Testament* (Grand Rapids: Zondervan, 2012), 282.

terms include sun, moon, stars, heavens, while the agricultural elements include the land, earth, pastures, wilderness, trees (and specifically fig trees), vines, the sea, grain, oil, locusts, and rain. Often these terms are in direct collocation in near back-to-back procession. For example, terms within celestial domains fill Joel 2:10[33] and 3:15 ET/4:15 MT, while terms within agricultural and natural domains fill Joel 2:20-25.

Joel 2:28 ET/3:1 MT provides a clear reference to God pouring out his Spirit on the people. There is debate whether Joel 2:28 ET/3:1 MT should be read with what comes before as a single unit. The phrase "then afterward" suggests a temporal shift to a later time. This shift involves a move from the presence of the Lord in verse 2:27 to the pouring out of God's Spirit on his people (Joel 2:28-29 ET/3:1-2 MT). Along with the coming of the Spirit come portents that appear similar to the exodus event (Joel 2:30-32 ET/3:3-5 MT), as in the earlier section of the chapter: columns of fire and smoke, shifting of celestial elements. A remnant will remain who calls on the name of the Lord in Mount Zion/Jerusalem. This leads to the restoration of Judah and Jerusalem (3:1 ET/4:1 MT).

Thus, lexical cohesion and deixis in Joel 2-3 ET/2-4 MT provide means to express links between the effects of God's presence on celestial and agricultural elements (thereby on the heavens and the earth). Temporal shifts provide opportunities for rhetorical and theological impact encouraging people to repentance and demonstrating a link between this repentance and God's exodus character. This makes the relational, spatial, and temporal work together toward one theological picture. The repeated use of lexemes related to the exodus event—clouds, fire, mountain, wilderness, and God's dwelling place—return the people again and again to God's actions in the exodus event as consistent with God's ability to reshape the current events of the Israelites. The Lord's presence becomes a means of refuge and protection (Joel 3:16 ET/4:16 MT). The repeated promise of God's presence in Joel 2 and 3 ET/2 and 4 MT bookend the account of God pouring out his Spirit at the end of Joel 2:28-32 ET/3:1-5 MT.

---

33. Van Ruiten points to the collocation of these celestial terms as part of Joel's rewriting of the Genesis account also found in Jeremiah 31:35, Isaiah 13:10, and Ezekiel 32:7. See Jacques T. A. G. M. van Ruiten, *Primaeval History Interpreted: The Rewriting of Genesis 1-11 in the Book of Jubilees* (Leiden: Brill, 2000), 38.

Micah: God's Spirit and Kingship

Micah's depiction of God's Spirit can be read in light of the larger traditions of Davidic kingship, which are frequently linked with God's kingship by way of the Spirit's anointing on David and David's role as shepherd being conceptually linked to his kingship, extending a shepherd-king motif consistent with ancient Near Eastern traditions of the time.[34] This conceptual framework then provides a basis for further discussion of later prophetic books, including the Book of the Twelve. While the dating of Micah is controversial (as is the dating of Isaiah), Micah appears to share the conceptual linking of God as shepherd and God as divine warrior via kingship that we find in Isaiah 40. As noted above, Joel links aspects of the divine warrior with Yahweh as king in Zion. Micah's emphasis is on Yahweh as divine warrior who is also shepherd to his people as he speaks of God's Spirit and presence.

A close reading of Micah 3–5 and of the shepherd passage in Micah 7 demonstrates several links to these themes of Spirit, God's revelation, kingship, and shepherding. In Micah 3, in contradiction to the false prophesies of peace, Micah the prophet is filled with power and the Spirit of the Lord (while anointing language is absent, this is probably built on the common notion of prophets as anointed by the Spirit). Micah 3:8 speaks of the prophet being "filled with power, with the Spirit of the LORD, and with justice and might to declare to Jacob his transgression, to Israel his sin."[35] The filling of the Spirit is matched with the filling of justice and might. The rulers are judged in Israel along with the destruction of the mountain of the house of the Lord—a picture of temple destruction.

---

34. For more on "shepherd" in relation to king metaphors, see Beth M. Stovell, "Yahweh as Shepherd-King in Ezekiel 34: Linguistic-Literary Analysis of Metaphors of Shepherding," in *Modeling Biblical Language: Papers from the McMaster Divinity College Linguistics Circle,* ed. Stanley Porter, Christopher Land, and Gregory Fewster (Leiden: Brill, 2016), 200–230.

35. Notably the language of the "filling" of the Spirit is also used in the exodus account. As Richard Hess explains, "In Exodus 31:3 the Lord tells Moses of how the Lord has filled Bezalel with the Spirit of God related to wisdom, understanding and knowledge associated with skills for production of the tabernacle. The story of this filling by God's Spirit in turn Moses echoes to the Israelites in Exodus 35:31." Hess argues that in Exodus 28:3 "God gives his spirit (*ruach*) to each of those engaged with the construction of the tabernacle." Hess appears to base this reading on the combination of the verb "fill" with "spirit." See Richard S. Hess, "Bezalel and Oholiab: Spirit and Creativity," in *Presence, Power and Promise: The Role of the Spirit of God in the Old Testament,* ed. David G. Firth and Paul D. Wegner (Downers Grove: IVP Academic, 2011), 161–72 (164–65).

Micah 4 shifts to a future time when all will come to the house of the Lord (linking the mountain of the Lord's house in 3:12 with 4:1); the Lord's word goes out. As in Micah 3, the Lord judges, but now it is between the peoples rather than against the rulers. This word is the word of the "mouth of the LORD of hosts" pointing to God as divine warrior. The reassembling of the people will point to the Lord's coming eternal reign (Mic 4:7).

Micah 5 shifts from the hope of God's Spirit upon the prophet in Micah 3 and the hope of the Lord's word coming from the temple in Micah 4 to a hope for a shepherd and coming ruler.[36] Micah 5:3–5 anticipates a ruler who will shepherd his flock "in the strength of the LORD, in the majesty of the name of the LORD his God."[37] This ruler like David will have a rule that extends to the "ends of the earth." This ruler gives peace and becomes the deliverance from Assyrian rule (5:6). This anticipated ruler shall come from Bethlehem (5:2). Micah 7 returns to the theme of a shepherd-king over the people, but this shepherd-king is Yahweh himself, who is light in Micah's darkness (7:8). Yahweh will shepherd his people, the flock of his inheritance (7:14), showing them wonders like those who came out of Egypt. Here the Lord's presence is experienced again as his presence was experienced during their coming out of Egypt (7:15); the Lord silences their oppressors and cares for them along their way out of enslavement as he did in the wilderness (7:14-16). The language of compassion, mercy, and a reduction of anger (7:18-19) along with the larger promise of faithfulness to Jacob via God's oath to them (7:20) echo the Sinai event and God's self-revelation in Exodus 34.[38]

36. There are debates on the inclusion of this prediction of Davidic kingship as part of Micah's earliest texts. Most scholars consider this a later redaction. However, as noted at the start of this chapter, while my approach does not deny such redaction, my focus is a synchronic rather than diachronic reading.

37. Micah 4 and 5 can be contrasted in terms of their pictures of birth. Micah 5:2 returns to the birthing metaphor found in Micah 4:9-10, except with a substantial change. Instead of birth being associated with the sounds and experiences of pain, depicting Israel's experience of crisis as occurs in Micah 4, Micah 5:2 focuses on Israel as a birthing mother who will bring new life that will provide hope to the people by the ruler whom she births. See Claudia D. Bergmann, *Childbirth as a Metaphor for Crisis: Evidence from the Ancient Near East, the Hebrew Bible, and 1QH XII, 1-18*, BZAW (Berlin, New York: de Gruyter, 2008), 111; Rick R. Marrs, "'Back to the Future': Zion in the Book of Micah," in *David and Zion*, ed. Bernard Batto and Kathryn Roberts (Winona Lake, IN: Eisenbrauns, 2004), 77–96 (93).

38. Goldingay speaks of the promises and the provision of God in the exodus event. See John Goldingay, *Israel's Gospel*, vol. 1 of *Old Testament Theology* (Downers Grove, IL: InterVarsity,

Examination of these passages demonstrates consistent links to other sections of Scripture. The filling of the Spirit of the Lord on Micah is similar to the depictions of Isaiah where the prophet is anointed by the Spirit (such as Isa 61).[39] The promise of the nations coming to the temple to worship God resounds with allusions to the Psalms and Isaiah. The shepherd-ruler of Micah 5 draws its depiction from Davidic themes in 2 Samuel and aspects of the Royal Psalms. Besides referencing the exodus event in Micah 7, the anticipated ruler depicted here echoes many of the same Davidic themes in Micah 5. In Micah 3–5 and 7, the word of the Lord comes to the people through the Spirit-filling of the prophet. Through this filling the prophet is able to describe the anticipated worship of God from all the nations (Mic 4) and an anticipated king who will free his people from oppression (Mic 5). This human king is mirrored in the deliverance brought by God, the great king, in Micah 7. Thus, it is the word of the Lord delivered by the Spirit with justice and might and strength that becomes the means of revelation of the Davidic future king and of the great king's deliverance of the people.

HAGGAI: GOD'S SPIRIT AND FILLING[40]

Besides the language of God's presence in this passage creating lexical cohesion, the language of God's Spirit also creates lexical cohesion in the passage. As noted in our examination of Exodus, notions of God's Spirit are often associated with the term "filling." In Haggai 2, this language of "filling" reverberates in verse 7, which speaks of the Lord filling the temple. Further in Exodus, God's Spirit with the people provides the means to act in accordance with God's goals. The work of the artisans, particularly the work of Bezalel and Oholiab, to build the tabernacle is empowered, directed, and accomplished by God's Spirit in these artisans. Haggai 2:4 points to the "work" of constructing the temple by means of God with the people. The call to work is enabled by God's Spirit abiding with the people.[41] Internal linguistic

---

2003), 313–20. Other scholars have noted the links between Micah 7 and Exodus. See Ehud Ben Zvi, *Micah*, FOTL (Grand Rapids: Eerdmans, 2000), 117, 146, 152.

39. John Levison draws comparisons between Micah's view of the Spirit's filling and Isaiah's view. See John R. Levison, *Filled with the Spirit* (Grand Rapids: Eerdmans, 2009), 44.

40. This section is dependent on my work on the use of Exodus in Joel and Haggai in relation to divine Spirit and presence. See Stovell, "Metaphors of Presence."

41. Mark Boda discusses the central place of work in this passage and its relationship to the Spirit and to Exodus understandings of the Spirit and the work of the people. See Mark J. Boda, *Haggai, Zechariah*, NIVAC (Grand Rapids: Zondervan, 2004).

structures of the promise of the people coming out of Egypt in verse 5 links to God's Spirit being among the people. In verse 5 the people going out from Egypt is paralleled with God being among the people by the similar formations of the words: *betsechem* and *betocchem*. In both cases the prefix *beh* is added to the beginning while the second-person masculine plural suffix *chem* is added to the end to form the new word. This same linguistic structure of *beh* + word + *chem* is found in verse 3, when "by their eye" the people see nothing. What looks like nothing "in their eyes" in verse 3 is transformed by the memory of the people's experience of God's promise "in their going out" from Egypt because now God's Spirit abides "in their midst" (2:5).

We can see that in both the case of God's presence and God's Spirit the exodus event becomes a linchpin that joins these two concepts via lexical cohesion. In both cases, the rhetorical emphasis is on the work at hand and God's equipping via his presence and Spirit to do this work. The theological emphasis is on the hope to move from the nothing that the people currently see to a future hope of God filling the temple with a greater glory than in former times and making this place one of peace.

ZECHARIAH: GIVING REST TO GOD'S SPIRIT

Zechariah's use of *ruach* is frequently associated with a possessive pronoun indicating relational deixis that provides the Spirit who is acting. In Zechariah 4:6, Zerubbabel is instructed that events will come not by might or power but by "my Spirit," referring to Yahweh. As will be discussed in more detail below, this contrast between might and power and Yahweh's Spirit plays into the larger contexts of the Twelve by linking to the language of God's Spirit in Micah 3–4.

The depiction of God's Spirit in Zechariah 6:8 appears to find symmetry with two other parts of Scripture. First, the depiction of giving rest to God's Spirit in Zechariah 6:8. הֵנִיחוּ אֶת־רוּחִי with the *hiphil* perfect third-person common plural of *nuach* ("to cause to rest or give rest to") + *ruach* with a first-person common singular, "my Spirit," has striking similarities to the exodus account, similar to the conceptual linking we noted in Haggai 2. Exodus 20:11 uses the same verb of Sabbath rest, while in Exodus 33:14 the Lord promises, "My Presence will go with you, and I will *give you rest*." Here the form of the verb is nearly the same except that in Exodus 33:14 God is the one who gives rest (first-person singular) rather than receiving this rest from the people of the north. This may be a way that Zechariah joins pictures of God's Spirit and God's presence in subtle ways.

In Zechariah 6:8 the conception of "my Spirit" plays with the word *ruach* as "these four winds" (*elah arbah ruchot*) several verses before in Zechariah 6:5. This way of linking winds to God's Spirit or presence appears to be also at play in Jonah's account where God hurls a great wind (*ruach gadolah*), pursuing Jonah (1:4) after he has tried to flee God's presence (1:3), a passage that will be discussed in greater detail below.

Zechariah 7:12 points to the people's lack of attention to the message the Lord sent by "his Spirit" via the earlier prophets. Zechariah 12 appears to focus on the Spirit given to man in comparison to the Spirit poured out by the Lord. It is not universally agreed upon whether this "spirit of grace and supplication" is a result of the divine Spirit upon the people. The language of "poured out" is used elsewhere of God's Spirit as are other metaphors of anointing, so this may connect to that tradition. But such a suggestion must then be balanced with the description of a "spirit of impurity" in Zechariah 13:2.

LINKING GOD'S SPIRIT AND PRESENCE IN THE TWELVE

With these core conceptions about God's Spirit and presence in the Twelve surveyed, it is now helpful to see how these conceptions blend in the Twelve as well. After a brief exploration of Joel and Haggai, I will focus on the linking of God's Spirit and presence in Amos, Jonah, Zechariah, and Micah.

HAGGAI 2 AND JOEL 2: SIMILARITIES IN CONCEPTUAL METAPHORICAL BLENDING OF GOD'S SPIRIT AND PRESENCE

We will now discuss the impact of conceptual metaphor blending on the conceptions of divine presence and divine Spirit in Haggai 2 and Joel 2. We have discussed the same major metaphors in Joel 2–3 ET/2–4 MT and Haggai 2. This may suggest a common linking of particular metaphors with conceptions of God's presence and Spirit. These two metaphors are God as divine warrior and God as creator.

Joel 2:10–11 presents the metaphor of God as divine warrior.[42] In the verse preceding verse 10, it seems that an army is coming to devour the people, yet

---

42. For further discussion on the divine warrior motif, see Patrick D. Miller, *The Divine Warrior in Early Israel* (Atlanta: SBL Press, 2006); Tremper Longman III, "The Divine Warrior: The New

in verses 10–11, the subject of that army shifts and it is God himself who is heading up this army. As in Haggai 2, God is depicted as divine warrior (Joel 2:11), causing the earth and heavens to quake and tremble (parallelism), sun and moon/stars to be darkened/withdraw their shining. As noted above, the celestial metaphors here are closely collocated for effect. All of creation is shaken and darkened as God the divine warrior heads up his army (Joel 2:10–11). Because of God as warrior among the people, the weakling among the people is also called a warrior (Joel 3:10 ET/4:10 MT). Because of God as warrior to his people and his mighty and wondrous deeds (Joel 2:26), the people will not be ashamed and the identity of God as the one who is in their midst is made known (Joel 2:27). Thus, God as divine warrior becomes a part of how God's presence is made known among the people. Similarly, when God pours out his Spirit upon the people, the portents that God shows in Joel 2:30–32 ET/3:2–3 MT echo the divine warrior imagery of Joel 2:10–11. Thus, God's Spirit and God's presence are both made manifest in part via God's depiction as divine warrior.

Joel 2:21–22 links the depiction of God as creator to God's presence. Joel 2:21–22 speaks to the soil and animals themselves with a promise of restoration (an echo of God's creational sovereignty), but also with a message of courage. As in Haggai 2, the message of courage resonates with its repeated reference: "do not fear." The people and land need not fear because God as creator of the universe is able to provide for all they have lost and all that they fear to lose.[43] David Baker argues that this depiction of God as creator points to the exodus story where God is the creator of light and darkness and therefore has power over them.[44] The list of these items that God will provide creates the collocation of language associated with nature described in the section on lexical cohesion above. God's gracious choice to

---

Testament Use of an Old Testament Motif," *WTJ* 44.2 (1982): 290–307; Martin Klingbeil, *Yahweh Fighting from Heaven: God as Warrior and as God of Heaven in the Hebrew Psalter and Ancient Near Eastern Iconography*, OBO Göttingen: Vandenhoeck & Ruprecht, 1999); Tremper Longman III and Daniel G. Reid, *God Is a Warrior*, Studies in Old Testament Biblical Theology (Grand Rapids: Zondervan, 1995).

43. See Marvin A. Sweeney, "The Place and Function of Joel in the Book of the Twelve," in *Thematic Threads in the Book of the Twelve*, ed. Paul L. Redditt and Aaron Schart, BZAW (Berlin: de Gruyter, 2003), 133–54 (147).

44. David W. Baker, T. Desmond Alexander, and Bruce K. Waltke, *Obadiah, Jonah, and Micah: An Introduction and Commentary*, TOTC (Downers Grove: InterVarsity Press, 2009), 102.

repay the people for the years the locusts have eaten (Joel 2:25)[45] acts in accordance with his Exodus 34 character and leads to a realization of further revelation of God's presence among the people in Joel 2:27.

Both God as divine warrior and God as creator ultimately lead toward the picture of God as the one who dwells in Zion and among his people. This picture of God resonates with the larger images of God's presence found elsewhere in Joel 2–3 ET/2–4 MT and also with the story of God dwelling in the tabernacle in the exodus account.

DEPICTIONS OF GOD'S PRESENCE AND SPIRIT IN RELATION TO JUSTICE IN THE TWELVE

Amos 5 and Micah 3 demonstrate intertextual links between the Twelve that join aspects of divine presence and divine Spirit. It appears that Micah 3 depends on Amos 5 for much of its language but also inverts aspects of the original language of Amos 5 to make a point about the rising levels of injustice among Israel's leaders. Both Amos 5 and Micah 3 demonstrate a tendency in the Twelve to speak about God's presence and God's Spirit in relation to justice.

Amos 5: God's Presence and Justice

Besides the many ways that Amos 5 depicts a relationship between worship and justice,[46] Amos 5 also shows how God's presence is linked to justice and worship. Scholars have noted a link between Amos's language of the Lord "passing by" ('avar) in 5:17 and the use of this verb in Exodus.[47] The language of the Lord "passing through/by" is found extensively in Exodus alongside pictures of God's presence in both positive and negative interactions. On the one hand, it is by passing that Moses experiences God's glory (Exod 33:19, 22), but it is also God's presence passing by that strikes down the Egyptians to execute judgment upon them (Exod 12:12, 23). Amos 5 seems to play on both uses

---

45. Duane Garrett discusses the complex theological value of the imagery of locusts in Duane Garrett, *Hosea, Joel: An Exegetical and Theological Exposition of Holy Scripture*, NAC 19A (Nashville: B&H, 1997), 298–99.

46. See my paper, Beth M. Stovell, "Handmade Images, Noisy Harps, and Rolling Waters: Mapping Kingship, Worship, and Justice in the Book of the Twelve" (presented at the Annual Meeting of the Canadian Society of Biblical Literature, Congress of Humanities and Social Sciences, University of Regina, May 28, 2018).

47. See James Richard Linville, *Amos and the Cosmic Imagination*, SOTSMS (Hampshire, England: Ashgate, 2008), 110.

by way of allusion. Amos 5:17 picks up on the picture of God's judgment as his presence passes through, using the repeated language of cries, weeping, and wailing to emphasize rhetorically the pain of this judgment, drawing on auditory imagery for the hearer/reader of the passage in verses 16–17. Unlike Exodus 33 where God's presence passes through to judge Israel's enemy Egypt, now God's presence passes through in Amos 5 to judge Israel, just as he has judged the foreign nations. This links to the larger theme in Amos 5 that the day of the Lord will not be one of peace for Israel and judgment for the oppressive nations, but rather one of wailing for Israel as well.

Yet the language of God's presence in Amos 5 is not only dire. Amos 5:14 also offers the promise of God's presence when the people "seek good, not evil." This presence is depicted in terms of spatial deixis: "the Lord God Almighty/Lord of Hosts will be with you." This idea of the Lord's presence based on the pursuit of good rather than evil has several overlapping aspects. First, such seeking leads to life. Second, verse 15 appears to invert the order of the statements in verse 14 with great emphasis and describes another experience of God's faithfulness to the people: to have mercy. Instead of simply seeking good rather than evil, the people are encouraged to hate evil and love good. Rather than using simple indicative verbs, this command is cast in the *qal* imperative, creating rhetorical force. Compared to the simple adverb "not" in verse 14 to speak of evil, verse 15 uses command force to encourage God's people to hate evil and add that they should maintain justice in their courts. Yet the promise of God's response is less sure. Rather than the strong language of "because" and "therefore" of verse 14, verse 15 states a "perhaps" in terms of whether God will have mercy on the remnant. Thus, while God's presence is promised in response to good and not evil, God's mercy to the remnant is less certain, but hoped for. Amos 5 demonstrates that the presence of the Lord can be either a response to seeking good (5:14) or a response to seeking evil (5:17). Yet for God's presence to be with the people and not pass through their midst in judgment, they must turn toward justice, seeking good as a response of right worship before their God.

Micah 3: God's Spirit and Justice
Like Amos 5, Micah 3 portrays justice as a key motivator for God's responses to the people. In this case, however, instead of speaking of God's presence, Micah 3 describes this in terms of God's Spirit, perhaps suggesting for us

one of the ways that God's presence and Spirit show similar capacities in the Twelve.

Like Amos 5, Micah 3 speaks of the injustice of its time, offering another direction. Micah 3:2 famously flips Amos's cry to the people in Amos 5:15 to "hate evil and love good." Instead, the people of Micah's time so lacked in their embrace of justice that they "hate good and love evil." What follows is a chilling depiction of the gross brutality of injustice among the leaders of Israel through the metaphor of cannibalism (Mic 3:2–3). In contrast to Amos 5, where the promise of the Lord's presence would be with the people if they hate evil, in Micah 3 the leaders' vicious cannibalistic violence against one another has led to God's intentional absence. Whereas Amos 5 spoke of the Lord who would be "with them," injustice in Micah 3 means that the Lord "will not answer them." Instead, giving his presence in language that mirrors Moses's experience of seeing God's face as in Amos 5, God "will hide his face from them" (Mic 3:4). The reason given for this divine hiddenness in terms of response to the people is stated plainly: "because of the evil they have done." Thus, Micah 3 provides a picture of the inverse relationship potential in Amos 5.[48] Amos 5 offered the possibility of God's presence via Israel's justice. Israel's proven injustice and love for evil has turned God's presence away.

Yet all is not utterly lost, for as Amos 5 speaks of injustice while offering a glimmer of hope, so also Micah 3 offers an alternative direction by way of the prophet. Amid a crumbling, unjust society surrounding the prophet, he declares in 3:8:

> But as for me, I am filled with power,
> > with the Spirit of the LORD,
> > and with justice and might,
> > to declare to Jacob his transgression,
> > to Israel his sin.

This language of "filling" (mahleh) in relation to the Spirit is found in other biblical texts that may be foundational for Micah 3, such as portions of Exodus. Many scholars have noted how prophets function as intermediaries between the divine and human beings. At times, they call out to God on

---

48. Warren Wiersbe, The Prophets: Isaiah-Malachi, The Bible Exposition Commentary: Old Testament (Colorado Springs: David C. Cook, 2002), 394.

behalf of the concerns or needs of humankind, while at other times they function as God's mouthpiece to speak God's words to the people and leaders. In this case, the prophet's voice cries out above the fray (and above the sounds of the false prophets described in verses 5–7). The use of the otherwise unnecessary first singular pronoun, "I" (anokhi), here adds to the emphasis. The prophet's voice calls out in this way because he has been empowered by God's Spirit. Here "power" and "the Spirit of the LORD" are placed in parallel structures along with "justice" and "might." Each share the verb "fill" (mahleh). Thus, one could argue that the filling of the Spirit of the Lord can bring about such characteristics as power, justice, and might. It is important to point out that justice is among this list in light of the context for the prophet's utterance. All around the prophet is injustice and now a filling of justice characterizes the filling of the prophet with God's Spirit. There is perhaps here the notion that where injustice stood before, now the Spirit brings justice in order to counter the injustice of the time.

Micah 4 connects these notions of God's Spirit in Micah 3 with conceptions of God's presence in Micah 4. Whereas in Micah 3, the focus is on the absence of the Lord through the turning away of his face—yet the Lord's Spirit is depicted as with the prophet Micah—Micah 4 depicts the return of the Lord's presence via God's voice and name as described above, joining aspects of God's reign as king to his depiction as shepherd to his people in Micah 4–5.

Jonah's Encounters God's Presence and Wind

There is some question whether one can speak of Jonah encountering God's Spirit, but it is possible that Jonah 1 pairs Jonah's intent to escape from God's presence with God's great wind (a potential play of the spirit-wind overlap in ruach). In Jonah 1, after Jonah has tried to flee God's presence (1:3), God hurls a great wind (ruach gadolah), pursuing Jonah (1:4). There is linguistic cohesive linking between these two verses by ending verse 3 with "from God's presence" and the final word Yahweh (lefne YHWH) and beginning verse 4 with "but Yahweh" (vaYHWH). Thus, Jonah's choice to flee from God's presence is joined to pictures of God's omnipresence not only via the similar language in Psalm 139, but also by actively demonstrating in the very next verse the force and power of God's wind/Spirit. In Jonah 1:4, "great wind" and "great storm" are placed in parallel phrases, and it is possible that we have an allusion to the larger creational themes associated with God's wind/Spirit elsewhere in Scripture, particularly in Genesis and Exodus, but also in Joel as noted above. Notably, the other two uses in the Hebrew Bible of a "great wind" are in 1 Kings 19:11 and Job 1:19. In 1 Kings 19:11, this "great wind" tears the mountains apart, coming directly after the Lord asks Elijah to stand on the mountain in the presence of the Lord so that the Lord can pass by.[49] If Jonah 1 is placing the wind/Spirit as a creative active force of God's making in verse 4, then we see the repeated theme that Jonah cannot truly flee from God's presence because God's Spirit is actively present.

d. Zechariah and Micah: Intertextual and Interweaving Divine Spirit and Presence

Micah 3:8 appears to have influenced Zechariah 4:6, which uses similar language of "power," "might," and the "Spirit" of the Lord, but for different ends. Whereas Micah 3:8 points to these as characteristics filled alongside or by the filling of Spirit of the Lord, in Zechariah these terms create a contrast between the use of might and power and the abilities of God's Spirit. Yet notably the kind of "might" described in Zechariah 4:6 is ha-yil, a word associated with army as well as might compared to gibburah ("might") in Micah 3:8. Both use the shared language of "power" (koach). Furthermore, a key word is completely absent from Zechariah's list: justice (mishpat). That is not to say that Zechariah on the whole is without reference to justice (mishpat). Zechariah 7:9 and 8:16 use language very similar to what is found in Amos 5 and Micah 3, calling for the administration of justice (Zech 7:9) and speaking truth to one another with justice in the courts (Zech 8:16). But this does not negate the considerable point that Zechariah 4:6 does not speak of justice. This is likely because the focus of Zechariah 4 is not on injustice, but on the rebuilding of the temple by means of God's Spirit. The emphasis in Zechariah 4 on the negation of power or might as a means of building the temple is not because power and might are in and of themselves the problem, but because Zerubbabel might be tempted to believe that it was by his own abilities that he was able to rebuild the temple rather

---

49. Notably, the text tells us that the Lord was not in this wind, but this use of great wind does follow a scene directly about the Lord's presence, similar to Jonah. In Job 1:19, the great wind that collapses the house is set in parallel to the fire of God which falls from the heavens and burns up the sheep and servants in Job 1:16. As wind and fire are often associated with the presence of God, it is possible that here we see another such link, if a rather gruesome one.

than by God's Spirit empowering him. Forgetting the power of God's Spirit threatens to undo the long history of Israel's lessons in exile, where they believed falsely in their own strength and power and were nearly destroyed because of it.

CONCLUSION: GOD'S SPIRIT AND PRESENCE AND THEMES WITHIN THE TWELVE

Nogalski has argued that there are four core themes in the Twelve: "the Day of YHWH, fertility of the land, the fate of God's people, and the theodicy problem."[50] One could additionally argue that in specific ways each of these themes is developed alongside an ongoing picture of God's Spirit and presence with God's people, at times punishing and pursuing, at times restoring the people to one another and to the land, and often demonstrating to them the answers to questions of theodicy.

Several key themes have arisen in this survey of the Twelve's depiction of God's Spirit and presence. As Micah and Amos demonstrate, both God's Spirit and God's presence are associated with the need for the people and their leaders to maintain justice. One cannot flee from God's presence because God will ultimately follow the person, such as Jonah, by different means, including God's creative Spirit/wind. Micah, Haggai, and Zechariah all demonstrate the renewal that comes from God's presence and the power of God's Spirit. Following the conceptual framing of Exodus, Haggai and Zechariah both depict the ability of God's presence to restore the sacred spaces to the people and protect their home despite all of what they have experienced in their previous exile. Yet this is explicitly not by the might or power of their leaders, but by God's Spirit alone. Joel along with Micah demonstrates that the outpouring of God's Spirit, like the giving of his presence, leads to transformation of a people filled with the Spirit. The conceptualization of God's presence may take the form of God's voice or his name, as we find in Micah and in Joel, following in earlier traditions in Exodus and Deuteronomy. Such experience of God's presence can set not only human beings trembling as in Nahum 1, but the world as well as in Joel 2. The reign of God and his role as divine warrior also play a role in depictions of God's

---

50. James Nogalski, "Recurring Themes in the Book of the Twelve: Creating Points of Contact for a Theological Reading," *Int* 61. 2 (2007): 125–36 (125).

Spirit and presence in the Twelve, as Zechariah, Micah, Haggai, and Joel all pick up these themes in a variety of ways.

Next Steps in Research

Such a brief overview of God's Spirit and presence in the Twelve is only an initial step to a larger project on divine Spirit and presence in Scripture. To fully explore such a topic, it would be helpful to demonstrate how these conceptions begin in other parts of Scripture and further develop in the Twelve and to also follow the trajectories that the Twelve begin, which are picked up in later writings of the Second Temple period and the New Testament. Research of this breadth is beyond the scope of this chapter, but my hope is that this has provided a starting point for such work.

9

Furry, Feathery, and Fishy Friends—and Insects— in the Book of the Twelve: Their Role and Characterization

Julie Woods

INTRODUCTION

This paper looks at the role and characterization of animals in the Book of the Twelve. Without exception, every book in the Twelve has some mention of an animal (usually more), and animals are an intrinsic, yet, I would suggest, an overlooked aspect of the text; where they are mute, we are silent.

The animals that appear with most frequency in the Book of the Twelve, apart from the general "beast" (בְּהֵמָה) are horses, flocks (mainly in Zephaniah), and lions. It would be unsurprising if the animals cited in the texts were those with which the Israelites would have been most familiar, but lions were not such a familiar sight and, to quote Edwin Firmage, "While the lion captured the imagination of biblical poets (as in Homer, most of the references to the lion occur in poetic similes), the leopard seems to have had a greater real impact on human society."[1] Horses, too, are significant players, given that the Israelites were not a horse people. Some animals, it seems, are chosen for rhetorical or literary purposes. We will take a brief look at some of the material on lions, horses, and herds (oh my!) as well

---

1. Edwin Firmage, "Zoology (Fauna)," *ABD*, 6:1109–67 (1143).

as the locust, which is the most commonly occurring insect in the Book of the Twelve, despite making an appearance in only three of the books. We will then consider the animals in Jonah and take a little glimpse at Hosea's, Micah's, and Amos's depictions of various animals.

LIONS

PREDATORS

In the Book of the Twelve, the lion (various Hebrew words are used) is usually characterized as one might imagine: a predator at the top of the food chain which kills, tears apart, and devours its prey. Elsewhere in the Prophets, the destroying enemy, or the nations, are likened to a lion which acts on behalf of God, but this is not a strong theme in the Book of the Twelve, where, generally, either God himself is the lion who comes against his people, or the nations are lions which come against God's people with his disapproval. Hosea is the book that most frequently likens God to a lion.

Hosea 5:14[2] reads, "I will be like a lion [שַׁחַל] to Ephraim and like a young lion [כְּפִיר] to the house of Judah. I, even I, will tear to pieces and go away, I will carry away, and there will be none to deliver." Hosea 13:7–8 adds other predatory animals to the list, and reads, "So I will be like a lion [שַׁחַל] to them; like a leopard [נָמֵר] I will lie in wait by the wayside; I will encounter them like a bear [דֹּב] robbed of her cubs [שַׁכּוּל (lit. "bereaved/robbed of offspring")], and I will tear open their chests; there I will also devour them like a lioness [לָבִיא], as a wild beast [חַיַּת הַשָּׂדֶה] would tear them." Lions were a familiar, even stereotypical motif, in ancient Near Eastern literature and art,[3] though Gordon Johnston argues that Hosea 5:14 is not simply using stereotypical lion imagery but alluding to the use of the royal lion motif used by Neo-Assyrian kings, whereby kings depicted their military victories as lions attacking their prey.[4] In Hosea, God was a greater lion who used those Assyrian lions for his own attacks. Hosea 5:14, according to Johnston, probably refers to the subjugation of Israel and Samaria by Tiglath-Pileser III

---

2. Scriptural quotations are from the New American Standard Bible (NASB) unless otherwise noted.

3. Gordon H. Johnston, "Nahum's Rhetorical Allusions to the Neo-Assyrian Lion Motif," *BSac* 158 (2001): 287–307 (290).

4. Johnston, "Nahum's Lion Motif," 294.

in 734-732 BCE, Shalmaneser V in 725-722, and Sargon II in 722.[5] However, it is Nahum who makes the most allusions to the lion motif of Assyria, argues Johnston.

Nahum 2:11(12)[6] asks rhetorically, "Where is the den of the lions [אֲרִי] and the feeding place of the young lions [כְּפִיר], where the lion [אַרְיֵה], lioness [לָבִיא] and lion's cub [גּוּר אַרְיֵה] prowled, with nothing to disturb them?" The implication is that the predators' safe places have been threatened/destroyed. A predator of the predators is attacking them. Nahum 2:12(13) continues, "The lion [אַרְיֵה] tore enough for his cubs [גּוּר], killed enough for his lionesses [לָבִיא], and filled his lairs with prey and his dens with torn flesh." The fat cats live securely, but that will soon change; "a sword will devour your young lions [כְּפִיר]; I will cut off your prey [טֶרֶף] from the land" (Nah 2:13(14)). Johnston points out that these verses against the Assyrian city of Nineveh allude both to the royal-lion motif and the lion hunt, which was also popular in Assyrian royal culture. For, here, God has become the lion hunter; in particular, God is hunting the last powerful Neo-Assyrian king, Ashurbanipal (668-627 BCE), who had the "reputation as the most illustrious lion hunter in Assyrian history."[7]

Judah is sometimes likened to lions, and in Zephaniah 3:3-4 her leaders are compared unfavorably so: "Her princes within her are roaring lions [אֲרִי], her judges are wolves [זְאֵב] at evening; They leave nothing for the morning. Her prophets are reckless, treacherous men; Her priests have profaned the sanctuary. They have done violence to the law." On the other hand, the remnant of Jacob is favorably likened to a lion in Micah 5:8(7) in order to portray its strength. In fact, there is a role reversal in this text for the nations of Israel and Judah, who are often depicted as sheep and vulnerable to attack: "Like a lion [אַרְיֵה] among the beasts of the forest [בְּהֲמוֹת יַעַר], like a young lion [כְּפִיר] among flocks of sheep [עֶדְרֵי־צֹאן], which if he passes through, tramples down and tears and there is none to rescue."

5. Johnston, "Nahum's Lion Motif," 295.
6. Where the Hebrew text delineates the text differently than the English, the Hebrew reference is given in parentheses.
7. Johnston, "Nahum's Lion Motif," 295-96 (301).

KING OF THE JUNGLE

Unusually, Hosea in one place uses the imagery of a lion not in terms of a predator about to kill its prey but in terms of the leader of the pride whose roar summons his sons to him. This is another instance in Hosea where the lion is a metaphor for God. "They will walk after the LORD. He will roar like a lion [אַרְיֵה]; Indeed He will roar and his sons will come trembling from the west. They will come trembling like birds [צִפּוֹר] from Egypt and like doves [יוֹנָה] from the land of Assyria; and I will settle them in their houses, declares the LORD" (Hos 11:10–11). Though lions do not call other animals to them, they do roar to let other lions know where they are (the roar can be heard up to five miles [eight kilometers] away[8]). When they call their young, however, lions—both males and females—roar softly,[9] so the lion here is depicted in more of a stylized way, akin to what we might think of as "the king of the jungle."

HORSES

Horses are unusual in that they are almost never envisaged apart from humans, and when horses are mentioned, it is normally in the context of their relationship to humans. That is, horses tend not to be treated as animals in their own right in the Book of the Twelve. The overriding portrayal of horses is as a trained, working animal, rather than in terms of natural characteristics. For instance, the horses neighing or grazing are not singled out for attention, though their speed and power are of interest, often implicitly, in a military context. Amos 6:12 is unusual when it depicts the horse as vulnerable with its rhetorical question that alludes to the fragility of horse's legs and their propensity to break: "Do horses [סוּס] run on rocks [lit. the rock]?" Furthermore, the horse here is not defined by its relationship to a human and may not even be a warhorse.

While horses are subservient to humans by nature of their being shackled to chariots and ridden by humans, their superior strength makes them necessary to humans, who become reliant on them. Indeed, in the Old Testament, humans are told not to trust in horses for deliverance. In the

8. Lion Alert, "How do Lions Communicate?" https://lionalert.org/african-lions, paragraph 2.

9. Lion Alert, paragraph 4; Teague Stubbington, "Why Do Lions Roar?," Daily Mail, http://www.dailymail.co.uk/femail/article-2646767/Why-DO-lions-roar-The-questions-child-ask-answered-experts.html.

first chapter of Hosea, God tells the house of Judah that he will deliver them, but not by horses (סוּס) or horsemen (פָּרָשׁ) (1:7), and in the final chapter, Israel is to say to the Lord: "Assyria will not save us, we will not ride on horses [סוּס]" (14:3). Thus, the first and the last mention of horses in Hosea is as a potential vehicle of deliverance (i.e., military might), which would not be used in the deliverance of Israel/Judah.[10]

While Judah is generally forbidden to trust in horses and is repeatedly reminded that horses are inadequate vehicles of salvation, there are occasions when she is commanded to bring out the horses for battle. One instance is in Micah 1:13 where Lachish is called to harness the chariot to the team of horses (רֶכֶשׁ) for the day of battle had arrived. Lachish was a fortified chariot city, and it seems that there is a wordplay on its name לָכִישׁ, and לָרֶכֶשׁ "to the team of horses."[11]

While in Nahum God castigates Assyria because of her devastating military campaigns, epitomized by the "galloping horses [סוּס]" (Nah 3:2), in Habakkuk, God claims that he is raising up the Chaldean cavalry. "Their horses [סוּס] are swifter than leopards [נָמֵר] and keener than wolves [זְאֵב] in the evening. Their horsemen [פָּרָשׁ "steed"] come galloping, their horsemen [פָּרָשׁ] from afar; they fly like an eagle [נֶשֶׁר] swooping down to devour" (Hab 1:8). Here, the horses are given characteristics of other animals (leopards, wolves, and eagles) to make them "super horses," even superhero horses. Top speeds for a horse are 25–30 mph (40–48 kmh), for a leopard 36 mph (58 kmh), and for an eagle in dive 200 mph (322 kmh). The top speed goes to peregrine falcons which dive at 242 mph (389 kmh). However, dives are not technically flying since this speed is the terminal velocity of the bird. At any rate, these fortified horses of Habakkuk are virtually invincible.

Later in Habakkuk, when God himself rides out on horses for the salvation of his people (Hab 3:8–13), we read, "was your wrath against the sea that you rode on your horses [סוּס]? On your chariots of salvation?" (3:8). In this text, the horses are not so much super horses, but embody the mythical element, for God is riding out the horses against the rivers and seas; see also Habakkuk 3:15 where God is described as trampling on the sea with his horses (סוּס). The stylistic presentation of horses is not peculiar to Habakkuk, however, and Zechariah 1 takes the mythological to a different

10. Douglas Stuart, *Hosea-Jonah*, WBC 31 (Waco, TX: Word, 1987), 213.

11. Ralph L. Smith, *Micah-Malachi*, WBC 32 (Waco, TX: Word, 1984), 21.

level with its apocalyptic visions of horses. Petersen's research convincing-ly shows that Zechariah's colors of horses (red, a different red, chestnut—or sorrel—and white) are normal colors for horses.[12] Although many have tried to find meanings for the colors, I would provisionally concur with Ralph Smith and others that there is no significance, either here in chap-ter 1 or in chapter 6 (where the colors are different).[13] Nevertheless, Carol Meyers and Eric Meyers point out that the colors would not have been able to have been seen in the setting of darkness,[14] which suggests they do have some rhetorical value.

When horses reappear in 6:2-3, they are hitched to chariots, and when Zechariah asks what these are (6:4), he is told that they are the four spir-its of heaven which are going forth after standing before the Lord of the earth (6:5). That is, these horses have had the privilege of being in the pres-ence of the Lord, an honor not usually associated with animals. As well, the bronze mountains of 6:1 (the only time that they are mentioned in the Old Testament), whence come the chariots, are often taken to mean God's dwell-ing place,[15] so these verses twice make the point that the horses are coming out from the Lord's presence. The privilege is extended in 14:20 where hors-es are described as wearing bells with "Holy to the LORD" inscribed on them—the inscription found on the miter of the high priest (Exod 28:36-38). This is particularly ironic given that horses were unclean animals.

In contrast to this military backdrop, the king in Zechariah 9:9 comes riding to Jerusalem, "humble and mounted on a donkey [חֲמוֹר], even on a colt [עַיִר], the foal of a donkey" (a young donkey, offspring of a she-donkey, אָתוֹן). When this verse is discussed, the attribute of the donkey that is often emphasized is that of humility.[16] I would argue, however, as others have done before me,[17] that the primary purpose is to demonstrate that when

12. David L. Petersen, *Haggai and Zechariah 1-8*, OTL (London: SCM Press, 1985), 140-41; see also Mark J. Boda, *Haggai, Zechariah*, NIVAC (Grand Rapids: Zondervan, 2004), 194-95, 320.

13. Smith, *Micah-Malachi*, 190.

14. Carol L. Myers and Eric M. Meyers, *Haggai, Zechariah 1-8*, AB (New York: Doubleday, 1987), 126.

15. Smith, *Micah-Malachi*, 213.

16. Petersen, *Haggai and Zechariah 1-8*, 58; Eugene H. Merrill, *An Exegetical Commentary: Haggai, Zechariah, Malachi* (Chicago: Moody, 1994), 253; Smith, *Micah-Malachi*, 256.

17. Douglas Rawlinson Jones, *Haggai, Zechariah and Malachi: Introduction and Commentary*, TBC (London: SCM, 1962), 131; Ben C. Ollenburger, "Zechariah," in *Introduction to Apocalyptic Literature, Daniel, The Twelve Prophets*, NIB 7 (Nashville: Abingdon, 1996), 807; Meyers and Meyers, *Haggai, Zechariah 1-8*, 129, 131.

the king comes there will be no overtone of war; the warhorse has been replaced with a donkey. This is accentuated by the next verse, where, in the context of war, God says that he will cut off the horse from Jerusalem and that the king will speak peace to the nations (Zech 9:10). That the donkey is a young donkey further highlights the non-military nature of the animal.

FLOCKS, CATTLE, HERDS, AND BEASTS OF THE FIELD

Also, in contrast to the powerful warhorse are the flocks, cattle, herds, and beasts of the field. One of the most employed metaphors of flocks (which may consist of sheep and/or goats) is that which likens God's people, Israel and Judah, to flocks—often flocks of (sometimes disobedient) sheep that need pasturing and shepherding (see Mic 7:14; Zech 9:16; 10:2; 11). In Micah, the idea of God's people as a flock is linked with restoration of the remnant (Mic 2:12). On occasion, for example, in Zechariah 11 (a chapter concerned with flocks and shepherds) the metaphor of the flock is abandoned or altered: for "the afflicted of the flock (צֹאן) who were watching me realized that it was the word of the LORD" (11:11). Here, in their watching, the flock exhibits human behavior.

In Zechariah 8:10, the herd animals are likewise represented in anthropomorphic terms, but the difference in this chapter is that the herd animals are not metaphors for humans. The writer laments that "before those days there was no wage for man or any wage for animal [בְּהֵמָה]." The translation is not straightforward and the sense of the construct (וּשְׂכַר הַבְּהֵמָה) unclear. The New Jewish Publication Society (NJPS) translates the text as "the earnings of men were nil, and profits from beasts were nothing," while Merrill argues that there was unemployment for both humans and animals.[18] שָׂכָר can mean "reward," but even so, it is strange terminology given that animals are not normally rewarded for work any more than they receive wages. Petersen understands to refer to animals that can be rented out.[19] I would tentatively suggest that the animals may be on par with humans in terms of their suffering—a reminder that animals are part of society and that human wickedness brings pain to them.

---

18. Merrill, *Haggai, Zechariah, Malachi*, 225.
19. Petersen, *Haggai and Zechariah 1–8*, 306; see also Meyers and Meyers, *Haggai, Zechariah 1–8*, 421; Merrill, *Haggai, Zechariah, Malachi*, 225.

Indeed, in Joel 1:18–19 the beasts (בְּהֵמָה) groan and the herds of cattle (עֶדְרֵי בָקָר) wander aimlessly because there are no "pastures of the wilderness" (נְאוֹת מִדְבָּר) for them. Even the flocks of the sheep (עֶדְרֵי הַצֹּאן) suffer. In fact, one way of indicating that God's judgment is severe is to make it clear that his punishment affects not just the humans but the animals too (e.g., Hag 1:11; see also Hab 3:17). Joel 1:20 goes further, however: "Even the beasts of the field [בַּהֲמוֹת שָׂדֶה] pant [עָרַג] for you." These animals are hungry for more than food—they are longing for God; the animal behavior has become stylized. In 2:22, in a passage where the land is also addressed, God addresses these beasts of the field (בַּהֲמוֹת שָׂדֶה) which panted for him. He tells them not to fear, for the "pastures of the wilderness" (נְאוֹת מִדְבָּר)—the same phrase used in 1:19—have now turned green. As God would make up to the people for the years that the locusts had eaten (Joel 2:25), he makes up to the animals for the pastures that the fire had eaten. It is not the only time in the Bible that the animals are addressed, but the occasions are rare. The beasts of the field are not merely grazing machines but have a semblance of a relationship with God, even if only in rhetoric; they have approached him in some way and God has responded. Furthermore, when nature springs forth, it is for the benefit of land and animals as well as humans.[20] It is thus evident that the welfare of the animals and land is important to God.

The land becoming desolate and only fit for animals, including unclean animals, to live in—or, at least, the land being overrun with animals—is a familiar motif. Often it is the wild animals that dwell in such places, such as the jackals (תַּן) (Mal 1:3), but in Zephaniah 2:14, it is the farm animals along with smaller animals who will possess the land, for flocks (עֵדֶר) will lie down in the midst of Nineveh with a range of herd beasts (חַיְתוֹ־גוֹי "creatures of every kind," lit. "of the nations"[21]) as well as the pelican (קָאַת), and the hedgehog/porcupine (קִפֹּד), which will lodge in the tops of her pillars (see also Zeph 2:6). To ask how all these animals would survive in a ruined desert city, or what a bird that consumes fish, such as a pelican, is doing in the desert,[22] is surely to push the metaphor too far.

---

20. Stuart, *Hosea–Jonah*, 259.

21. כָּל־חַיְתוֹ־גוֹי is an unusual phrase; see Adele Berlin, *Zephaniah*, AYBC (New Haven: Yale University Press, 1994), 114–15.

22. John Merlin Powis Smith, "Zephaniah," in *Micah, Zephaniah, Nahum, Habakkuk, Obadiah, Joel*, ICC (Edinburgh: T&T Clark, 1911), 233–34.

HOSEA'S BEASTS

Given that "flock" is often used as a metaphor for God's people, it is unsurprising that both Obadiah and Nahum, oracles against the foreign nations, do not use the term. Additionally, both are short books, as are Haggai and Malachi, books which also do not mention flocks. Where one might expect to see flocks, however, is in Hosea, a longer book which contains a wide array of animals across all animal classes (horses, beasts of the fields, various birds, creeping things of the ground, fish of the sea, a heifer, a lamb, a moth, a variety of lions, a donkey, a leopard, a bear, cubs, and wild beasts). Flocks are mentioned in Hosea 5:6, but only in the context of sacrifice.

It is surely overreading the text to say that in Hosea God's people are not passive flocks, scattered without a shepherd, but active idolaters who take the initiative in committing adultery—particularly as other prophetic books portray them as such. Nevertheless, they are likened to a stubborn heifer (פָּרָה סֹרֵרָה) with the apparent sense that the Lord cannot therefore pasture them as a lamb (כֶּבֶשׂ) (4:16). Later, they are described as a wild donkey (פֶּרֶא) which goes up to Assyria alone (8:9), which most see as denoting a donkey in heat that is looking for a mate.[23] Providing some balance is 10:11 which describes Ephraim as a "trained heifer [עֶגְלָה] that loves to thresh" and whom God will lead by putting a yoke (implicit to the text) over her neck.

Hosea does use a phrase, however, that is employed particularly in the Pentateuch and the Major Prophets but not the rest of the Twelve: חַיַּת הַשָּׂדֶה "beast(s) of the field." This is a generic term that seems to encompass both predatory and non-predatory animals, often to differentiate the mammals from the birds, fish, and creeping things (Hos 2:18[20]; 4:3). בַּהֲמוֹת שָׂדֶה is a term used in Joel (1:20; 2:22) which, like Hosea's phrase, חַיַּת הַשָּׂדֶה, is sometimes also translated "beasts of the field" (e.g., NASB).

COVENANT WITH THE ANIMALS IN HOSEA 2:18(20)

In Hosea 2:18(20) God makes a covenant for his people with the animal kingdom: the beasts of the field (חַיַּת הַשָּׂדֶה), birds of the sky (עוֹף הַשָּׁמַיִם), and creeping things of the ground (רֶמֶשׂ הָאֲדָמָה). This verse has generated discussion regarding whether there are links to the creation story in Genesis and/or to God's words to Noah after the flood in Genesis 9. Some see the covenant

23. Stuart, Hosea-Jonah, 135.

as between Israel and the animals (e.g., Luther Mays) with God as either the proxy for Israel (e.g., Francis Landy) or as the mediator (e.g., Hans Wolff), and others view the covenant as between God and the animals (e.g., Andrew Dearman, Francis Andersen, and David Freedman).[24] Whichever view one takes, it seems clear that the covenant with the animals is for "them," rather than for the sake of the animals themselves. That is, God provides reassurance to his people that he will shut the lions' mouths, so they will not harm them.[25]

Although God's covenant of protection of animals is for the people and it seems that no human response is required, the Old Testament repeatedly emphasizes the need for humans to behave justly. In addition, there are texts that indicate that animal welfare should not be neglected (e.g., the animals were to be included in the Sabbath rest in Deut 5 and Exod 20). Thus, it would not be surprising if the human response to the covenant with the animals here should be one of respect toward the animals. Mays stresses that the covenant is a local one with Israel, "not the whole earth,"[26] but Landy thinks the text is unclear on this point.[27] In a world where many animals are on the endangered list (including some lions), if there is to be a more eschatological and universal fulfillment of this peculiar covenant in Hosea 2:18(20), then I hope that one day the lion will be safe to lie down with the man.

LOCUSTS

In the meantime, humans need protecting from locusts, and in Amos 7:1 where God is forming a locust-swarm (גֹּבַי) to devour the vegetation of the land, Amos responds to God (7:2), "How can Jacob stand, for he is small?" A locust is a small creature, but Jacob is too small against them, for it is not a single locust that is the threat. The swarm of locusts is clearly powerful enough to crumble this nation and God changes his mind about bringing

---

24. James Luther Mays, *Hosea: A Commentary*, OTL (Philadelphia: Westminster, 1969), 49; Francis Landy, *Hosea*, A New Biblical Commentary (Sheffield: Sheffield Academic, 1995), 43; Hans Walter Wolff, *Hosea*, Hermeneia (Philadelphia: Fortress, 1974), 50–51. See also Francis I. Andersen and David Noel Freedman, *Hosea*, AB (Garden City, NY: Doubleday, 1980), 265, 280–81; J. Andrew Dearman, *The Book of Hosea*, NICOT (Grand Rapids: Eerdmans, 2010), 126.
25. I am paraphrasing two lines from the children's song, "Daniel Was a Man of Prayer," https://bibletruthpublishers.com/daniel-was-a-man-of-prayer/lets-sing-about-Jesus-24/lkh24LSAJ.
26. Mays, *Hosea*, 49–50.
27. Landy, *Hosea*, 44.

the locust swarm against Jacob (Amos 7:3). This characterization of locusts as part of a devastating swarm that strips vegetation is frequently employed to denote God's punishment on his people (e.g., Amos 4:9) or on Israel's enemies (Nah 3:15). The only depiction in the Old Testament of ineffective locusts is in Nahum, where in 3:16–17 the locusts sit on a cold wall doing nothing until the sun comes up, when they flee (נָדַד), leaving the city unguarded.

While Hosea includes more animals than most (though one must remember that Hosea is the longest book of the Twelve), locusts are not among the animals named. Joel, on the other hand, seems to have a bit of a penchant for locusts, despite talking about them in only two passages, for he names four different sorts, or phases, of the locust, which the NASB translates as the gnawing locust (גָּזָם), the swarming locust (אַרְבֶּה), the creeping locust (יֶלֶק), and the stripping locust (חָסִיל) (1:4 and 2:25). That the translations for these locusts is not too precise can be shown by the way that the various versions translate them. The dictionaries, too, do not present a cohesive picture. BDB considers that גָּזָם and אַרְבֶּה are the collective nouns for locusts (i.e., a swarm), while יֶלֶק and חָסִיל are both "a kind of locust." The ABD lists all of these words as "locust." NIDOTTE describes יֶלֶק as the first larval stage when the larva is black and hops, being wingless, חָסִיל as the next stage when the larva is black and yellow with partially developed wings and jaws, גָּזָם as the next stage when the insect is yellow and has developed wings and jaws that eventually dry, and אַרְבֶּה as the sexually mature adult as well as אַרְבֶּה being the generic term for locust. It then continues, "If these terms do not represent developmental stages, they may refer to different species, colors, regional names, or simply be synonyms used rhetorically."[28] In other words, if you did not know that the locust is the migratory phase of the grasshopper, then all is not lost. You could just as easily call them A, B, C, and D; the point is that the locusts, between them, will have utterly destroyed God's land. If one understands the locusts as at different stages then, to quote Stuart, "The picture given is highly figurative, rather than literal,

---

28. Robert C. Stallman, "אַרְבֶּה," in *New International Dictionary of Old Testament Theology and Exegesis*, ed. Willem A. VanGemeren, vol. 1 (Carlisle: Paternoster, 1997), 491–95 (494).

since all the stages of locusts do not work together at once."[29] The same can be said of different kinds of locusts.[30]

In a similar way to Habakkuk's super horses, the locusts in Joel 1:4–7 are described hyperbolically in terms of other animals, having the teeth of a lion (אַרְיֵה) and the fangs of a lioness (לָבִיא) (1:6). Although it has been argued that locusts are not symbolic of human invaders,[31] it seems clear that in Joel 1:4–7 they represent the "nation that has invaded my land" (1:6), namely Babylon. If one wants to further the metaphor in the manner of Jerome, the four locusts can be identified with the empires of Assyria and Babylon, followed by the Medes and Persians, followed by Greece, and then finally by Rome; the last two being the ghosts of locusts yet to come.[32]

JONAH

If Joel's locusts are sometimes larger than life, then they are in good company with the characters in Jonah. Jonah's characters also behave atypically, or, to put it more Hebraically, every character in Jonah is a great character who acts greatly. So, the pagan sailors pray and make sacrifices to God, the prophet runs away rather than speak the word that God has given him (no fire in the bones is God's word to Jonah!), and the fish swallows a human.

Fish

We are introduced to the fish in 1:17(2:1) when the Lord appoints a great fish (דָּג גָּדוֹל) to swallow Jonah. There are debates about whether 1:17 belongs to the previous or the next chapter, but most commentators, wherever they split the chapter, treat 1:17 as a separate idea from the preceding passage and do not consider the possibility that the fish might be an answer to the

---

29. Stuart, Hosea–Jonah, 241.

30. In informal email conversations John A. Gatehouse, professor in the department of biosciences at Durham University, and Dr. Val Standen, retired ecologist whose interest is insects, confirmed that, due to the mechanics of how swarms form (one species has out-competed the others), one can assume that a swarm consists of one species of locust, though the question is probably unanswerable. I am grateful to them both for responding to my question.

31. Stuart, Hosea–Jonah, 241–42.

32. Cited in Josef Lössl, "When Is a Locust Just a Locust? Patristic Exegesis of Joel 1:4 in the Light of Ancient Literary Theory," JTS 55 (2004): 575–99 (588). Lössl gives a fuller study of the reception history of this verse. Or, with Julian of Aeclanum, we may see them as the four emotional states of the soul: hope, joy, fear, and pain (cited in Lössl, "When Is a Locust Just a Locust?", 594–95 [596]).

FURRY, FEATHERY, AND FISHY FRIENDS

sailors' prayer.[33] I prefer to break the chapter after 1:17 as our English versions have it.[34]

The sailors ask in 1:14 that innocent blood not be put on them, then throw Jonah overboard as he has commanded them to do in order to quell the storm, but then they pray and make vows to God whom they fear with a great fear. It makes sense, according to the narrative and according to God's normal response to human intercession, that the great fish is sent to swallow Jonah as God's response to their prayers and vows. That is, the men feared the Lord with a great fear and the Lord appointed a great fish for Jonah. There is no innocent blood upon the heads of the sailors. Furthermore, while the sailors prayed, there is no record of Jonah having done likewise at this point. Thus, I propose that the *vav* in 1:17(2:1) be translated "so," as an answer to the sailors' prayer. Verses 16 and 17 then read, "Then the men feared the LORD greatly, and they offered a sacrifice to the LORD and made vows. [So] the LORD appointed a great fish to swallow Jonah." The next section then starts with 2:1(2): "Then Jonah prayed."

My reading also provides balance (in a swim-bladder way of providing equilibrium) to the narrative of the fish, for it is when the sailors pray and make vows that the great fish swallows Jonah and it is when Jonah prays and makes vows in 2:9(10) (the same words as were used for the sailors) that the fish (דָּג) (not described as a great fish on this occasion) vomits Jonah onto dry land in 2:10(11). Or, if one wishes to read Jonah's prayer suspiciously, the fish cannot stomach Jonah's words and vomits him out.[35] Either way, it is interesting that as the readers heard nothing of Jonah's prayer for salvation, neither do they hear anything of Jonah making the sacrifices and offerings that he has vowed, so if God had brought Jonah to dry land in order to receive Jonah's offerings, he may have been disappointed. Elsewhere, as

---

33. Stuart, *Hosea-Jonah*, 469; T. Desmond Alexander, "Jonah," in *Obadiah, Jonah and Micah*, ed. David W. Baker, T. Desmond Alexander, and Bruce K. Waltke (Leicester: Inter-Varsity Press, 1988), 110; Julius A. Bewer, "Jonah," in *Haggai, Zechariah, Malachi and Jonah*, ed. Hinckley G. Mitchell, John Merlin Powis Smith, and Julius A. Bewer, ICC (Edinburgh: T&T Clark, 1911), 41–42; Phyllis Trible, "Jonah," in *Introduction to Apocalyptic Literature, Daniel, The Twelve Prophets*, 503; James D. Smart and William Scarlett, "Jonah," in *Lamentations, Ezekiel, Daniel, Twelve Prophets*, IB 6 (New York: Abingdon, 1956), 885–88; John D. Watts, *The Books of Joel, Obadiah, Jonah, Nahum, Habakkuk and Zephaniah*, CBC (Cambridge: Cambridge University Press, 1975), 82; Stuart, *Hosea-Jonah*, 469.

34. See also Smart and Scarlett, "Jonah," 885; Bewer, "Jonah," 41; Watts, *The Books of Joel*, 84.

35. Trible also draws attention to the negative word used in this verse. "Jonah," 504, cf. 507; see also Phillip Cary, *Jonah*, SCM Theological Commentary on the Bible (London: SCM, 2008), 104.

we have seen, the people are warned against putting their trust in horses for deliverance. Nowhere are they warned about putting their trust in fish for deliverance.

The fish that has been presented to us so far is male—that is, the masculine word for "fish" (דָּג) is used for the fish that swallows Jonah and then spits him out. However, the feminine noun is used for the fish in whose stomach Jonah resides (דָּגָה) (2:1(2)). When the fish swallows Jonah, Jonah goes down the digestive tract to (one of) the stomach(s), and "stomach" is indeed how some English versions translate מֵעֶה,[36] though a number translate it "belly."[37] However, מֵעֶה can also be used to mean "womb," as others have pointed out, indicating, according to Phyllis Trible, that Jonah has gone from death to life.[38] Rashi notes that Jonah spent three days in the male fish's big stomach before he prayed, so God made the fish spew Jonah into the mouth of a female fish full of offspring in order to make Jonah less comfortable in the restricted space and force him to pray.[39]

Another thought is that Jonah becomes the offspring of this great fish and being vomited out is analogous to birth. When God first called Jonah, in Jonah 1:1, the word of the Lord came to Jonah, the son of Amittai. Perhaps mischievously, we can think that when Jonah is called a second time (Jonah 3:1), he is Jonah, meaning "dove," son of the fish.

Some fish do change sex for mating purposes, but great fish tend not to swap sex. As well, of course, great fish do not have a track record of swallowing humans and then spitting them out—on land—three days later.

HERDS AND FLOCKS

In Jonah 3, humans make the animals behave out of character. The immediate and thorough repentance of the Assyrians is larger than life, but lest we not recognize a grotesque when we see one, the king of Nineveh commands the people not to let any man, beast (בְּהֵמָה), herd (בָּקָר), or flock (צֹאן) taste a thing (3:7) and orders both man and beast (בְּהֵמָה) to be covered with sackcloth (3:8). The animals are not to behave like grazing animals but like repentant humans. How one can stop a grazing animal from grazing

---

36. E.g., NASB, NEB.
37. E.g., AV, NRSV, JPS.
38. E.g., Trible, "Jonah," 505.
39. Rashi's commentary on Jonah 2:1, https://www.chabad.org/library/bible_cdo/aid/16184/jewish/Chapter-2.htm#showrashi=true.

is another issue. Having clothed man and animal in sackcloth, the Hebrew text goes on to say, וְיִקְרְאוּ אֶל־אֱלֹהִים בְּחָזְקָה ("And let them call on God with strength"). Although the NASB translates the first part of verse 8 as "let men call on God earnestly" and the NIV "let everyone call urgently on God," I would prefer to follow the translations that keep "them" as "them" (e.g., ASV, ERV, JPS, and RSV; see also NRSV, NAB, NET, and AV), so that "them" includes the animals. That is, "Let them [humans and animals] call urgently on God." Indeed, it makes sense from the narrative that the animals as well as the humans should call on God—what is the point of fasting and wearing sackcloth if not? If the beasts of the field panted for God in Joel 1:20, the beasts in Jonah have gone several steps further.

WORM

The worm (תּוֹלָעָה/תּוֹלַעַת) that God appoints to attack the plant in Jonah 4:7 is not described as a great worm, but it is the next larger than life animal in this story. The plant, incidentally, has a phenomenal growth rate; if you can see bamboo growing and hear rhubarb growing, you could undoubtedly both see and hear this plant growing. The worm's job is to attack that plant, which is large enough to be a shade over Jonah. This worm is on a deadline. God brings it into the story at dawn, and before the sun comes up it needs to have chomped through enough of the plant to have brought it to its knees, so to speak. Many commentators have discussed the size of the great fish's belly, but I have yet to see discussion on the size of the belly of the grub which eats like a horse.

The word for a male or female worm (kermes insect) is a feminine form (תּוֹלַעַת), and the word for "smite" (root: נָכָה) is also a feminine form, so I like to think that this is a she-worm. In destroying the plant in a few hours, perhaps this caterpillar is a wannabe locust, but whatever her desires, she has behaved, like the fish, a little out of character. In Jonah, the animals (all of which have strange eating habits) play different roles: the fish saves, the herds and flocks repent, and the she-worm—the only one to play a negative role—executes punishment.

GOD

Although all the other actors in Jonah have tended toward the grotesque, God has acted as one might expect. He calls his prophet, he demonstrates his power over the wind and the waves, he calms the storm, he provides deliverance, he threatens punishment, he relents when he sees repentance, he responds to prayers and vows, he provides for his prophet, and he teaches his prophet a lesson. Jonah had said that salvation comes from the Lord (2:9) and that God is gracious and compassionate, slow to anger, and abundant in lovingkindness, and God has behaved according to type.

In the final verse, God tells Jonah that he should have compassion on Nineveh, the great city in which there are more than 120,000 persons who do not know their right hand from their left, but then he adds, "and many animals," a humorous reference back to the animals who fasted and wore sackcloth. "And many animals" (וּבְהֵמָה רַבָּה) are the final words of the book in which animals have played a more active role than animals often do in biblical narratives. And this is how Jonah ends. With an uncharacteristic, humorous wink from God—a rare glimpse into what seems to me to be the wry sense of humor of God. It is, in my view, a wonderful ending to this quirky book of Jonah.

HOSEA

BIRDS

If Jonah (יוֹנָה) has a great fish in it, Hosea has a silly dove, for Ephraim is likened to a dove (יוֹנָה) without sense in Hosea 7:11. Her silliness is in forsaking God and going to Egypt and Assyria. The next verse says that when they go, God will spread his net over them and will bring them down like the birds of the sky (עוֹף הַשָּׁמַיִם). Though the generic term for birds, עוֹף, is used, the context is that of the dove (יוֹנָה). Might the difference in terminology be due to the fact that the domestic dove[40] that belongs to God has become a wild bird when she flees from him? At any rate, the silly dove, יוֹנָה, did not realize that she would be caught by God as soon as she fled from him. The prophet Jonah (יוֹנָה) might think there was a sermon in there somewhere!

---

40. Bones of small animals are hard to find in excavation and can only be retrieved by fine sieving. However, while the Bible does not explicitly talk about doves and pigeons being domestic, the amount needed in sacrifices would suggest that they were, so the assumption is that they were domestic. By Hellenistic times, they began to be raised in large, industrial installations (Firmage, "Zoology," 1117, 1144–45).

Hosea's bird motif continues into chapter 8, for in 8:1, Ephraim's enemy is a depicted as an eagle (נֶשֶׁר), which comes against the house of the Lord. Interestingly, it is not the bird of prey who is described in pejorative terms, for it is the prey (the "silly dove" of 7:11), not the predator, who is out of line here. Later, Ephraim's glory will fly away like a bird (עוֹף) (9:11) and she herself will fly back "like birds [צִפּוֹר] from Egypt and like doves [יוֹנָה] from the land of Assyria" (11:11).

MOTH

Hosea employs an unusual metaphor in describing God as "like a moth [עָשׁ] to Ephraim" (Hos 5:12), the moth, or the larvae, being paralleled with "rottenness" in the second half of the verse. When the people ignore the lesser force—God as a moth—God becomes a force that cannot be ignored; a lion (שַׁחַל), a young lion (כְּפִיר), who tears to pieces and carries away (Hos 5:14). We are familiar with, "Behold, the Lion that is from the tribe of Judah. ... And I saw ... a lamb" (Rev 5:5–6), but here it is more like "Behold the moth ... and I saw a lion."

MICAH

Micah tends to portray animals in a more stylistic way than most. For instance, Micah 1:8 reads, "I must make a lament like the jackals [תַּן] and a mourning like the ostriches [יַעֲנָה]." Jackals do not lament, nor ostriches mourn. Jackals call, particularly when they are hunting, but ostriches have no vocal chords, though ostrich chicks can make a weak, chirping sound, adult female ostriches can hiss, and the adult male "booms and grunts during the mating season."[41] Highgate Ostrich Show Farm states that "The Arabian Ostriches in the Near and Middle East [Micah's ostriches] were hunted to extinction by the middle of the 20th century."[42]

There is more stylized animal behavior in Micah 7:17 where Micah declares that the nations "will lick the dust like a serpent [נָחָשׁ], like reptiles of the earth [כְּזֹחֲלֵי אֶרֶץ]." Snakes do not lick the dust as such; they smell

---

41. "Ostrich Facts," Highgate Ostrich Show Farm, South Africa, https://web.archive.org/web/20181026152612/http://www.highgate.co.za/ostrich-facts/.

42. "About Ostriches," Highgate Ostrich Show Farm. https://web.archive.org/web/20181106060055/http://www.highgate.co.za/-the-history-of-the-ostrich.

through their tongues, by taking particles from the air, ground, and water, which they then press against two hollows in the roof of their mouth, called the Jacobson's organ.[43] Some other reptiles do similarly.

Micah 4:13 also employs stylized animal imagery: "Arise and thresh, daughter of Zion, for your horn I will make iron and your hoofs I will make bronze, that you may pulverize many peoples." Cattle threshed wheat and corn in ancient societies, so in this verse, it seems that Daughter Jerusalem is being likened to threshing cattle. However, the metaphor is extended because she is then given horns of iron and hooves of bronze that seem to turn her into a bull that tramples its enemies. While ancient Near Eastern iconography frequently shows bulls trampling enemies, this is not characteristic behavior of bulls.[44] Malachi 4:2(3:20) does similarly, for verse 2 paints a picture that sounds as if it would fit well with the opening scenes of *The Sound of Music*: "You will go forth and skip about like calves [עֵגֶל] from the stall." Verse 3, however, rectifies any thoughts that this might be the rollicking of a young animal which we might anthropomorphize as joyful, for it reads, "'You will tread down the wicked, for they will be ashes under the soles of your feet on the day which I am preparing,' says the LORD of hosts."

AMOS'S SNAKES

Amos 5:19 portrays the futility in fleeing from God: "'As when a man flees from a lion [אֲרִי] and a bear [דֹּב] meets him, or goes home, leans his hand against the wall and a snake [נָחָשׁ] bites him." This verse may depict one or two events (depending on whether the man is caught by the bear or escapes it), but if it is one event, then it is ironic that once he reached the safer place (home), having escaped the ferocious mammals, the man finally falls to a reptile. God brings out his reptilian weapons again in Amos 9:3: "I will command the serpent [נָחָשׁ] and it will bite them." As in chapter 5, chapter 9 is talking about not being able to flee from God's judgment. While God is implicitly behind the activity in chapter 5, in chapter 9, he is the active agent who commands the serpent. In Amos 5 it seems that the man's demise is caused by "natural" causes in a "natural" environment. In 9:3, though, the

---

43. "Chemoreception," Britannica, https://www.britannica.com/animal/reptile/Chemoreception.
44. Stephen G. Dempster, *Micah*, Two Horizons Commentary (Grand Rapids: Eerdmans, 2017), 137.

people are hiding from God on the bottom of the sea, and it is from there that God commands the serpent which bites them. This is far from a natural scene. It is an impossible scene, seemingly constructed to make the point that it is impossible to flee from God.

Obadiah makes a similar point, in just as fantastical terms, in verse 4, though here God brings down from the stars those who flee, rather than pulls them up from the floor of the ocean: "'Though you build high like the eagle [נֶשֶׁר], though you set your nest among the stars, from there I will bring you down,' declares the LORD." The eagle is a strong bird at the top of the food chain, but these qualities of power, speed, and freedom, along with a safe dwelling in the heights is ineffectual when escaping from God.[45] The predator has become the prey.

HABAKKUK'S LEADERLESS CREATURES

There is also reversal in Habakkuk, for 1:14 concludes a series of rhetorical questions with, "Why have you made men like the fish [דָּג] of the sea, like creeping things [רֶמֶשׂ] without a ruler over them?" Such animals are easily caught. The Bible does not have the same zoological classifications as we do now, and רֶמֶשׂ, or "creeping things" are "called by us reptiles" according to Burton in 1836,[46] while Sheldon recently (2017) considered רֶמֶשׂ to include both reptiles and amphibians.[47] It is ironic that humans who should have ruled over the fish of the sea (Gen 1:28) have now been brought down to their level.[48] This position of having no leader is the consequence of God being silent, Habakkuk argues, as part of his appeal to God. As a result, the Chaldeans can bring them up with a hook, drag them away with their net, and gather them in their fishing net, as easily as they would do fish (1:15).

---

45. See also Stuart, *Hosea–Jonah*, 417.

46. Charles James Burton, *A View of the Creation of the World in Illustration of the Mosaic Record* (London, 1836), 97.

47. Robert Sheldon, *The Long Ascent: Genesis 1–11 in Science and Myth*, vol. 1, Resource Publications (Eugene, OR: Wipf & Stock, 2017), 197.

48. See David W. Baker, *Nahum, Habakkuk and Zephaniah*, TOTC (Leicester: IVP, 1988), 56; O. Palmer Robertson, *The Books of Nahum, Habakkuk, and Zephaniah*, NICOT (Grand Rapids: Eerdmans, 1990), 162.

CONCLUSION

In the Book of the Twelve, therefore, animals may play an active or a passive role and be viewed in a positive or negative way (depending on the metaphor). Animal metaphors may denote the tools of God's punishment or indicate the results of such punishment, such as when they inhabit cities. They suffer with humans, suffer due to humans, cause humans to suffer, and at times provide salvation. They may be depicted according to natural traits or in stylized terms—on occasion both (e.g., Joel's locusts). They may take on mythical qualities or play a comic role. Sometimes they may act as a foil to the overall plot, such as the horses—unclean animals—in Zechariah who appear in God's presence or wearing bells with "Holy to the LORD" inscribed on them, a phrase associated with high priests. Rarely, though significantly, animals are shown to have a relationship with God, and in one instance God makes a covenant with them.

Different books within the Twelve have their distinct perspective or use of animals. Hosea, for instance, does not mention flocks (outside of the context of sacrifice) or locusts, but employs a term not found elsewhere in the Twelve: "beast(s) of the field," חַיַּת הַשָּׂדֶה. Joel uses four different kinds of locusts to make its point and Micah tends to depict animals stylistically. Jonah's animals behave, like the rest of the cast in the book, out of character. Habakkuk presents God with a picture of fish and creeping things that have no leader to demonstrate that God's silence reduces humans to the level of such beasts. The same animals may be depicted differently, according to the context and rhetoric. Thus, the animals in the Book of the Twelve are given full and free treatment: they howl, they hunt, they hide. Far from a few animals being consigned to stereotypical metaphors, a wide variety of animals mount up from the pages with wings like eagles.

10

Twelve Books, One Theology?

John Goldingay

The Twelve Prophets comprise twelve works each bearing the name of a different prophet, but in some contexts they have been treated as one book alongside Isaiah, Jeremiah, and Ezekiel; in length, they are comparable to Ezekiel.[1] Thus, in manuscripts from Qumran and from Nahal Hever, they come on one scroll. In Josephus (*Against Apion* 1.8), they count as one book out of the twenty-two that comprise the Torah, Prophets, and Writings, and in the Talmud (Baba Batra 14b) as one of the twenty-four books. In the 1990s there developed a scholarly interest in understanding them as one book that might reflect a process of mutual redaction.[2] In what way do they hold together in substance?

The other prophetic books provide three possible models for thinking about the theology of a prophetic scroll. Ezekiel is the nearest to constituting the deposit of one stream of religious, ethical, and theological thinking, though the Gog and Magog chapters especially suggest expanding from another stream. The book of Isaiah has a consistent understanding of God and Israel, but chapters 24–27 and 40–55 and 56–66 nuance it further than Gog and Magog do for Ezekiel. The book of Jeremiah is more complex, so multi-hued that it has been thought not capable of being read as a unit. It

---

1. Scripture quotations are my own translation unless otherwise noted; I have sometimes presupposed exegesis from J. Goldingay, *Hosea to Micah* (Grand Rapids: Baker, 2020) and J. Goldingay and P. J. Scalise, *Minor Prophets II* (repr., Grand Rapids: Baker, 2012).

2. See especially James D. Nogalski, *Literary Precursors to the Book of the Twelve*, BZAW 217 (Berlin: de Gruyter, 1993) and *Redactional Processes in the Book of the Twelve*, BZAW 218 (Berlin: de Gruyter, 1993).

can assert both that disaster is inevitable and that escape is possible, that disaster is deserved and that it is to be protested, that disaster will be the end and that restoration will come about.

While this diversity in Jeremiah might reflect a redactional process whereby different voices have added their perspectives to Jeremiah's, it appears to me more likely that it reflects the breadth of Jeremiah's own thinking. Either way, the diverse material has become one scroll. And Jeremiah provides a plausible model for thinking about the Twelve in their diversity. If they came into being by a redactional process, then process and end result have something in common with Jeremiah. But the Twelve remain also separate works within their more substantial whole, and they came together by a more serendipitous process than the deliberate one that generated the one Jeremiah scroll (even in its two major recensions, MT and LXX).

The Megilloth provide another model for thinking about the compilation and theology of the Twelve. Song of Songs, Ruth, Lamentations, Qoheleth, and Esther were of independent origin, but they came to be treated as a collection. That development has led to the possibility of asking about theological links between them. In some ways, the Megilloth are further away from each other than the Twelve are. Their collocation happened only in the Middle Ages; they are an adoptive family. In some ways they are closer. They have theological features in common: they have God working behind the scenes of it all, make no reference to the great story of Yahweh's dealings with Israel, and focus more on everyday life.[3] If the Twelve are a family, while naturally they do not share all the family resemblances, they do have overlapping features. One might also understand the formulating of a theology of Jeremiah, of the Megilloth, or of the Twelve, as a construction project. Given the diversity of the rocks that they comprise, what building might they form together—perhaps something greater than the parts but doing justice to them all? In considering the theology of the Twelve here, I look at their portrayal of Yahweh in light of their attachment to his self-description in Exodus 34:6–7, at the complexity of the way they affirm both Yahweh's attachment to Israel and his being the God of all the nations, at the theme of Yahweh's Day, at their promises concerning David, and (in the

---

3. See Brittany N. Melton, *Where Is God in the Megilloth? A Dialogue on the Ambiguity of Divine Presence and Absence*, OTS 73 (Leiden: Brill, 2018).

most overt exercise of rock assembly) at a spirituality of sacredness that might emerge from them.

GRACIOUS BUT NOT TOO EASYGOING

At Sinai Yahweh announces himself as

> God compassionate and gracious, long-tempered, vast in commitment and truthfulness, preserving commitment toward the thousands, carrying waywardness, rebellion, and wrongdoing; he certainly doesn't treat people as free of guilt, attending to parents' waywardness in connection with children and with grandchildren, with thirds and with fourths. (Exod 34:6–7)

Elements of this description of Yahweh recur in the Twelve.[4]

> I shall marry you to me permanently,
> > marry you to me with faithfulness and with the exercise of
> > > authority,
> With commitment and with compassion,
> > marry you to me with truth. (Hos 2:19–20 [21–22])

> Tear your mind, not your clothes,
> > and turn back to Yahweh your God,
> Because he is gracious and compassionate,
> > long-tempered and vast in commitment,
> > and relenting about something bad. (Joel 2:13)

> Oh, Yahweh, isn't this what I said when I was in my country? ... I knew that you're a God gracious, compassionate, long-tempered, vast in commitment, and relenting about something bad. (Jonah 4:2)

> Who is a God like you, carrying waywardness,
> > passing over rebellion for the remainder of his domain?
> He doesn't keep hold of his anger permanently,
> > because he delights in commitment.

---

4. Jacob Wöhrle sees this recurrence as redactionally significant; see, e.g., *Der Abschluss des Zwölfprophetenbuches*, BZAW 389 (Berlin: de Gruyter, 2008), 363–419. Paul R. House closes with this passage in "The Character of God in the Book of the Twelve," in *Reading and Hearing the Book of the Twelve*, ed. James D. Nogalski and Marvin A. Sweeney, SBL Symposium Series 15 (Atlanta: SBL Press, 2000), 125–45 (145).

When he has compassion on us again, he'll trample on our wayward
      acts;
   he'll throw all our wrongdoings into the depths of the sea.
You will show truthfulness to Jacob,
      commitment to Abraham. (Mic 7:18–20)

Yahweh is a God who is passionate and takes redress;
      Yahweh takes redress and is a possessor of wrath.
Yahweh takes redress on his adversaries,
      maintains it toward his enemies.
Yahweh is long-tempered but big in energy;
      he certainly doesn't treat people as free of guilt. (Nah 1:2–3)

Although Isaiah, Jeremiah, and Ezekiel don't directly reflect Exodus 34:6–7,
a different formulation implying a similar theology appears in Isaiah 28:21:

Yahweh will arise as on Mount Perisim,
      he will be astir as in Gibeon Vale,
To do his deed—strange is his deed,
      to perform his service—foreign is his service.

Lamentations 3:31–33 has its own formulation, implying it:

Because the Lord
      doesn't reject permanently.
Rather he brings suffering, but has compassion,
      in the vastness of his acts of commitment.
Because it's not from his heart that he humbles
      and brings suffering to human beings.

Yahweh's self-revelation at Sinai, mirrored in the Twelve and paralleled
in Isaiah and Lamentations, affirms that his character combines graciousness and sternness, but also that the two aspects are not equally balanced
in Yahweh. Graciousness is closer to his heart than sternness. In Exodus 34
he speaks of being compassionate (the noun is the plural of the word for a
womb, so it suggests motherly), gracious (acting on the basis of generosity
and favor for reasons that come from himself rather than because of the re-
cipient's merit), long-tempered (rather than taking quick punitive action),
vast in commitment (faithful in a way that persists despite the object's abandoning faithfulness), vast in truthfulness (staying true to his word), and

carrying offenses (forgiving rather than requiring the wrongdoer to pay for them). Yet Yahweh does hold people responsible for their offenses and lets these offenses have a negative effect on their family, though he places a limit on how long that happens compared with the long-lasting nature of his commitment. I assume that the tension between the two statements implies that the compassion and grace look for a turning from waywardness; it is when people decline to do so that he attends to their wrongdoing.

The prophets use the Exodus formulation in ways that can be creative and subtle, even droll. Yahweh's self-revelation explained what had happened at Sinai and made a promise regarding how things would be in the future. In Hosea and Micah, the promise relates to a threat to act again as he did at Sinai; this chastisement will not be the end of the story. In Joel, the promise opens up the possibility of Yahweh preventing the invasion(s) that Joel has portrayed. Jonah takes up the formulation with irony, in a way fitting his story: he knows Yahweh has this character and is happy for Yahweh to relate to Israel and to him on that basis but doesn't wish to see compassion extended to an oppressive superpower. Nahum also takes up the formulation with subtlety and irony in relation to the superpower that is oppressing Judah; while Jonah objects to the formulation, Nahum turns it upside down, and with further irony, whereas Yahweh critiques Jonah for his attitude to Nineveh, Nahum reassures people that Yahweh will take redress on Nineveh.

The other books among the Twelve imply the same theology as Exodus 34:6–7, even without reflecting the formulation. Amos urges Yahweh to carry Ephraim in its waywardness, and Yahweh relents of the action he had announced, though while he is long-tempered, he eventually acts (7:1–9). Then he promises eventually to restore Ephraim, as he does through Hosea when he reflects the formulation. Yahweh's chastising but then restoring is another way Yahweh squares the circle of acting in character by being gracious but not too easygoing.[5] Zephaniah works in a similar way to Amos.

---

5. Raymond C. van der Leeuwen thus reframes the use of Exodus 34:6–7 in the Twelve in terms of the modern notion of theodicy in "Scribal Wisdom and Theodicy in the Book of the Twelve," in *In Search of Wisdom: Essays in Memory of John G. Gammie*, ed. Leo G. Perdue et al. (Louisville: Westminster John Knox, 1993), 31–49; cf. James L. Crenshaw, "Theodicy in the Book of the Twelve," in *Thematic Threads in the Book of the Twelve*, ed. Paul L. Redditt and Aaron Schart, BZAW 325 (Berlin: de Gruyter, 2003), 175–91; Joel Barker, "From Where Does My Hope Come?" *JETS* 61 (2018): 697–715.

Obadiah's words about Edom parallel Nahum's about Nineveh. Habakkuk's words about Judah and Babylon compare with Hosea and Amos on one hand and with Nahum and Obadiah on the other, and Habakkuk (3:2) appeals to Yahweh to keep in mind compassion (to Judah and Babylon?). Yahweh tells Zechariah that he is impassioned and compassionate toward Jerusalem, will remove the country's waywardness, and will be God for Israel in truthfulness and faithfulness (Zech 1:14, 16; 3:9; 8:2, 8; 10:6); and Zechariah talks about Yahweh's anger with the present generation's parents/ancestors (1:2; 8:14).

YAHWEH GOT ISRAEL UP FROM EGYPT AND THE PHILISTINES FROM CAPHTOR

In explaining how God had always intended to draw the nations into acknowledging him, Paul quotes Hosea 1:10:

> I will call "not-my-people" my people, and "not-loved" loved. And in the place where it was said to them, "You are not my people," there they will be called "children of the living God." (Rom 9:25–26)

Amusingly, Paul is turning a promise about Ephraim (whom Yahweh is about to cast off) into a promise about the nations. Paul changes the reference of the words but does so in a way that matches the perspective of the Scriptures as a whole, even though making this particular promise denotes something different from what God was saying through Hosea. It happens in many New Testament quotations from the Scriptures. One can thus be relaxed about this inspired reapplication of God's promise;[6] many scriptural texts speak of Yahweh's intention that the nations should come to recognize him along with Israel, even though Hosea 1 isn't one of them. Paul's reapplication of Hosea 1 encapsulates a scriptural insight, an insight that is one aspect of the vision of the Twelve.[7]

Its neatest articulation comes as the promise that brings to a climax the first half of Zechariah.

---

6. See further John Goldingay, *Reading Jesus's Bible* (Grand Rapids: Eerdmans, 2017).
7. See Daniel C. Timmer, *The Non-Israelite Nations in the Book of the Twelve*, Biblical Interpretation Series 135 (Leiden: Brill, 2015).

> Peoples and inhabitants of many towns will yet come, and the inhab-
> itants of one will go to one another saying, "Let's go, let's go to seek
> Yahweh's goodwill and seek Yahweh Armies. I myself intend to go, yes."
> Many peoples will come, numerous nations, to seek Yahweh Armies
> in Jerusalem and to seek Yahweh's goodwill. ... In those days, when
> ten people from all the nations' tongues will take hold, they will take
> hold of the hem of a Judahite individual's coat, saying, "We want to go
> with you, because we've heard that God is with you." (Zech 8:20-23)

Like many promises of this kind in both Testaments, these words constitute an encouragement to the people of God itself; but they can fulfill that
function only insofar as they truly affirm that Yahweh intends the nations
to recognize him. But Zechariah combines this vision with a promise of a
kind that appears in other Prophets: Yahweh will put down imperial powers (1:18-21 [2:1-4]). Whereas Isaiah 40-55 sees Cyrus as Yahweh's anointed
and Yahweh's shepherd and points to Persia as Yahweh's means of fulfilling
his promises (as 2 Chr 36:20-23 and Ezra 1:1-2 confirm), Zechariah cannot
rest with that assumption a couple of decades later, even though (or precisely because) he opens by noting that Darius is king.

A related but different double perspective on the nations appears
in Amos. Amos begins in 1:3-2:3 by declaring that Yahweh intends to act
against Ephraim's neighbors for committing what we might call war crimes.
Like us when we use that category, and like Paul in Romans, Amos assumes
that the nations know the basics about right and wrong. They don't need
the Torah to tell them that enslaving people, tearing open pregnant wom-
en, and dishonoring someone's dead body are unethical. Acting thus, the
nations ignore the awareness they have as human beings. Obadiah extends
the argument regarding Edom in particular, which knows that success and
illustriousness are dangerous, but can deceive itself, and knows that brotherhood imposes obligations, but has ignored them (3, 10-14). Nahum knows
that Nineveh is guilty because of its bloodshed and for the plunder it has
gained through its killing operations (3:1) and can assume that Nineveh
does not need a special revelation to establish this guilt. In a paradoxical
way, Jonah makes the same assumption about Nineveh.

But the Jonah story shows that this assumption is not the totality of
Yahweh's attitude toward Nineveh. Yahweh's grace applies to Nineveh too.
And Amos, toward the end, has a surprising declaration about two of the

peoples with whom he began: Yahweh has taken the Philistines and Syrians to their present homes from their original locations (9:7). In terms of God's sovereignty, God's provision, God's expectations, and God's chastisement, the nations and Israel are in the same position. Here, too, Amos makes his points to remind Israel about facts concerning itself, but the validity of his argument depends on the truth of those points about Yahweh's relationship with the nations. Hosea argues in a similar way when he indicts the inhabitants of the earth (which I take to be the meaning of *hā'āreṣ* in 4:1-3, not "the land"), to entrap Ephraim for an indictment that will follow. Micah 1:2-5 and Zephaniah 2:4-3:7 work in the same way.

Even nearer the end of Amos, Yahweh takes up his opening comments about other nations and declares that Israel will gain possession of the remains of those nations over which his name had been called (9:12); the logic parallels that of the Torah and Joshua, that Israel finds collateral gain from Yahweh's attending to the wrongdoing of nations into whose territory Israel can enter and take possession (the verb is *yāraš*, as in Deuteronomy and Joshua). Yahweh specifically mentions Edom, the focus in Obadiah, which follows in the MT. The background to Obadiah is arguably Edom's takeover of Judahite territory in the sixth century; Yahweh will crush Edom in order to restore Judah. In Nahum, similarly, Nineveh is doomed both because of its violence and plunder, and because Judah as Yahweh's people is Nineveh's victim. Further, for Israel there is another aspect to these declarations. Hosea recurrently names Assyria and Egypt as the objects of Ephraim's false trust. These nations are not to be Israel's resources for support and defense. They are doomed.

A double attitude to the nations reappears in Micah. The promises in 4:1-5 follow an indictment of the Judahite leaders, also appearing in a variant form in Isaiah 2:2-5.[8]

> Because of you,
>
> Zion—as open country it will be plowed,
> Jerusalem—it will become ruins,
> the mountain of the house—a great shrine in a forest.

---

8. We do not know whether they are original to either prophet, or whether Yahweh gave them to an anonymous prophet and they found their way independently into the two books. So, by "Micah" I mean Micah the book rather than necessarily Micah the person, and something similar applies to my other references to the books that make up the Twelve.

But it will come about, at the end of the time:
The mountain of Yahweh's house will become established
at the head of the mountains,
Raised above the hills,
and peoples will stream to it.
Many nations will go,
and will say, "Come,
Let's go up to Yahweh's mountain,
to the house of Jacob's God,
So he may instruct us from his ways,
and we may walk in his paths."
Because from Zion instruction will go out,
Yahweh's message from Jerusalem.
He will exercise authority among many peoples
and reprove massive nations far and wide.
They will beat their swords into hoes,
their lances into pruning knives.
Nation will not carry sword against nation;
they will not learn battle again.
They will sit, each one, under his vine
and under his fig tree,
And there will be no one disturbing,
because the mouth of Yahweh Armies—it has spoken.
Because all the peoples—they walk
each in the name of its god.
But we—we will walk in the name of Yahweh our God,
for all time, forever. (Mic 3:12–4:5)

In Micah, the promise reverses the preceding threat, and it is again good news for Israel as for the nations, who don't know about it. Through their flocking to the temple in Jerusalem as a place where priests instruct people in Torah, Yahweh's message is to go out from Jerusalem. Through that process Yahweh will come to exercise authority in the world and cause the nations to give up war-making in favor of improving their farming. They find a collateral gain and a peace dividend. When the work is done, they share in the ideal image of a relaxed life. The closing line is a surprise, but it presupposes Israel having to wait for Yahweh to fulfill his promise: "It will come about, at the end of the time"; perhaps not this week or next week, but neither is the implication that it may take centuries. In the meantime, the nations will continue to recognize their gods rather than turning to Yahweh, and Israel's job is to walk before Yahweh, with Yahweh, and like Yahweh.

Also, in the meantime, before showing up for Yahweh to teach them things, the nations will show up to attack Jerusalem (4:11-13). And then Jerusalem will give them what for; for Judah, Micah would not disagree with Joel's ironic bidding of the nations to turn their hoes into swords (Joel 3:10). Judah will "devote" the nations (ḥāram hiphil and another verb from Deuteronomy and Joshua). It is conventionally under-translated "utterly destroy," but its meaning is closer to "sacrifice." It indicates that Zion's action does not issue in Judah's gain; it will gain nothing.

The figure among the Twelve who most worries Western readers is Nahum with his relentless declarations that Yahweh is about to take redress on Nineveh, the city of bloodshed, and bring its empire to an end. There might be two reasons why Nahum gained a place in the Scriptures. First, it brought good news to Judah as Assyria's underling, which links to a reason for readers in Britain and the United States finding Nahum troublesome. We have had a position in the world like Assyria's. Nineveh stands for London or New York. Conversely, Nahum seemed like good news in South Africa in the context of apartheid.[9] Nahum is divinely inspired resistance literature. It does not urge Judah to take up arms against Assyria; it does promise that Yahweh will. The book's nature thereby links with the second possible reason why it found a place in the Scriptures. It was proved true by events. Although the prophecy did not find fulfillment in a literal implementing of its pictorial portrait of Nineveh's destiny (as also happens with messianic promises), city and empire did fall. Nahum proved to be a true prophet. Something similar is true of Habakkuk with its promises about the fall of Babylon.

The double perspective on the nations in the Twelve compares with and is related to the portrayal of Yahweh as gracious but not too easygoing. Yahweh is the God of the nations and is at work in their lives. The Twelve do not come as close as Genesis does to indicating that Yahweh has the nations' benefit in

---

9. See Wilhelm Wessels, "Nahum: An Uneasy Expression of Yahweh's Power," *Old Testament Essays* 11 (1998): 615-28.

mind when God gets involved with Israel for its benefit, but they do indicate that he is concerned about the nations and that Israel's blessing can become their blessing. His design for them is good but they commonly surrender the fruits of that good design and experience his action as bringing trouble. Yet that need not be the end of their story.

YAHWEH'S DAY

In discussion of the possible redaction of the Twelve, the "Day of Yahweh" has had a significant place.[10] While the word *yôm* indeed *denotes* a "day," the phrase "the Day of the Lord" requires defamiliarizing. Yahweh's Day is not a twenty-four-hour period, and we might do better to think of it as "Yahweh's moment" or "Yahweh's time."

The precise expression "Yahweh's Day" appears twelve times in the Twelve (Joel 1:15; 2:1, 11; 2:31 [3:4]; 3:14 [4:14]; Amos 5:18a, 18b, 20; Obad 15; Zeph 1:7, 14a, 14b; Mal 4:5 [3:23]). The theological ideas it expresses are not unique to the Twelve over against Isaiah, Jeremiah, and Ezekiel (see Isa 13:6, 9; Ezek 13:5), but its prominence is distinctive. Similar phrases such as "a day for Yahweh" and "the day of Yahweh's anger/fury/sacrifice" also recur more often in the Twelve than elsewhere (e.g., Zech 14:1; Zeph 1:8; 1:18; 2:2, 3). It is sometimes accompanied by other allusions to a "day" that gloss these references retrospectively (e.g., Joel 2:2), sometimes by describing it as "that day" (e.g., Zeph 1:9, 10; Zech 14:4, 6, 8, 9, 13, 20, 21). This vaguer expression is more common throughout the Prophets. It can refer back to a particular day that has just been mentioned (e.g., Zech 6:10), but it may commonly carry the connotation of "that [well-known] day," Yahweh's Day (e.g., Amos 8:3, 9; Mic 5:10 [9]; Zech 12:1–14), particularly where it has no antecedent temporal expression to which it could be referring back (e.g., Obad 8). Although the precise phrase comes in only five of the Twelve, all but Jonah use expressions that may be related.[11]

---

10. See Rolf Rendtorff, "How to Read the Book of the Twelve as a Theological Unity," in *Reading and Hearing the Book of the Twelve*, ed. James D. Nogalski and M. A. Sweeney, SBL Symposium Series 15 (Atlanta: SBL, 2000), 75–90.

11. For Hosea, Joel, Amos, and Obadiah in this connection, see James D. Nogalski, "The Day(s) of YHWH in the Book of the Twelve," in *Thematic Threads in the Book of the Twelve*, ed. Paul L. Redditt and Aaron Schart, BZAW 325 (Berlin: de Gruyter, 2003), 192–213; more broadly, James D. Nogalski, "Recurring Themes in the Book of the Twelve," *Int* 61 (2007): 125–36 (125–27).

Chronologically, the expression leaps onto the stage fully-formed in Amos 5:18–20. In the Masoretic Text order of the Twelve, Joel with its multiplicity of occurrences precedes Amos, as do Isaiah and Ezekiel with their references. In the LXX, Amos precedes Joel, and the Twelve precede Isaiah, Jeremiah, and Ezekiel, so there the Amos references come first in the Scriptures. We do not know the background or origin of the expression, but it evidently denoted a time when things would be light and bright. In Amos's day things likely were light and bright for many people, at least for the sort of people who write and read papers like this one. And Amos's audience knew that Yahweh was a God who loved to bless his people and intended to open the storehouses in the heavens for them, and that Yahweh's moment would mean an even fuller experience of those realities. Amos's message about Yahweh's Day appears in conjunction with observations about festivals in a sanctuary such as Bethel, when people's worship might remind them of those intentions on Yahweh's part. Amos turns their expectations upside down in declaring that Yahweh's moment will mean gloom not brightness. On either side of the threat are exhortations to have recourse to Yahweh himself rather than to a sanctuary such as Bethel, and to see that authority is exercised in a faithful way in the community to ensure that ordinary people do as well in their lives as professors and pastors. By implication, however, Yahweh's threat can be forestalled.

Joel makes the same assumption and gives the same warnings but elaborates on the point; Yahweh's Day is the distinctive focus of his prophecy. As a key aspect of his exposition, he spells out two sets of events to which Yahweh's Day can refer; he does not clash with Amos, but he may go beyond Amos's implications. Joel 1 describes a locust epidemic that in the prophet's vision has apparently already happened but that is in prospect for his audience. The threat of this epidemic means that "a day of Yahweh is near" (1:15). The vision might imply a literal epidemic or might be a figure for military invasion. Joel 2 then relates a further vision that certainly describes military invasion. Both visions seek to press people into turning to Yahweh with fasting and prayer. The two visions, then, portray Yahweh's moment as one or more events that are to overwhelm the community.

Joel speaks further about Yahweh's Day in 2:28–32, which forms a new paragraph in the Masoretic Text and constitutes chapter 3 in printed Hebrew Bibles. The variation from the English chapter division matches the way Joel now speaks differently of Yahweh's Day, describing cosmic portents that will herald it. The description of the day itself follows as a new chapter in printed Bibles (3:1–21 English, 4:1–21 Hebrew), though not in the Masoretic Text.

Joel's distinctive insight is that Yahweh's Day in its catastrophic reality can happen in the course of regular human experience, taking the form of a natural calamity or a military calamity. Or it can constitute an ultimate exercise of divine authority after which nothing will be the same. "Yahweh's Day" need not always refer to the same actual moment, as the conventional English translation "*the* day of the Lord" implies. When a construct noun links to a name, the construct noun can be indefinite.[12] So *yôm yhwh* is open to meaning "*a* day of Yahweh."

The closing verses of Joel suggest another insight. Following on from the declaration that a Day of Yahweh is near, in Determination Vale (3:14 [4:14]), Joel adds:

> And it will happen on that day:
> > the mountains will drop treading.
> The hills will run with milk,
> > all the channels in Judah will run with water.
> A fountain will go out from Yahweh's house,
> > and water Acacias Wadi. (Joel 3:18 [4:18])

Here, "that day" refers back to Yahweh's Day (3:14 [4:14]), but that day is now a day of blessing. The assumptions countered by Amos and by himself were not so wrong after all. Amos agrees:

> On that day:
> I will raise up David's fallen bivouac
> > and repair its breaches;
> I will raise its ruins,
> > and build it up as in days of old. (Amos 9:11)

"That day" with positive implications in passages such as Hosea 1:5; 2:16, 18, 21 [18, 20, 23]; Haggai 2:23, and a phrase such as "the day of Jezreel" in Hosea 1:11, likewise look like a reference to Yahweh's Day as a day of restoration and blessing.

---

12. See, e.g., Bruce K. Waltke and Michael Patrick O'Connor, *An Introduction to Biblical Hebrew Syntax* (Winona Lake, IN: Eisenbrauns, 1990), 241.

Joel, then, puts us on the track of two double significances about Yahweh's Day that run through the Twelve and constitute one of the themes that unites the Twelve. There can be a Day of Yahweh (maybe more than one) that embodies in history a final epoch-changing day still to come. And whereas people thought of Yahweh's Day as simply a destined moment of blessing, in the short term it will be a day of catastrophe, unless they reorder their community life and reaffirm their commitment to Yahweh. But on the other side of catastrophe, Yahweh's Day can be the day of blessing that Yahweh intended. The alternatives that the Twelve put before Israel are actually the ones laid out in Deuteronomy 28 in the promises and threats attached to Yahweh's covenant.

A NEW DAVID

Like Paul interpreting God's purpose for the nations with a reference to Hosea 1:10, Matthew interprets the Lord telling Joseph to take Jesus and his mother to Egypt with a reference to Hosea 11:1. Joseph thereby "fulfilled" Yahweh's reminder that he had called his son from Egypt. Originally, that reminder was not a message about the future but a recollection concerning the past. God fulfilled it in the story of Jesus in the sense of filling it out, giving it a new significance. Further, in Hosea Yahweh had more precisely called *to* his son, which suggests his calling to Israel ever since Egypt. The LXX has "called my son," a version more directly open to reapplication to Jesus.

Hosea's actual prophecy concerning David comes at the climax of the book's opening three chapters, which form an introduction to the book as a whole with more focus on promise than on the warning that dominates Hosea 4–14. On the other side of Yahweh's chastisement, "the Israelites will turn back and have recourse to Yahweh their God and David their king" (3:5). "David" stands for whoever is the Davidic king at the time, and "Israelites" means the Ephraimites who are Hosea's people and the people among whom he operates. Turning back to the right way will mean returning to an association with Judah and Jerusalem and recognizing David's line. Presumably the formation of Hosea 1–3 as the book's introduction postdates the fall of Samaria, the taking of a collection of Hosea's messages to Judah, and their shaping into a message for the future there; hence the book beginning with dates in terms of Judahite kings and its applying Hosea's message to Judah from time to time.

We have noted that Amos ends in a related fashion with a promise about restoring David's fallen bivouac "on that day" (Amos 9:11). Here, too, a prophet who worked in Ephraim (though he was a Judahite) makes a promise concerning the monarchy based in Jerusalem. David's fallen bivouac is likely a figure for the twelve-clan "household" over which David was head, which had been in an emaciated state since the northern clans' departure. Amos goes on to describe the household also taking possession of Edom, which might presuppose either Edom's declaration of independence from Judah not long before Amos's day (2 Kgs 8:20-22) or Edom's later occupying much of Judah. Either way, Yahweh promises to rebuild the Davidic nation. After the felling of the Davidic tree in 587 BCE and the promise that Yahweh would revive it, the Davidic bivouac suggests David's line itself, and the promise came to suggest the restoration of David's line. An anthology of Old Testament texts from Qumran, *4QFlorilegium* (4Q174), seems to interpret it in connection with an expected Davidic messiah and speaks of some fulfillment in its own community as a "human sanctuary." James does the same in Acts 15:16.

Micah's promises refer most explicitly to an individual Davidic king.

You, Bethlehem Epratah,
    little to be among Judah's clans,
From you there will emerge for me
    someone to be ruler in Israel,
Though his emergings are from long ago,
    from days of old.
Therefore he will give them up
    until the time when the one who is going to give birth has given
    birth.
When the rest of his brothers turn back
    to the Israelites,
He will stand and shepherd in Yahweh's power,
    in the majesty of the name of Yahweh his God.
So they will settle, because now he will be great, right to the ends of
    the earth,
    and he will be the one of peace. (Mic 5:2-5 [1-4])

The promise does not name David, though the one from long ago must surely be a descendant of that son of Bethlehem to whom God made promises centuries previously. Nor does Yahweh call this ruler a king. He does declare, as he does in Hosea, that people who have turned away from David, even though they were his brothers, will return to him. Together they will settle down in peace. Matthew again picks up this promise to apply to the one actually born in Bethlehem, though he (or someone he follows) modifies the text in light of its fulfillment: Bethlehem is now "not at all" least among Judah's clans.

There is a family resemblance between these three promises in Hosea, Amos, and Micah, and then a different family resemblance between promises in Haggai and Zechariah 1–8. Zerubbabel, a descendant of David, now rules in Jerusalem, as governor. He is in some measure a fulfillment of promises about David, though Yahweh has much more to do before things in Judah count as real fulfillment. He now makes promises concerning when he does act. Haggai begins by recognizing that Darius is king, but he closes by declaring Yahweh's intention to overturn the throne of the nations' kingdoms (2:22). Yahweh says: "I will take you, Zerubbabel ben Shealtiel my servant ... and make you like a signet, because I have chosen you" (2:23). He doesn't call Zerubbabel king or note his Davidic lineage, but everyone would know the implications of his being the son of Shealtiel. "My servant" and "I have chosen you" are Davidic designations, and "my signet ring," my seal, was Yahweh's designation in connection with David's grandfather (Jer 22:24–27). The negative implications of the reference in Jehoiachin's story find a contrast in connection with his grandson.

In Zechariah, Zerubbabel is the person who initiated the temple building and will complete it (4:6–9).

> There is the man whose name is Branch. From his place he will branch out and build Yahweh's palace. He is the one who will build Yahweh's palace. He is the one who will put on majesty and sit and rule on his throne. (Zech 6:12–13)

Like Haggai, Zechariah does not refer to David or use "king" language, but describing Zerubbabel as Branch (ṣemaḥ; cf. 3:8) associates him with the Davidic tree in language that appears in Jeremiah just after the signet ring passage (Jer 23:5; cf. 33:15). In Isaianic terms, he will prove that felling the Davidic tree does not mean it cannot generate new growth (nēṣer in Isa 11:1).

And he will put on the majesty that his great-grandfather lost (Jer 22:18) and will sit and rule on his throne. Further, unlike the book of Haggai, the book of Zechariah has pointedly not called Darius king (1:1), though it will do so momentarily (7:1).

While the Judahites did rebuild the temple, as far as we know Zerubbabel never sat on a throne in Jerusalem. Apparently, Yahweh had a change of mind about this possibility, though the preservation of the unfulfilled promise suggests that the community was not fazed by it.

Perhaps Zerubbabel is the unnamed shepherd in Zechariah 13:7. In Zechariah 9–14 as a whole, the allusions to David and to kingship are ambivalent and ambiguous. They begin with a vision of Zion having a king who is faithful and finds deliverance, but who is lowly and riding on a donkey, as anyone else does if they are lucky; he is not given a link with David (9:9). The notion of David and of kingship is more understated in Zechariah 12–14. The splendor of David's household and of Jerusalem's people is not to be greater than Judah's or too great for Judah, and the feeblest among the people is to be like David (12:7–10). The household of David is to be like God, like Yahweh's messenger at their head. There will be cleansing for the household of David (13:1). It is Yahweh who will be king (14:9, 16, 17). The ambivalence in Zechariah 9–14 over Davidic kingship extends to other forms of leadership. Yahweh's anger burns against the "shepherds," the "he-goats" (10:3; cf. 11:5), who might be Davidic leaders or would-be leaders, and/or other officials, and/or the prophets who explicitly feature later (13:2–6), and if they don't include priests, Malachi is keen to add them (Mal 1:6; 2:1, 7).

While Haggai and Zechariah 1–8 are explicit on the context of their promises, uncertainty is attached to the historical context of the prophecies on either side. Historical-critical study sees the promises in Hosea, Amos, and Micah as later than their day, while the setting and reference of the passages in Zechariah 9–14 are purely guesswork. There is not one clear vision of David in the Twelve.[13] The diversity recalls the other three prophetic scrolls, especially Isaiah, where there is an individual embodiment of David, a corporate embodiment, and a Persian embodiment. The

---

13. But contrast Anthony R. Petterson's argument in "The Shape of the Davidic Hope across the Book of the Twelve," *JSOT* 35 (2010): 225–46.

David of Hosea 3:5 has been called "a messianic figure,"[14] but this terminology risks being more confusing than illuminating. It's no coincidence that the Old Testament never applies the word *māšîaḥ* to the future David it speaks of. The Messiah of later Jewish and Christian thinking stands in continuity with the David of the Twelve, but he is a development from that figure. The prominence of the David theme in the Twelve may again link with the process of their redaction. Theologically, the significance of David and of Yahweh's promise to David meant prophets could not get away from David, but the implications of his image can vary through the Twelve.

A SPIRITUALITY OF SACREDNESS

How might the Twelve shape the community's life with God? In this connection, no distinctive motif runs through them, though a number have their own distinctive or characteristic motifs. In discussing their spirituality, I shall proceed by picking out one motif from each book. It will be a different kind of intertextual or canonical exercise, and not one making any redactional assumptions.

Eleven of the books do use the word "sacred" or "holy": the adjective *qādôš*, the noun *qōdeš*, and the verb *qādaš* (Nahum is the exception, but one could easily argue that sacredness is part of its thinking). "Be sacred like me," Yahweh urges in the Torah (e.g., Lev 11:44, 45; 19:2). "I'm sacred, which expresses itself in the fact that I needn't act in my anger toward you," Yahweh says in the first book in the Twelve (Hos 11:9); "My mountain is sacred," he says in the second (Joel 2:1); he swears an oath by his sacredness in the third book (Amos 4:2); and so on.

Yahweh's sacredness is his distinctiveness. It marks the difference between him and human beings. "I'm God, not a human being, among you as the sacred one," he says in that declaration in the first of the Twelve. Now Yahweh is not the only embodiment of sacredness; he has an entourage of sacred beings, and the horses and pots associated with him can be sacred (Zech 14:5, 20, 21). Further, sacredness need not imply positive qualities; there are heavenly sacred beings that lack such qualities, and there

---

14. Ehud Ben Zvi, *Hosea*, Forms of the Old Testament Literature 21A/1 (Grand Rapids: Eerdmans, 2005), 89.

are apparently *qədēšôt*, hierodules, in Ephraim who lack them (Hos 4:14). But Yahweh's sacredness expresses itself in that positive personal quality of not needing to act in anger (Hos 11:9). And the positive qualities for which Yahweh looks in Israel will constitute its sacredness.

In Hosea, the quality for which Yahweh looks is acknowledgment of him as God. The verb *yāda'* runs throughout Hosea. The traditional translation "know" misses the way the word denotes recognition expressed in action not merely a close personal relationship or an awareness of facts about Yahweh. Yahweh wants acknowledgment rather than burnt offerings, commitment (*ḥesed*) not sacrifices (Hos 6:6; cf. 8:13). The reminder might puzzle Ephraimites who thought they were acknowledging him with their offerings, but the acknowledgment he seeks finds expression in life outside worship as well as inside. Hosea makes clear elsewhere that we should not be literalistic in interpreting his declaration about acknowledgment rather than offerings; he assumes the propriety and necessity of worship. But the problem is that swearing oaths (falsely), lying, murder, stealing, and adultery replace acknowledgment, truthfulness, and commitment (4:1-2). A spirituality of sacredness means acknowledging that it is Yahweh who gives us food (2:8 [10]), who bandages us when we are wounded (11:9), who delivers us from bondage, thirst, and hunger (13:4-6). Acknowledging Yahweh is the opposite of whoring, a faithlessness that treats other agencies as key to having something to eat (5:4), and of putting Yahweh out of mind as we enjoy his blessings (13:6). It means a faithfulness that looks to him alone in the way a wife looks to her husband alone (1:2-3:5; 4:1-19; 10:12). It means not abandoning him and looking to other nations, to strongholds, to military resources (4:10, 12; 5:13; 7:11; 8:9-10, 14; 10:13; 12:1 [2]). It means keeping faith, keeping the covenant pledge, staying on the way (4:10, 12; 5:7; 6:4-7; 7:1, 13; 8:1; 10:12). It means having recourse to Yahweh and being awestruck by Yahweh (3:5).

In Joel, the key verb is turn (*šûb*), which runs throughout Joel 1-2. Turning to Yahweh is a way of describing acknowledgment of Yahweh (see Joel 3:17 [4:17]), though in Joel, turning eventually leads to that acknowledgment (2:27). Joel shares his visions of the epidemic, and the army aims to get people to turn to Yahweh. Whereas turning in Hosea implies turning from wrongdoing and from having recourse to other deities and resources (e.g., Hos 5:4; 12:6 [7]; 14:1 [2]), and thus could be translated "repentance," Joel does not imply that the community has sin to repent of. It seems simply to need to turn to Yahweh as deliverer and protector in a coming crisis. Turning might still contrast with confidence about taking responsibility for yourself and making your own decisions (Hos 5:5; 7:10, 13). And, whereas Hosea emphasizes the inadequacy of sacramental actions—such as offering sacrifices when it is unaccompanied by a turning of the whole person—Joel calls for sacramental action, for fasting, weeping, and mourning (Joel 1:14; 2:12, 15-17), for crying out (1:5, 8, 11, 13, 14), for trembling and being in anguish (2:1, 6), for calling on Yahweh (2:32 [3:5]). Rip your heart, your inner being, your thinking, not your clothes, Yahweh urges (2:13); the context indicates that he means your heart as well as your clothes. People need to turn with their whole being, inward as well as outward, symbolic as well as substantial. Similarly, Hosea is not reluctant to urge people to turn to Yahweh with words (Hos 14:2 [3]).

Amos makes distinctive use of the idea of pursuing or seeking or looking to (dāraš), which appears in connection with the priorities he urges. "Pursue me. ... Don't pursue Bethel. ... Pursue Yahweh. ... Pursue the good and not the bad. ... Repudiate the bad, be loyal to the good, establish the proper exercise of authority at the gate" (Amos 5:4-6, 14-15). Among the Twelve, only Amos issues this bidding to pursue as his term for acknowledging or turning. Like the other prophets, he expects turning to express itself in action; his verb distinctively suggests energy.

Obadiah speaks of brotherhood (Obad 12). It parallels the reference to brotherhood in the Edom passage in Amos 1:11 and the stress on brotherhood as a principle for community life in the Torah, especially in Deuteronomy. There is (presumably unintentional) irony in the Obadiah reference, since the prophet critiques Edom for a failure of brotherhood but doesn't seem very brotherly in his promises about Edom's destiny.

Jonah ends up with a double reference to pity (Jonah 4:10-12). Jonah feels sorry for the bush that grew but withered, yet he has not shown pity for the Ninevites. The reference suggests a different irony: it is Ezekiel who talks most about pity (ḥûs) in order to deny that Yahweh will show any to Judah (e.g., Ezek 7:4, 9), though Joel invites Judah to make it an object of appeal (Joel 2:17), and the Old Testament also makes it a principle for the king's relationship with the needy (Ps 72:13).

The well-known bidding in Micah concerns (conventionally) justice, kindness, and a humble walk with God (Mic 6:8). Actually, Micah is concerned about mišpāṭ, which implies the proper exercise of authority by people who have authority, such as kings, officials, elders, and heads of households. If we wonder what the proper exercise of authority means, then Micah clarifies the point by glossing mišpāṭ with ḥesed, which denotes the faithfulness that persists when the other party has forfeited any right to it. Lastly, Micah wants people to walk circumspectly with Yahweh (ṣānaʿ, hiphil). The verb appears only here, but the related adjective contrasts with presumptuousness (zādôn; Prov 11:2). It suggests being deferential about thinking we know what Yahweh wants us to do or what Yahweh is doing. Micah's trinity of words compares with Hosea's vision for a turning to Yahweh that will issue in mišpāṭ, ḥesed, and a willingness to wait for Yahweh to act (Hos 12:6 [7]), and with his warning about making our own political decisions (Hos 8:4).

"Celebrate your festivals" (ḥoggǝgî ḥāggayik) Nahum bids (1:15 [2:1]) in a neat contrast with Hosea 2:11 [13]; Amos 5:21; 8:10 (but cf. Zech 14:16). It illustrates further how the Twelve can both critique and affirm worship. Nahum would no doubt oppose the innovative worship that Hosea confronts though (Hos 8:4-6, 11; 10:1; 13:2).

"How long?" is Habakkuk's first word, and "why?" follows. Habakkuk models a spirituality that comes to Yahweh with straight questions, like the Psalms, though it then allows for listening to Yahweh's answers, like Job.

Like Nahum but going further, Zephaniah urges Zion to chant and shout, to rejoice and exult (3:14).

In Haggai, three times Yahweh urges people who should be rebuilding the temple to "take courage" or "be strong" (ḥāzaq; Hag 2:4); Zechariah uses the same verb in the jussive (Zech 8:9, 13). In connection with the rebuilding, Haggai and Zechariah complement each other in their respective stresses on Israel's obligation and Yahweh's promise. You must take action; he will ensure you succeed.

It is thus tempting to link Haggai and Zechariah 1-8, but working with the book of Zechariah makes it possible to note the motif of mindfulness—what is usually translated "remembering" (zākar, zikkārôn; Zech 6:14; 10:9; 13:2). A key theme in Old Testament spirituality is an attentiveness that gives its mind to the past (so it is remembering) but also in the present to Yahweh and not images.

In Malachi, revering or being in awe (*yārē'*, verb and adjective) recurs more than anywhere else in the Twelve (Mal 1:14; 2:5; 3:5, 16a, 16b; 4:5 [3:23]). And awe for Yahweh has been described as the Old Testament way of denoting spirituality.[15]

Through a process of redaction and/or some other process, then, the Twelve came to have a mutually overlapping theology that also shared common ground with the other three prophetic scrolls. In their understanding of Yahweh this overlapping theology is symbolized by the recurrence of motifs from Exodus 34:6-7, though the prophets who do not incorporate an allusion to that text do have a similar understanding of Yahweh as gracious but not too easygoing. The overlap is also symbolized by the distinctive recurrence of allusion to Yahweh's Day with its reference to a final ultimate event that would turn out to be embodied in the meantime partially but not finally in a particular historical event; again, the prophets who do not use the expression Yahweh's Day imply a similar theology. Without sharing another comparable form of words, the Twelve as a group suggest that Yahweh was involved with Israel in a distinctive way but was also involved with all the nations, and they look forward to the arrival of a new David through whom Yahweh's purpose will be fulfilled. And out of the Twelve it is possible to articulate a spirituality of sacredness that involves being in awe of Yahweh, being mindful of Yahweh, questioning Yahweh, acknowledging Yahweh, turning to Yahweh, pursuing Yahweh, celebrating, chanting and shouting, being circumspect yet courageous in doing what Yahweh says and promises to support, and living in brotherhood, in pity, and in an exercise of authority that manifests in commitment.

---

15. See Rolf Knierim, "The Spirituality of the Old Testament," in *The Task of Old Testament Theology* (Grand Rapids: Eerdmans, 1995), 269-97.

Index of Subjects

U
unfaithfulness, 15, 18, 22, 27, 106, 107, 108, 121

W
woe
  oracles from Habakkuk, 54–57, 59, 62
worship
  of false gods, 9, 21, 34, 50, 59
  and festivals, 191
  of God, 90, 140, 145, 182
  and justice, 144
  necessity of, 189
  as ritual, 40

Y
Yahweh
  dialogue with Habakkuk, 94–95, 99–102
  dialogue with Malachi, 96–98, 99–102
  as divine warrior, 138
  glory of, 55, 92, 132

and judgment of Israel (see Israel, judgment)
  lament of, 7–29
  and the new covenant, 111
  plan for humanity, 91
  portrayal in the Book of the Twelve, 171–92
Yahweh's Day, 98
Yahweh's Spirit, 141, 147

Z
Zechariah (biblical character), 156, 176–77
Zechariah (book), 115–19, 123–24, 133–34, 141–42, 148–49, 176, 186–87, 191
Zephaniah (biblical character)
Zephaniah (book), 175, 191
Zerubbabel (biblical character), 113, 128, 141, 148, 186, 187
Zion, 34, 41, 55, 62, 112, 117, 134–38, 144, 178–79, 187, 191
  election of, 32–33
  role in Amos, 36–37

Index of Authors

Index of Scripture and Other Ancient Literature

Old Testament

New Testament

Deuterocanonical Books

Ancient Jewish Writers

Josephus

Against Apion 1.8 171

Rabbinic Works

Talmud

Baba Batra 14b 171

Luther's Works

TO LEARN A DEAD LANGUAGE
PRETEND IT'S ALIVE